# POST-BUBBLE BLUES

## How Japan Responded to Asset Price Collapse

Editors
**Tamim Bayoumi**
**Charles Collyns**

International Monetary Fund

© 2000 International Monetary Fund

Production: IMF Graphics Section
Cover design: Massoud Etemadi
Figures: Theodore F. Peters, Jr.
Typesetting: Choon Lee


**Library of Congress Cataloging-in-Publication Data**

Post-bubble blues : how Japan responded to asset price collapse / editors,
Tamim Bayoumi, Charles Collyns.
    p.   cm.
Includes bibliographical references.
ISBN 1-55775-872-7

1. Stocks—Prices—Japan.  2. Financial crises—Japan.  3. Japan—
Economic conditions—1989– .  4. Monetary policy—Japan  I. Bayoumi,
Tamim A.  II. Collyns, Charles.
HG5773.P67   1999
330.952′049—dc21                                                    99-058930
                                                                         CIP


Price: $26.00


Address orders to:
International Monetary Fund, Publication Services
700 19th Street, N.W., Washington D.C. 20431, U.S.A.
Telephone: (202) 623-7430
Telefax: (202) 623-7201
E-mail: publications@imf.org
Internet: http://www.imf.org

# Contents

The following symbols have been used throughout this book:

...   to indicate that data are not available;

—   to indicate that the figure is zero or less than half the final digit shown, or that the item does not exist;

–   between years or months (for example, 1997–98 or January–June) to indicate the years or months covered, including the beginning and ending years or months;

/   between years or months (for example, 1997/98) to indicate a crop or fiscal (financial) year.

"Billion" means a thousand million; "trillion" means a thousand billion.

Minor discrepancies between constituent figures and totals are due to rounding.

The term "country," as used in this book, does not in all cases refer to a territorial entity that is a state as understood by international law and practice; the term also covers some territorial entities that are not states, but for which statistical data are maintained and provided internationally on a separate and independent basis.

# Preface

The research papers presented in this book were prepared by members of the Japan team in the IMF, working under the direction of Charles Collyns and Tamim Bayoumi, during 1998 and the first half of 1999. The papers complement the policy analysis provided in *Japan—Staff Report for the 1999 Article IV Consultation* (IMF Staff Country Report No. 99/93) and the overview of recent trends provided in *Japan—Economic and Policy Developments* (IMF Staff Country Report No. 99/114). Support and encouragement from senior members of the Asia and Pacific Department—especially Hubert Neiss, Yusuke Horiguchi, and David Goldsbrough—are gratefully acknowledged. The papers also benefit from useful comments from participants in seminars at the IMF and at the Japan Group of the National Bureau of Economic Research and the Tokyo Center for Economic Research. The authors would like to thank the stalwart assistance of Anita Jupp in preparing the text, Youkyong Kwon and Fritz Pierre-Louis for research assistance, and Jeremy Clift of the IMF's External Relations Department for editing and producing this book.

The views expressed in this volume are those of the authors, and do not necessarily represent those of the Japanese authorities, IMF Executive Directors, or other IMF staff.

# 1

# Overview

*Tamim Bayoumi and Charles Collyns*

The 1990s were very difficult for the Japanese economy. Toward the end of the decade, Japan experienced a recession of a depth and duration virtually unprecedented for a major industrial country since the Second World War, a recession from which it has only recently begun to recover. Moreover, this sharp downturn followed a prolonged period of economic weakness dating back to the bursting of the asset price bubble in 1991. In fact, from 1991 to 1999, output growth averaged only a little over 1 percent, compared with around 4 percent achieved in the 1980s. This experience has led macroeconomic policymaking into uncharted territory and called into question many of the most basic tenets about the behavior of Japan's economy, including the growth rate of potential output, the effectiveness of fiscal and monetary policies, and the strength of the Japanese system of corporate governance.[1]

The research in this book was undertaken by IMF staff during 1998 and 1999 in response to this rapidly changing and uncertain situation. It provided an analytical framework for the IMF's assessment and policy advice related to the Japanese economy over this period when the difficulties in Japan were an important factor contributing to global economic and financial strains.

---

[1]The report for the 1999 IMF Article IV consultation with Japan (IMF, 1999) provides the IMF staff's most recent overall assessment of Japanese macroeconomic policies and prospects. It is available on the Internet at http://www.imf.org/external/pubind.htm.

The roots of the story lie at least as far back as the overheating of the Japanese economy that occurred during the late 1980s. As is well known, the rapid growth achieved during this period was associated with the development of a major asset price bubble. Economic growth slowed markedly from 1991 as a tightening in monetary policy prompted the collapse of equity and land prices. The continued appreciation of the yen through early 1995 was an additional factor depressing activity, contributing to a period of stagnation that lasted through most of the early 1990s and left the economy significantly below its estimated level of potential output.

Spurred by a combination of fiscal stimulus, a monetary easing, and deregulation initiatives, activity started to recover in late 1995, and in 1996 the Japanese economy grew by 5 percent, the fastest among the Group of Seven industrial countries. Growth was further boosted in early 1997 by anticipation of a hike in the consumption tax rate from 3 percent to 5 percent at the beginning of April—an initial step towards fiscal consolidation—which caused individuals to bring their purchases forward to avoid the additional taxes. Although a temporary lull in activity was anticipated following the introduction of the higher tax rate, most forecasters—including those at the IMF—expected growth to recommence quickly, as would be expected in a normal cyclical recovery.

In the event, however, the economy failed to revive. Although there was an initial recovery in spending as the immediate impact of the consumption tax hike wore off, output fell again in late 1997 and continued to fall through the whole of 1998. This recession, the worst experienced by Japan since quarterly GDP figures started to be published in the mid-1950s, left output in the last quarter of 1998 5 percent below its peak in early 1997. This downturn was by far Japan's worst recession of the postwar period and involved all components of private demand (Figure 1.1).

The immediate triggers of the downturn in 1997 are readily identified. The initial shock was a larger-than-expected drop in household spending after the April 1997 consumption tax hike. Later in the year, the weakness was exacerbated by financial factors, namely the disruptive impact of the failures of a major bank and two large securities firms in November 1997 and tighter bank credit in advance of a strengthening of bank regulations planned for April 1998. Moreover, the growing crisis in Asian emerging mar-

**Figure 1.1. Comparison of Five Japanese Cyclical Downturns**
*(Index peak = 100)*

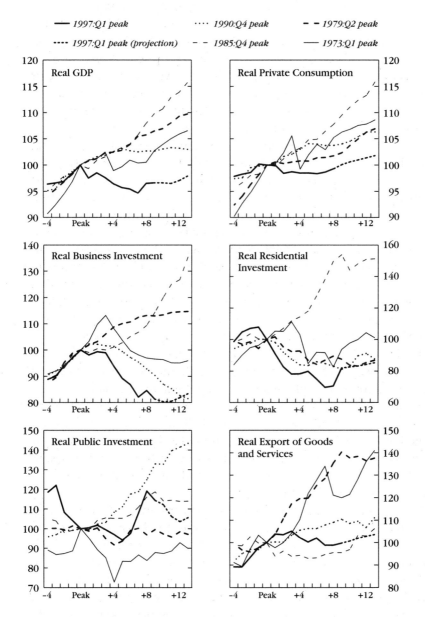

Source: Nikkei Telecom.
[1]Three-quarter moving averages (centered).

3

kets hurt external demand, as well as striking a further blow to confidence.

The recession continued through 1998, despite a further shift toward stimulative macroeconomic policies. Short-term interest rates were brought down to virtually zero by early 1999 and repeated doses of fiscal stimulus raised the general government fiscal deficit (excluding social security) to almost 10 percent of GDP. The weakness of business investment was particularly acute, notwithstanding determined government action to reduce risks of further financial disruptions and relieve credit constraints.

Finally, in 1999 the economy again began to recover. The turnaround was initiated by a burst of public investment spending early in the year and a recovery of consumer confidence as forceful action by the government to deal with weak banks and inject public capital into the banking system alleviated fears of financial crisis. However, a rapid rise in the yen from its low point in mid-1998—linked in part to external developments as well as improving sentiment about the Japanese economy—has raised concerns about the impact on the still fragile recovery and led to calls for further easing of monetary policy even though short-term interest rates are already virtually at zero.

Recent experience and the striking contrast between Japan's weak macroeconomic performance during the 1990s and the dynamic performance in some other industrial countries—notably the United States, which completed its eighth year of expansion in 1999—have put a spotlight on deeper structural problems in Japan. Two main themes can be identified:

- First, the slow pace at which the economy, and more particularly the corporate and financial sectors, worked through the problems of excessive investment and excessive indebtedness that built up during the asset price bubble period. The "post-bubble blues" were thus allowed to linger for the whole decade, rather than being shrugged off after a sharp adjustment as might have occurred if the imbalances had been faced directly at an early point.
- Second, more fundamental weaknesses in corporate governance. Until recently, Japanese businesses and markets have moved only gradually to make the necessary transition from reliance on heavy capital accumulation and rapid export growth

4

that had successfully delivered high quality growth for 40 years following the Second World War to one placing greater emphasis on innovation, productivity growth, and efficient use of resources. Particular problems include an excessive emphasis on size and market share rather than profitability, an employment system that encouraged an immobile labor force, and still limited competition in many domestic markets for goods and services despite efforts to deregulate.

Against this background, the research presented in this book is aimed at answering three sets of questions. The first issue is to identify the constraining forces underlying the weakness of activity in the 1990s. The work on this is contained in Part I of the book "Explaining the 1990s." The second part, "Financial and Fiscal Transmission Mechanisms," seeks to understand why highly stimulative macroeconomic policies failed to prevent the prolonged stagnation. Finally, Part III "The Challenge of Corporate Restructuring," investigates why, until recently, Japanese businesses have not responded more dynamically to their deteriorating economic performance.

Chapter 2, "The Morning After: Explaining the Slowdown in Japanese Growth," by Tamim Bayoumi, uses vector autoregressions (VARs) to examine the reasons for the fall in Japan's output gap (output relative to potential) since 1991.[2] Four possible explanations are considered: the absence of bold and consistent fiscal stimulus, the limited room for expansionary monetary policy because of a liquidity trap, overinvestment and debt overhang, and the disruption of financial intermediation. The results point to disruption of financial intermediation, largely caused by falling asset prices and feeding through into business investment, as the major factor behind the disappointing macroeconomic performance. In addition, the model implies smaller multipliers for macroeconomic policies than has generally been assumed in the past, at least by the IMF, plausibly reflecting the impact of banking problems on the monetary transmission mechanism and the extensive use of temporary fiscal

---

[2]The VAR approach—an econometric technique used quite heavily in this book—provides a means of assessing a range of competing explanations within a single empirical framework and of examining the often complex interactions among variables without being required to fully specify a formal macroeconometric model of the economy.

policy tools (both issues are examined in more detail in subsequent chapters).

In Chapter 3, "Identifying the Shocks: Japan's Economic Performance in the 1990s," Ramana Ramaswamy and Christel Rendu also use VARs, but focus on rather different techniques and objectives. Structural VARs are used to identify the underlying shocks to the components of aggregate demand (consumption, business investment, residential investment, exports and imports, and government spending), with the aim of identifying which components of demand showed particular weakness over the last decade. The results indicate that business investment was the main source of weakness, followed (more surprisingly) by government consumption. The stimulative impact of fiscal policy, which is examined through an extension of the basic model, is also found to be quite limited, consistent with the results reported in Chapter 2.

The causes of the weakness in business investment are examined in more detail in "Explaining the Slump in Japanese Business Investment," by Ramana Ramaswamy. The chapter considers a wide range of possible explanations, including overinvestment over the bubble period caused by weak corporate governance, the impact of the debt overhang after the bubble burst, the effects of falling stock prices, and cyclical factors. It first examines underlying theoretical issues associated with each of these explanations, and then uses the insights from this discussion to estimate an investment function designed to differentiate between these hypotheses. The results indicate that past overinvestment is the major factor in explaining the current weakness in business investment, along with falling stock prices and debt overhang. By contrast, cyclical factors and falls in bank lending appear to have had only a smaller impact. The implication is that long-term structural weaknesses may need to be worked out before a strong recovery in business investment is likely to get under way.

The final contribution to the first section of the book is "Where Are We Going? The Output Gap and Potential Growth" by Tamim Bayoumi. This chapter examines the relative roles of reductions in the growth of potential output and an expanding output gap as actual output falls below potential, and finds that they are about equally important in explaining the disappointing macroeconomic performance of Japan since 1991. It also finds that when estimates of economic slack (such as unemployment or excess capacity) are used to estimate the current output gap, the results are consistently smaller than the output gaps derived indirectly from estimates of potential output, but that this result does not hold during the height of the bubble in the early 1990s. It is suggested that this dichotomy of 1–2 percentage points of GDP reflects the temporary effect of problems in financial intermediation on output potential, an effect that can be seen in direct estimates of economic slack but not in estimates of potential output based on physical productive capacity.

The dilemmas posed by fiscal policy over the 1990s are examined in the following chapter. Many commentators have argued that fiscal stimulus has been limited because the headline figures for government stimulus packages are much larger than their real content. The general government deficit, however, has expanded by almost 10 percentage points of GDP over this period. In "Too Much of a Good Thing? The Effectiveness of Fiscal Stimulus," Martin Mühleisen tackles this conundrum by examining the "real water" content of past stimulative packages (that is, the proportion of the packages that have a direct impact on activity). He finds that, although stimulus packages have had significant levels of "real water," their effects on the deficit (and, by implication, activity) have generally been temporary because the institutional structure mitigates against incorporating stimulus packages into future budget baselines. Stimulus packages thus played a relatively minor role in the expansion of the budget deficit in the 1990s, which is largely accounted for by an unexplained fall in tax elasticity in the early 1990s, apparently related to the bursting of the bubble, and the impact of the slump of activity on tax revenues.

The effects of monetary policy on the real economy are examined in detail in Chapter 7, "Monetary Policy Transmission in Japan," by James Morsink and Tamim Bayoumi. Small monetary VARs are used to examine how interest rates and credit variables affect private sector activity. Short-term interest rates are found to have a significant impact on activity, in particular business investment, with the main conduit being private sector bank lending. Indeed, such lending is also found to have an important independent role in explaining output fluctuations, largely reflecting the lack of alternative sources of credit to businesses. The chapter concludes that banking sector problems have exerted significant downward pressure on activity throughout the 1990s and that this has tended to obscure the impact of more stimulative monetary policy.[3]

Looking to the future, it is clear that Japan's corporate structure is in need of an overhaul. The next chapter, "Financial Reorganization and Corporate Restructuring in Japan," by Joaquim Levy, examines the increasing signs of strain in the corporate sector, the recent steps toward restructuring and how much more will be needed, the institutional constraints on restructuring efforts, and government initiatives that could accelerate the process. It concludes that while genuine restructuring has now begun—particularly in large corporations—plans need to be followed through resolutely and need to extend broadly across the economy. The government can play an important part in this process by establishing an environment conducive to restructuring, and recent initiatives have been in this direction.

As in other Asian countries, unwieldy bankruptcy procedures have been an important impediment in limiting corporate restructuring. The final chapter of the book—"Reform of Japan's Insolvency Laws" also by Joaquim Levy—looks at the existing system and evaluates current plans for reform. It describes how the basis for the traditional out-of-court approach to corporate financial reorganization has been eroded since the 1980s, and how the Japanese government is considering reforms similar to those in other industrial countries to create more workable legal procedures for corporate rehabilitation.

Together, these studies present a compelling and consistent story of the Japanese economy. Financial system problems, largely triggered by the bursting of the asset price bubble in the early 1990s, caused a fall in demand that worsened in 1997 due to increased banking regulation and a premature shift toward fiscal tightening. Banking problems and lack of fiscal transparency blunted the impact of macroeconomic policies aimed at reviving the economy, and the

---

[3]A more detailed examination of bank behavior can be found in Woo (1999), which uses cross-sectional regressions on individual banks to look at bank behavior with respect to capital adequacy. It finds a change in behavior in 1997, when capital adequacy (measured either by the official numbers or market perceptions of the strength of banks) started to affect bank lending. This shows how the microeconomic behavior of banks changed over time and helps explain why the "credit crunch" started in 1997. See references of end of Chapter 7.

sustained period of weakness exposed latent problems with corporate structure and corporate governance.

The overall message is, in sum, that continued progress with the banking reform now under way and vigorous corporate restructuring are central to any sustained revival of the economy. It is very encouraging that this process now seems to be gathering considerable momentum as a number of major Japanese business corporations and financial institutions have announced ambitious restructuring and merger plans. In the short term, such restructuring may involve transitional costs in terms of higher unemployment and bankruptcies that could imply that the emerging recovery will initially be gradual—as in fact was the case with the U.S. economy as it underwent a similar period of corporate restructuring in the early 1990s. Thus, macroeconomic policies will need to remain supportive of activity (including by avoiding a premature withdrawal of fiscal stimulus or a too early tightening of monetary conditions) during this period.

# 2

# The Morning After: Explaining the Slowdown in Japanese Growth

*Tamim Bayoumi*

What explains the Japanese economic slump of the 1990s? This question has gained importance since the economy's plunge into recession in early 1997. Before the latest bout of weakness, many regarded the downturn in activity that followed the bursting of the asset price bubble in 1991 as following a normal cyclical pattern, although somewhat longer than usual due to the size of the asset deflation. In particular, the nascent signs of economic expansion through much of 1996 and early 1997 appeared to confirm that the economy was regaining its balance (albeit assisted by some demand shifting in anticipation of the consumption tax hike in April 1997), and could be expected to recover steadily over the next few years.

Rather than recovering, however, in 1997 the economy entered its first recession since the early 1970s from which activity has still not fully rebounded. Combined with the earlier weakness, this means that by 1999 Japan has been in a slump for almost eight years. Growth averaged only slightly over 1 percent a year over the 1991–99 period, and the output gap is estimated to have moved from plus 4½ percentage points of potential output in late 1990 to minus 7½ percent by late 1998.[1] This amounted to the most serious economic

---

[1]Based on IMF estimates at the time of writing. The adjustments discussed in Chapter 5 have not been incorporated into these data. However, for reasons discussed below, these revisions are unlikely to materially affect the results.

slowdown experienced by any major industrial country since the early 1950s. Furthermore, this slump occurred despite significant countercyclical policies, involving a considerable expansion in the fiscal deficit (partly through packages aimed at fiscal expansion) and a reduction in the official discount rate to a record low of ½ of 1 percent in September 1995.

The proximate causes of the initial slowdown in output in the early 1990s are generally agreed. In mid-1989 the Bank of Japan started to raise interest rates so as to cool the asset price inflation that had started in the mid-1980s. The tightening of monetary policy pricked what was later identified as an asset price bubble, and stock and land prices started falling rapidly. Just as the run-up of asset prices in the upswing of the bubble had encouraged domestic spending and driven the economy significantly above potential output, so the collapse of asset prices lowered domestic demand and output, and the economy grew at an annual rate of 1 percent or less through 1994.

As the Japanese slowdown turned from temporary slowdown to slump, however, its causes came under further scrutiny, and a number of competing hypotheses emerged. They fall into four main categories. The first is that the slump reflected *inadequate policy responses*, particularly as regards fiscal expansion (Posen, 1998). Although the Japanese government unveiled a number of fiscal packages aimed at reviving the economy over the 1990s, the argument goes, most of these packages contained limited amounts of "real water" (that is measures that have a direct impact on activity). The main exception was the September 1995 stimulus package, to which the economy responded vigorously until the recovery was derailed by a switch to fiscal contraction in early 1997.[2] The implications of this analysis is that fiscal policy is effective, the downturn reflects the normal cyclical factors, and it is the absence of sufficiently bold fiscal policies that explains the length of the Japanese recession.

An alternative view, which focuses on monetary policy, holds that Japan has been stuck in a *liquidity trap* (Krugman, 1998).[3] Consumption is historically low in Japan, creating a high structural saving rate, which was offset during the golden years by high investment. How-

---

[2]See Chapter 6 for a more detailed discussion of fiscal policy over the 1990s.
[3]See Keynes (1936) and Hicks (1937).

11

ever, a slowdown in anticipated growth has led to a sufficiently large imbalance between saving and investment that the equilibrium real interest is now negative. The anti-inflationary reputation of the Bank of Japan is sufficiently strong that expectations of future inflation are low. As a result, despite record low nominal short- and long-term interest rates, the monetary authorities are unable to reduce the real interest rate sufficiently far to bring the economy back to full employment. Under this analysis, monetary policy is the most effective instrument for countercyclical policy (while past fiscal stimulus has had limited impact because of Ricardian effects), but as a result of the anti-inflationary credentials of the Bank of Japan it has lost traction and is hence unable to pull the economy out of its slump.[4]

A third view holds that the slowdown has reflected the *low rate of return to capital owing to overinvestment* (Ando, 1998). Japan is in a vicious cycle, in which past overinvestment is reducing the rate of return on capital, which both lowers current investment and spurs saving, as consumers fail to achieve their desired level of asset accumulation. The usual wealth effects that cause cyclical downturns are being elongated by the inefficiency of the corporate sector, exacerbated by a significant corporate debt overhang that further reduces the incentive to invest. In the absence of wealth-creating investment opportunities, the economy will remain depressed.[5] This view gives primacy to wealth effects (largely through the stock market, as land prices have divergent effects on property owners and those with no land) in explaining the prolonged slowdown in Japan, while the structural nature of the imbalance between saving and investment explains and the inability of countercyclical policies produces a significant private sector response.

A final view holds that the slump reflects *problems with financial intermediation*. Banks play a much more important role in financial intermediation in Japan than in Anglo-Saxon financial systems such as the United States or United Kingdom,[6] and are the main providers

---

[4]Traditional monetarists, however, argue that the liquidity trap is an illusion, and that the problem with policy has been the lack of expansion of the monetary base. This hypothesis will also be considered below.

[5]Some have also pointed to demographic effects in this connection, with the aging population depressing investment more than saving.

[6]See Borio (1996) for a cross-country comparison of financial systems.

of loans to small and medium-sized enterprises. During the asset price bubble, the banks lent large amounts of money to firms using land as collateral. With the dramatic fall in land prices since the bursting of the asset price bubble, many of these loans have stopped performing. The bubble in stock prices further exacerbated these effects by first boosting and then reducing bank capital.[7] Lax accounting rules and a permissive regulatory environment have allowed banks to survive, but with only limited ability to lend to companies because of the competing need to write off bad loans and maintain capital adequacy ratios.[8] As a result, the most productive parts of the corporate sector have been starved of new loans, and small and medium-sized companies in particular have thus been unable to play their usual role as leading sectors in the economic recovery.[9] Under this view, lending constraints have been the major constraint on the economy, and the inability to obtain finance has limited the effectiveness of monetary policy (which largely operates through banks) and the ability of the private sector to respond to fiscal stimulus.[10]

These explanations are not mutually exclusive. Indeed, it would be unlikely that a slump of the type experienced in Japan would have a single cause. However, each explanation points to a different set of variables as the major factor explaining the slump.[11] They also point to different explanations of the mini-revival in 1996 and early 1997, with the fiscal and liquidity trap explanations pointing to fiscal stimulus and falling real interest rates (and real exchange rates), respec-

---

[7]Bank capital is susceptible to changes in stock prices because Japanese banks typically hold large amounts of stock in industrial companies. Kwon (1998) explores the relationship between monetary policy, land prices, bank lending, and output using a VAR.

[8]See Ogawa and others (1996) and Ogawa and Suzuki (1998) for evidence on how land collateral has affected investment by Japanese firms.

[9]See Ogawa and Kitasaka (1998) for a discussion of the determinants of bank lending and its possible impact on investment, and Wescott (1996) for a discussion of the role of small and medium-sized companies in the 1995–96 upturn in activity.

[10]Monetary policy transmission is discussed further in Chapter 7.

[11]These explanations also correspond to the alternative explanations of the recovery of the United States from the 1930s' depression. The fiscal explanation, for example, is favored by Gordon (1988), the liquidity trap by Romer (1992), while the role of financial intermediation is discussed in Bernanke (1983). For a comparison of the role of banks and monetary policy in the two periods, see Bordo, Ito, and Iwaisako (1997).

tively, as the main cause of this upturn. The other two explanations, on the other hand, imply that the economy continued its stagnation over this period. The logical corollary is that the upturn was largely illusory, with continuing weakness being obscured by a shift in demand in anticipation of the April 1997 consumption tax hike. These "structural" explanations also imply weakness in different components of domestic demand. If wealth effects are a major cause of the slump, one would expect to see significant movements in consumption in addition to investment, while if the problems are mainly due to financial intermediation, it is more likely to be seen in business investment and, to a lesser extent, residential investment given the limited access of Japanese consumers to bank loans.

This chapter examines the reasons for the slowdown in activity in Japan empirically using vector-autoregressions (VARs) involving the main competing explanations: fiscal policy, monetary policy (including the exchange rate), domestic asset prices, and lending to the private sector. A VAR approach was chosen for a number of reasons. It allows the variables underlying the alternative explanations to be incorporated into a single empirical approach. For example, their impacts on output can be compared using the relevant impulse response functions. In addition, estimating a system of equations allows interactions between different variables to be examined, in particular the relationship between domestic asset prices, lending, and output, as well as allowing changes in underlying behavior to be assessed through examination of the residuals from individual equations. Finally, the historical role of each variable can be examined using the decomposition of past movements in output implied by the VAR.

## Past Trends

Before discussing more formal analysis of the causes of the slowdown in Japan in the 1990s, it may be useful to look at the underlying data for output and for domestic demand and its components over the period since 1980.[12] As can be seen in Figure 2.1, output has gone

---

[12]The year 1980 was chosen as a start for the empirical analysis to ensure that there was a significant period before the bubble economy of the mid-1980s, allowing the extended cycle in output since 1987 to be put in context. As discussed

Figure 2.1. Output and Demand Developments

*(Trillions of 1990 yen; Logarithmic scale)*

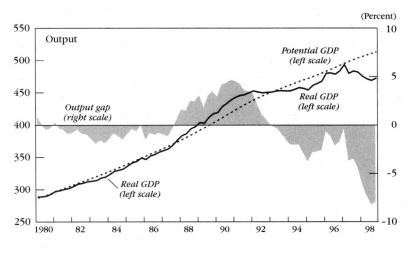

Sources: Nikkei Telecom; WEFA; and IMF staff estimates.

through a number of cycles over the last two decades, following a relatively stable growth path from 1980 through 1987, expanding rapidly through the next few years to 1991, and then stagnating from then through early 1995. This is followed by a very limited recovery through early 1997, and a renewed collapse in output that was still continuing in late 1998.[13] The figure also shows the IMF's estimate of potential output based on a Cobb-Douglas production function and the resulting path for the gap.[14] The path shows the cyclical path of the economy even more clearly, including the cyclical peaks in 1990–91 and 1997, and troughs in 1983, 1995, and the current downturn.

---

later in the text, extending the period back to 1973 (to the golden period of exceptionally vigorous Japanese economic growth, in which the underlying forces shaping the economy were probably somewhat different than they were subsequently) has little impact on the results.

[13]The data for total domestic demand have a similar pattern, although the period before 1987 looks somewhat less buoyant.

[14]See Chapter 5 for a more detailed discussion of the IMF's estimate of the output gap. This study was completed before the revisions discussed in that chapter were completed.

The advantage of correcting for potential output is that it provides a path for the cyclical element in output, which is primarily affected by short-term factors such as changes in aggregate demand. Given the prolonged stagnation of output in Japan, however, any estimate of the path of potential output is highly uncertain. The IMF staff estimate takes account of the impact of changes in business investment on underlying growth, and of demographic changes, in particular, the slowing of growth in the workforce over recent years. Because the calculation is based on a production function, it is less affected by the end-point of the data than other, more statistical approaches, such as a Hodrick-Prescott filter. This is particularly important in this exercise, as the data set ends in 1998 with the Japanese economy in the midst of a recession, so that any procedure that attempts to detrend based solely on the path of output will tend to underestimate the size of the output gap.[15] Indeed, the concern with the IMF staff estimate of the output gap used here is the opposite, namely that it may take too little account of certain underlying factors that may have lowered the growth in potential output over the 1990s, such as reductions in the rate of return on capital caused by the excesses of the investment boom over the bubble years or the possible slowing of the rate of technological progress because of inefficiencies in the allocation of capital.[16] Despite such uncertainties, the path of potential output provides a useful way of eliminating the underlying supply factors affecting the economy and is used as such in the formal analysis. In any case, the VAR is estimated in first differences, which minimizes the impact of errors in estimating potential output.

The behavior of individual components of demand can also provide insight as to the sources of the recent slowdown in demand. Figures 2.2 and 2.3 graph paths of private consumption, business investment, net exports, government consumption, government investment, and residential investment, measured as a ratio to output.[17] If the

---

[15]Krugman (1998) makes a similar point.

[16]See Chapter 5.

[17]Each component of demand is measured in three ways: nominal spending as a percentage of observed nominal GDP; real demand as a percentage of observed real GDP, which adjusts for changes in relative prices over time; and real demand as a percentage of potential output, which takes account of both relative prices and the cycle.

## Figure 2.2. Major Demand Components

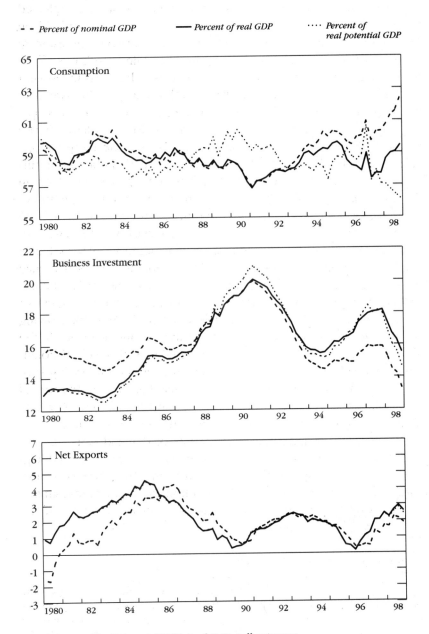

Sources: Nikkei Telecom; WEFA; and IMF staff estimates.

## Figure 2.3.  Minor Demand Components

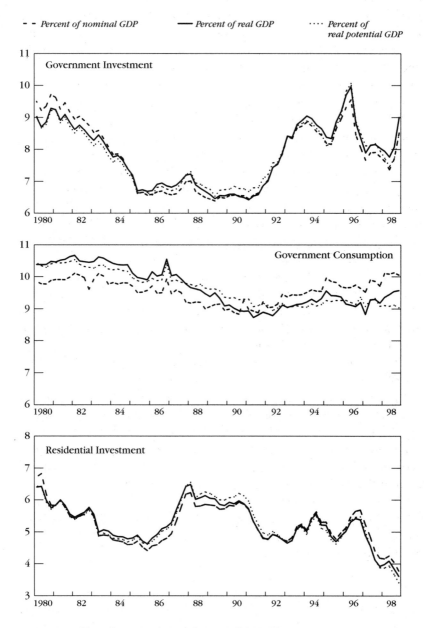

Sources: Nikkei Telecom; WEFA; and IMF staff estimates.

downturn in output during the 1990s largely tracks consumption, then one would assume that it reflected wealth effects of some form, while weakness in business investment would point more toward financial intermediation. To aid comparison, movements in the three major components of demand (private consumption, business investment, and net exports) are measured on the same scale, as are movements in the three more minor components of demand (government consumption, government investment, and residential investment).

Business investment is clearly the most cyclical element of demand since 1980, increasing markedly as a percentage of GDP over the bubble years compared with the period before or since. The underlying trend in investment is also significantly affected by movements in relative prices, with nominal spending staying fairly constant as a ratio to nominal GDP between the early 1980s and the later 1990s, but the corresponding ratio using real values has increased significantly, reflecting a decline in the relative price of investment goods (a reverse trend of this type holds for net exports).[18] By contrast, private consumption has been relatively stable as a ratio to GDP over the last two decades, fluctuating within a relatively narrow range between 57 percent and 61 percent of GDP. The alternative calculations illustrate this stability. Measured as a percentage of observed output, consumption is relatively low over the bubble years, while it is relatively high as a percentage of potential output, because most of the variation is in the denominator rather than the numerator. The source of this stability may well be the limited access of individual Japanese to the stock market (household assets are generally held in bank deposits, while banks are important owners of stocks) and to bank loans, the main factors that fueled consumption booms in other economies with asset bubbles and crashes, such as the United Kingdom in the mid-1980s or the Nordic countries in the late 1980s.[19]

Like their private sector counterparts, government investment has been significantly more variable than government consumption, although in this case it reflects government policies rather than maximizing behavior. The rapid increase in the ratio of government in-

---

[18]See also Chapter 3 for discussion of the behavior of components of aggregate demand.

[19]For a more detailed discussion of the experience of the Nordic countries, see Drees and Pazarbaşioğlu (1998).

Table 2.1. Comparison of the United States in the 1920–1930s and Japan in the 1980–1990s

| | United States | | | Japan | | |
|---|---|---|---|---|---|---|
| | 1920–29 | 1930–33 | 1934–37 | 1981–90 | 1991–94 | 1995–98[1] |
| Growth of real output | 4.4 | –8.6 | 8.7 | 4.5 | 1.4 | 0.9 |
| Inflation rate | –1.7 | –8.2 | 2.7 | 1.7 | 1.7 | 0.6 |
| Commercial paper rate[2] | 5.0 | 2.6 | 0.8 | 5.8 | 3.7 | 0.5 |
| Government bond rate | 4.1 | 3.4 | 2.8 | 6.6 | 4.9 | 2.6 |
| Central government balance/output | 0.1 | –0.2 | –0.4 | –3.1 | –2.2 | –4.0[3] |
| Share price | 12.8 | –8.7 | 15.1 | 16.4 | –9.3 | –6.2 |
| Bank loans | 2.6 | –14.1 | 1.0 | 10.0 | 2.8 | –0.2 |

Sources: Japanese data from IMF, U.S. data from the National Bureau of Economic Research (NBER) supplied by Michael Bordo.
[1]1995:Q1–1998:Q2 unless otherwise indicated.
[2]Gensaki rate for Japan.
[3]FY1996 and FY1997. The FY1997 data are IMF estimates.

vestment to GDP over most of the 1990s reflects the conscious use of government spending to counter weakness in the private sector, with the spike in spending after the September 1995 fiscal package being particularly notable. As might be expected, residential investment shows a significant increase over the bubble period, encouraged by increases in the relative price of land. Also notable is the spike in residential investment associated with anticipation of the consumption tax hike on April 1, 1997, an increase that finds no parallel at the time of the introduction of the consumption tax in early 1989.

It is also instructive to compare Japan's current slump with that of the United States in the 1930s. As can be seen in Table 2.1, the period leading up to the decline in asset prices and output were quite similar in both countries in terms of economic growth and interest rates, although bank lending grew significantly faster in Japan. The United States then experienced a very rapid fall in output and prices over 1930–33, followed by an equally vigorous recovery associated with higher share prices, increases in bank loans, and negative short-term interest rates. By contrast, in Japan the slump gathered steam over eight years, with growth and inflation declining over the second half of the period compared with the first, together with most financial indicators continuing to deteriorate. The most striking feature of the Japanese slump is not its severity (it has been relatively mild in many respects) but its length, which seems to have been extended far beyond that of a "normal" business cycle.

## Econometric Analysis

This section reports the results from VARs using output, two fiscal variables (the structural general government deficit is divided into direct government spending and taxes net of transfers[20]), two monetary variables (the real short-term interest rate and the real exchange rate), two domestic asset prices (real stock prices and real land prices[21]), and financial intermediation. (Data sources are provided in the appendix.) Financial intermediation was measured as lending to the private sector by banks, public institutions, and capital markets. As private bank lending turns out to be the most important component, representing over 70 percent of all lending and dominating quarter-to-quarter changes, this series will be simply referred to as bank lending below.[22] Output and real bank lending were divided by potential output to eliminate the trends caused by expanding supply, and logarithms were taken of those variables with no clear unit of measurement (the real exchange rate, real stock prices, real land prices, and real lending). In addition to a constant term, the VARs also included two dummy variables aimed at capturing the short-term shifting of demand seen the quarter before and after the introduction of the consumption tax in 1989 and the consumption tax hike in April 1997, with each variable being designed so that the impact sums to zero over time.

---

[20]The fiscal variables are adjusted for the cycle using the IMF's standard approach, which involves correcting taxes and social security contributions for the impact of the output gap using a buoyancy ratio, government spending for the impact of unemployment (a relatively unimportant effect in Japan, with its limited social safety net), and dividing the relevant totals by potential output.

[21]The role of real land prices in wealth is tricky, as changes in prices affect homeowners very differently from prospective buyers. Land prices can have an aggregate impact on the household sector in some circumstances, even if these groups behave differently from each other. In addition, the price of land is an important consideration for bank loans, as it provides the main form of collateral.

[22]As discussed later, the results are not sensitive to alternative measures of lending.

Figure 2.4. Underlying Variables

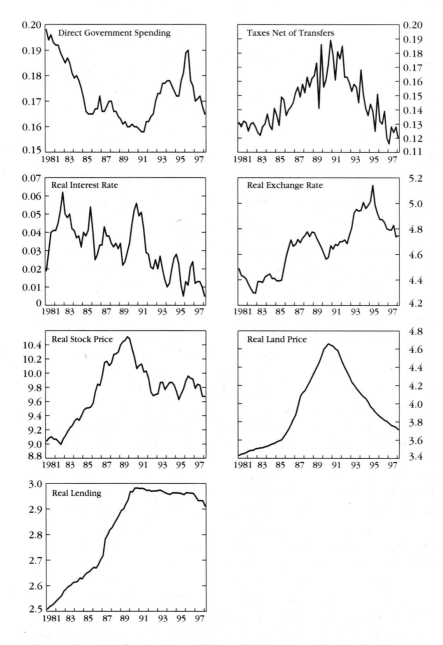

Sources: Economic Planning Agency (EPA) and WEFA. See text for more details.

## Table 2.2. Dickey-Fuller Test Results

| | Level | | First | Second |
| --- | --- | --- | --- | --- |
| | No trend | Trend | Difference | Difference |
| Output | 0.80 | 0.95 | 0.00 | 0.00 |
| Direct government spending | 0.25 | 0.76 | 0.00 | 0.00 |
| Taxes net of transfers | 0.03 | 0.11 | 0.00 | 0.00 |
| Real interest rate | 0.55 | 0.07 | 0.00 | 0.00 |
| Real exchange rate | 0.76 | 0.84 | 0.00 | 0.00 |
| Real land prices | 0.62 | 1.00 | 0.43 | 0.00 |
| Real stock prices | 0.51 | 0.96 | 0.00 | 0.00 |
| Real bank lending | 0.05 | 1.00 | 0.00 | 0.00 |
| *Memorandum items:* | | | | |
| Private consumption | 0.38 | 0.63 | 0.00 | 0.00 |
| Business investment | 0.79 | 0.98 | 0.00 | 0.00 |
| Residential investment | 0.48 | 0.82 | 0.00 | 0.00 |

Source: Author's calculations.

The first stage in the analysis involved investigating the statistical properties of the underlying series. The output gap is shown in Figure 2.1, while those of the other explanatory variables are shown in Figure 2.4. Even though most of the series are adjusted by potential output, many still appear nonstationary, with no tendency to revert to an underlying mean value or trend. This even appears to be true of the output gap, despite the fact that output should at some point revert to its level of potential. As discussed earlier, this presumably reflects the depth of the current recession, which makes it appear that deviations from trend can be permanent.

Formal analysis confirms these visual impressions. Table 2.2 shows the results from running Dickey-Fuller tests on the various components of the VARs. Almost all of the variables, including the output gap, fail to accept stationarity (without the inclusion of a time trend). Even the two exceptions, bank lending and taxes net of transfers, fail the test when a time trend is included, spectacularly so in the case of real lending. When the variables are first differenced, however, the opposite result holds true, with almost all of the variables accepting stationarity. The exception is real land prices, where the test cannot reject nonstationarity. After some experimentation using both first and second differences, the first difference of land prices was used in the VARs, as this did not appear to cause problems in the estimation.

It remains possible that there are cointegrating relationships between the levels of the variables, which would imply estimating the

Table 2.3. Results from the Johansen Procedure

| Number of Cointegrating Relationships | Trace Test | 90% Critical Value | λ Max | 90% Critical Value |
|---|---|---|---|---|
| 1 | 237.8 | 150.0 | 61.5 | 32.3 |
| 2 | 176.3 | 117.7 | 55.6 | 38.4 |
| 3 | 120.7 | 89.4 | 39.6 | 24.6 |
| 4 | 81.1 | 64.7 | 29.9 | 20.9 |
| 5 | 51.2 | 43.8 | 23.0 | 17.2 |
| 6 | 28.3 | 26.7 | 15.2 | 13.4 |

Notes: The test assumes that all variables have integration one and that there are two lags in the underlying VAR.

equation in levels terms. To investigate this, the model was estimated using the Johansen (1991) procedure, in which the number of cointegrating variables can be tested, although the tests are asymptotic and may not be very robust in the current context given the relatively short sample (under 20 years) and large number of variables. The results of such a test, shown in Table 2.3, indicate a large number of cointegrating relationships. However, none have particularly intuitive properties when normalized with respect to output.[23] As an alternative approach, the VAR was estimated in levels terms, which is equivalent to assuming there is one cointegrating relationships for each equation. Again, the estimated cointegrating relationship for output were unsatisfactory and, in addition, the impulse responses from this system exhibited considerable cycling and instability.[24] Accordingly, it was decided to focus on VARs using only first differences. Such an approach has the additional advantage that the constant terms in the estimation act as trends, making the estimation less dependent on the assumptions made about the path of potential output.

Accordingly, a VAR involving the first difference of the output gap, the other explanatory variables, a constant term, and dummy variables for the consumption tax changes of 1989 and 1997 was esti-

---

[23]Different assumptions about the number of lags and the deterministic trends produced similar results.

[24]These results probably reflect the fact that including a levels relationship in a VAR that already has two lags (to provide reasonable flexibility in the dynamic responses) implies estimating a high ratio of parameters to observation (27 parameters from 67 observations). This inevitably lowers the precision of the estimates.

mated from the first quarter of 1981 to the first quarter of 1998.[25] Two lags were used in the estimation as this was the lag length indicated by the Akaiki Information Criterion.[26] A Choleski decomposition was used to orthogonalize the underlying errors using the ordering: direct government spending, taxes net of transfers, the output gap, the real exchange rate, real stock prices, real land prices, and real bank lending. The ordering determines the level of exogeneity of the variables, with changes in government spending being assumed independent of all other explanatory variables, while current changes in bank lending are assumed to be affected by changes in all of the other explanatory variables. The ordering was chosen on the basis of the speed with which the variables respond to current events, with fiscal variables assumed to be the least responsive, followed by output, then monetary policy, asset prices, and bank lending.

The estimated impulse responses for output, shown in Figure 2.5, are generally intuitive.[27] The top left panel of the figure, for example, reports the impulse response of the level of output to a one standard deviation shock in direct government spending, together with the level response of direct government spending to its own shock (all of the variables are measured in such a manner that a change of 0.01 represents a 1 percent changes in the relevant variable[28]). An increase in direct government spending provides the expected temporary boost to the economy while an increase in taxes lowers activity. The dynamic multiplier for direct government spending, calculated using the ratio between the response of output and the response of government investment, indicates that in the short term a ¥100 increase in government spending raises output by about ¥65.[29] This stimulus

---

[25]The start date of 1981 reflects the need to accommodate transformations of the underlying data and lags in the VAR.

[26]The Schwartz Bayesian information criterion implied an optimal lag length of three. VARs using a third lag were also estimated, as discussed later.

[27]Note that these responses refer to the levels of output, and so on. As the model was estimated in first differences, underlying disturbances can result in permanent changes in the underlying variables.

[28]This is achieved through measuring the variable in logarithms, as a ratio to potential output or, in the case of the real interest rate, by dividing the percentage value by 100.

[29]These estimates are significantly smaller than the multipliers produced from large models (the IMF, for example, has estimated a multiplier of 1–1.2 in its analysis, see Lipworth and Meredith, 1998).

## Figure 2.5. Impulse Response Functions

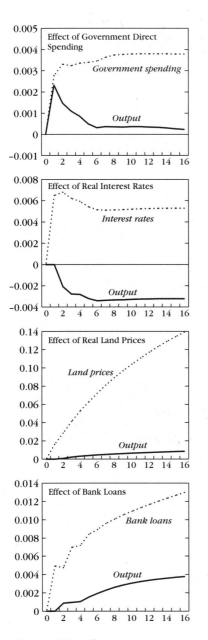
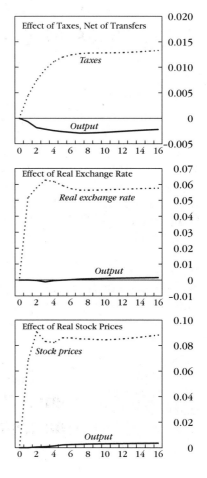

Source: IMF staff estimates.

wears off quite rapidly, and after about a year output is estimated to be roughly unchanged. This is consistent with those who have argued that higher government spending has been relatively ineffective over time because uncertainty about the timing and "real water" content of stimulus packages, and the choice of projects with low social rates of return. The implied multiplier from a tax increase, which peaks at −0.2 (in absolute value) after two quarters, is again quite small. This is consistent with the view that Japanese consumers are relatively Ricardian, although the focus on temporary tax cuts in the stimulus packages of the 1990s, rather than permanent changes in the tax system, is also likely to have lowered the multiplier.[30] In short, while fiscal policy is effective in stimulating output, the estimated impact is muted.

An increase in the real interest rate of 1 percentage point lowers output by about 0.6 percent. This is consistent with, although at the lower end of, the wide range of estimates from large models (see Krugman, 1998).[31] An increase in the real exchange rate also lowers output in the short term, although the effect is quite small—a 10 percent increase in the real exchange rate lowering output by about 0.2 percent, reflecting the relatively closed nature of the Japanese economy. Output rises in response to an increase in the real price of land and, to a lesser extent, to an increase in the price of stocks. Notably, it also rises quite significantly in response to an increase in bank lending, with a 3 percent increase in such lending leading to a 1 percent rise in output. The absolute size of the various impulse response functions is also illuminating, as they illustrate the impact of a "typical" disturbance in each variable on output. The largest response is associated with land prices, where a typical quarterly disturbance changes output by about 1 percent over time, compared with a value of 0.3 percent for real interest rates.

Figure 2.6 reports the standard errors around the responses of output (calculated using Monte Carlo methods with 500 replications), which indicate that the short-term responses are reasonably well identified. Over longer periods, however, the degree of precision deteriorates, because the underlying impulse responses are cumulated over time, compounding uncertainty.

---

[30]Bayoumi, Towe, and Oishi (1998) discuss in more detail various reasons how the implementation of fiscal stimulus may have muted its effects over the 1990s.

[31]When the real interest rate was divided into the nominal rate and inflation, it was found that each component was correctly signed and contributed about one-half to the estimated impact.

Figure 2.6. Impulse Response Functions: Output and
Standard Errors

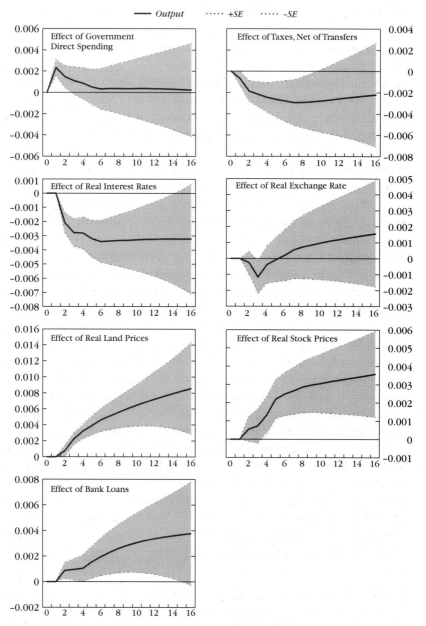

Source: IMF staff estimates.

Tests indicate that the results are relatively invariant to alternative orderings of most of the variables. This, however, is not the case for the relative position of land prices to stock prices or to bank lending, because of a significant colinearity between the residuals. If land prices are placed after the other two variables in the ordering, the estimated long-term impact on output becomes similar across all three variables. The ordering chosen was felt to be the most "reasonable," in that land prices are the least likely variable to be immediately affected by other developments. The nexus of domestic asset prices and bank lending is discussed further below.

To this point, the analysis has focused on the output responses implied by the system. It is also of interest to examine the most important interrelationships between the individual equations comprising the VAR, as these provide information as to the transmission mechanisms at work. These interrelationships can be analyzed through F-tests of the significance of each variable in each equation (Granger causality tests). The results from this exercise again are in accord with intuition. Output is most affected by past changes in real interest rates (note that the main impact of direct government spending is contemporaneous, as government consumption and investment feed through directly into GDP), and least affected by own shocks and real stock prices. Fiscal policy and the real interest rate are relatively independent of the other variables in the model, indicating that government policy decisions are made relatively autonomously, while the real exchange rate is also largely independent of the rest of the model.

By contrast, there are important interactions between stock prices, land prices, and bank lending. As can be seen from the impulse responses in Figure 2.7, positive disturbances in any one of these variables produce increases in all of them. This mutually reinforcing interaction helps explain the asset bubble of the late 1980s. It reflects, at least in part, the importance of domestic asset prices in the behavior of banks, with land being used as the most usual form of collateral, and shareholdings being an important source of bank capital.[32] In the 1990s, this process apparently went into reverse, hurting the economy

---

[32]Kwon (1998), also using a VAR approach, finds that collateral effects increase the impact of monetary policy on the economy, but does not explore the wider set of interactions examined in this paper. Lincoln (1998) provides a detailed discussion of the Japanese system of financial intermediation.

## Figure 2.7. Impulse Response of Financial Variables

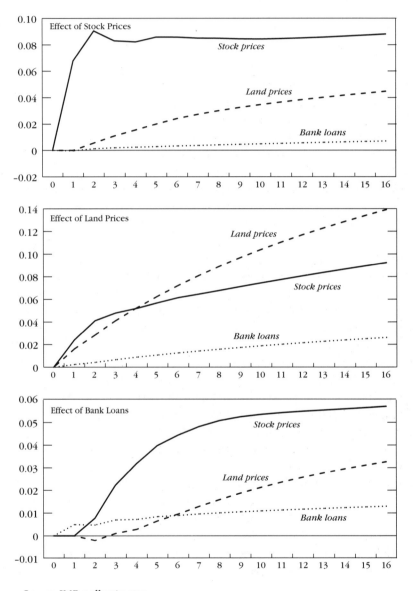

Source: IMF staff estimates.

through a reinforcing erosion of bank collateral, capital, and loans (called by some of the more melodramatic commentators the Japanese "death spiral").

The importance of these interactions can be examined by rerunning the VAR with one of the variables exogenized. This is done by excluding the chosen variable from the VAR, but including its first two lags as exogenous variables. The estimated equations for the remaining variables are identical to the main case, but any interactions involving the exogenized variable are no longer identified. When bank lending is exogenized in this manner, the impulse response of land price on output is lowered by almost 90 percent while the impulse response of stock prices falls by two-thirds, implying that the vast majority of the estimated impact of asset prices on output comes through financial intermediation.[33] Exogenizing land prices and stock prices in a similar manner also produces significant, if somewhat less spectacular, reductions in the impulse responses of the remaining financial variables with respect to output. In short, there appears to be a close and highly interwoven interrelationship between domestic asset prices and bank lending, an interrelationship that helps to explain the size and longevity of the estimated effects of each of these variables on output.

The cumulated residuals from each equation, shown in Figure 2.8, help to illustrate the direction of the underlying shocks (assuming the shocks are random, they should cumulate to random walks, which have apparent trends over time). In addition to illustrating policy changes (such as the spike in government spending after the September 1995 stimulus package was announced and the tightening of monetary policy in late 1989), the results also illustrate the rise and fall in domestic asset prices over the bubble and subsequent crash, the increase in bank lending in the early 1980s (a time of significant deregulation) and more recent weakness, and the large positive shocks to output in 1996, prior to the consumption tax hike.

The decomposition of past movements in output implied by the model is shown in Figure 2.9. Past changes in the output gap are divided into those parts explained by innovations in fiscal policy (the

---

[33]Reversing the ordering of land and stock prices in the VAR leads to a fall of about three-quarters in both impulse responses, when bank lending is exogenized.

Figure 2.8. Cumulative Residuals

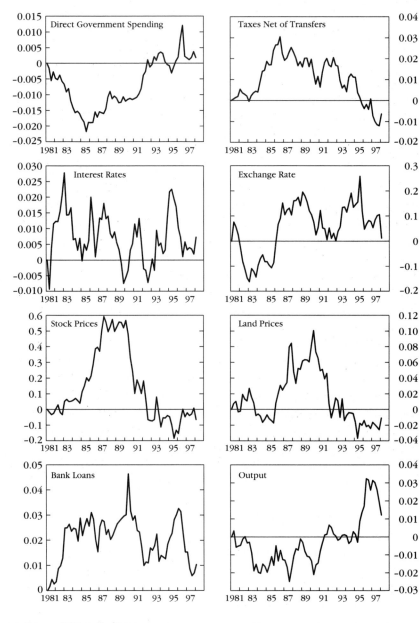

Source: IMF staff estimates.

Figure 2.9. Decomposition of Output

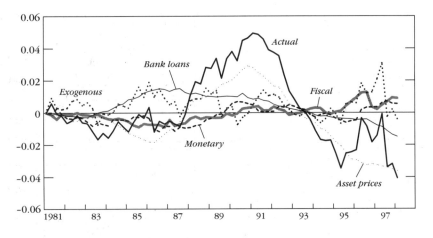

Source: IMF staff estimates.

sum of direct government spending and taxes net of transfers), monetary policy (the sum of real interest rates and the real exchange rate), asset prices (the sum of land prices and share prices), bank lending, and exogenous disturbances (the sum of independent shocks to output, the dummy variables, and any effects due to unidentified disturbances prior to the estimation period). Note that, as unidentified disturbances to output are included in the "exogenous" term, it is possible to conclude that past movements in output are not very well explained by any of the explanatory variables in the model—the underlying hypotheses can all be refuted.

The decomposition indicates that the most important factor explaining past movements in output is innovations in asset prices, accounting for most of the hump in the output gap over the bubble period and subsequent weakness. Changes in bank lending help to explain the rise in output in the early- to mid-1980s and more recent weakness in activity, indicating that shocks to bank lending can also generate significant movements in output. Monetary policy was supportive though the bubble period, restrictive through much of the 1990s, and more recently again providing a significant boost to the economy. Fiscal policy provided a significant boost to the economy in 1995 and early 1996, but this support was rapidly with-

33

**Figure 2.10. Decomposition of Output: Detailed Results**

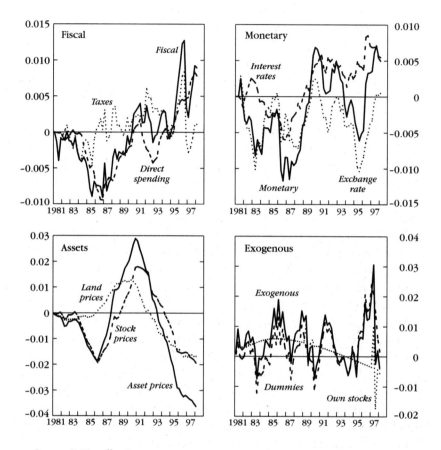

Source: IMF staff estimates.

drawn in the later part of 1996. While exogenous factors play an important role in explaining quarter-to-quarter variation in output, they only matter for overall movements in output over the more recent period.

Figure 2.10 decomposes the aggregate fiscal, monetary, asset price, and exogenous effects into their constituent parts (in the case of fiscal policy, for example, the effects of direct government spending and taxes net of transfers are distinguished). They indicate that the fiscal expansion of 1996 was largely fueled by direct government spending,[34] mirroring the sharp increase and subsequent fall in government investment, that changes in real interest rates have been the most important monetary policy channel, and that changes in land prices have been generally more important than stock prices in explaining movements in output.

Possibly the most striking result, particularly when compared with the bubble period, is the significant role played by own shocks in increasing output in late 1996 and early 1997 and reducing it subsequently. The most intuitive interpretation of this is that it reflects longer-term demand shifting from the consumption tax hike rather than that captured by the existing dummy variable, particularly for residential investment (Figure 2.3). This hypothesis is supported by the results from adding a third dummy variable to the model, allowing the 1997 tax hike to affect demand from the beginning of 1996. These estimates (not reported for the sake of brevity) indicate there was a substantial boost to output from early 1996 to early 1997 because of the consumption tax hike, followed by a fall in 1997 and early 1998 (this change in the specification had little impact on other responses).

The historical decomposition also has implications for the differing explanations for the mini-revival of output in 1996. The results shown in Figure 2.9 indicate that fiscal policy and monetary policy both contributed, each providing a boost of about 1 percent to output. However, the underlying situation appears to have started worsening in late 1996 (in part because of a sharp fall in public investment), an underlying weakness that was obscured by demand shifting in anticipation of the consumption tax hike.

The importance of bank lending as a conduit for asset price effects is illustrated in Figure 2.11, which graphs the estimated impact of land prices and stock prices on output once bank lending has been exogenized as described earlier. In this experiment, asset prices produce very limited movements in output, indicating that the "pure" effects of changes in wealth are quite limited.[35] A comparison of Figure 2.9 and

---

[34]By contrast, fiscal contraction in the 1980s largely operated through tax increases.

[35]When the ordering of land and stock prices in the VAR is reversed, the impact of stock prices increases, but still only accounts for a variation in the output gap of around 1 percentage point of GDP over the 1990s.

Figure 2.11. Decomposition of Output with Lending Exogenized

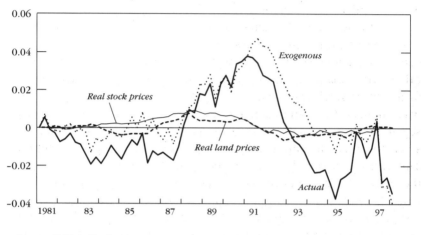

Source: IMF staff estimates.

2.11 vividly illustrates the central role played by financial intermediation in transmitting asset price shocks to the real economy.

The discussion to this point has focused on a single specification. To examine the robustness of the model, the VAR was reestimated under a number of alternative assumptions. The lag length of the VAR was extended from two lags to three lags, which produced very similar results (with more complex impulse responses). Next, the impact of changing the estimation period was examined, both by truncating the sample at the first quarter of 1996 to avoid the distortions associated with the consumption tax hike in 1997, and by extending the estimation period back to 1973. The VAR was rerun using nominal variables instead of their real equivalents, to examine whether nominal asset price changes produce a more significant impact on the model. Finally, experiments using different proxies for financial intermediation (restricting the variable to cover only bank lending or only lending to the corporate sector) were also conducted. None of these experiments changed the qualitative nature of the results.[36]

In another type of experiment, additional variables were included in the estimation. First, the old-age dependency ratio was added to

---

[36]Detailed results can be obtained from the author.

the VAR, in order to examine the role of demographic changes in explaining the bubble and subsequent slump. Demographic changes were found to increase output by about ½ of 1 percent over the 1980s and lower it by the same amount over the 1990s. At least some of this effect comes through asset prices, in that increases in the old-age dependency ratio were found to lower domestic stock and land prices, presumably reflecting the reduced demand for such assets from older individuals. The impact on the remainder of the model was minimal. Next, the capital stock was also added to the VAR, to see if a direct measure of overinvestment (the ratio of the capital stock to potential output) helps to explain past changes in output. This variable also had minimal effects either on output or the rest of the model. Finally, real narrow money (M1) was substituted for the real interest rate to see if a different measure of monetary policy had a significant effect on the results. The money supply provides a good substitute for the real interest rates within the estimation, but has very little impact on the other impulse responses. Exogenizing bank loans in this system still generates significant reductions in the impact on output of shocks to land prices (down by two-thirds) and stock prices (down by one-third), although these effects are somewhat smaller than when real interest rates are used. Hence, even with the money supply included, bank loans still appear to be an important conduit for asset price effects.[37]

An alternative way of examining the robustness of the results is to consider what happens when variables other than output are used in the VAR. In particular, if the conclusions from this analysis are valid, one would expect that same types of patterns found for output to be apparent in an analysis using the major components of aggregate demand. Accordingly, the VAR was reestimated three times, with output each time being replaced by a different major component of demand (private consumption, business fixed investment, and residential investment).[38]

The estimated impulse responses for each component of demand are shown in Figure 2.12. The impulse response functions for output from the various shocks appear generally sensible. Increases in gov-

---

[37]Very similar results were also found using real broad money (M2 + CDs).

[38]Like output, these variables were normalized by dividing by potential output.

Figure 2.12. Impulse Response Components of Demand

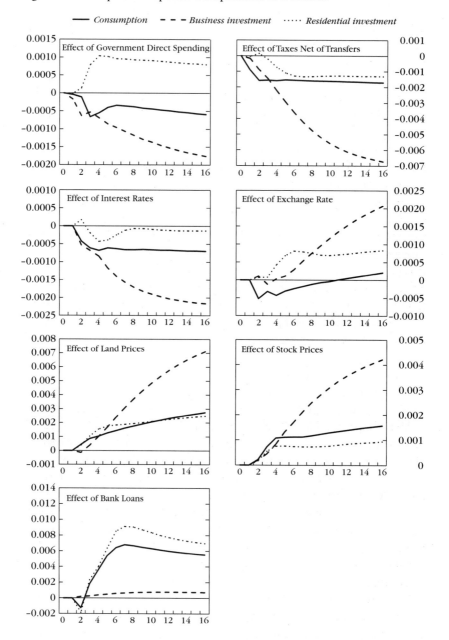

Source: IMF staff estimates.

ernment direct spending crowd out private consumption and business investment, but crowd in residential investment, which is what might be expected given the concentration in government investment projections on infrastructure projects of doubtful overall efficiency. Increases in taxes and interest rates lower all of the components of demand, again as might be expected, while the impact of the real exchange rate on domestic demand is small. Finally, increases in stock prices, land prices, and bank loans all raise demand.

The decomposition of historical movements in private consumption, business investment, and residential investment can be seen in Figure 2.13. The dominant factor explaining movements in business investment and consumption has been asset prices, while residential investment has been largely affected by bank loans, partly offset by expansionary fiscal policy, plausibly reflecting higher government investment (the panels are all produced on the same scale to aid comparisons across different components). Further analysis (not reported) indicates that land prices continue to be at least as important as share prices in explaining the behavior of output, and that bank lending remains an important channel for asset price movements. Hence, the analysis of the components of demand broadly confirms the conclusions of the original analysis.

## Conclusions

This chapter has examined the reasons for the marked slowing of growth in Japan in the 1990s in the context of a VAR analysis that includes the impact of fiscal policy, monetary policy, domestic asset prices, and bank loans. The results are used to attempt to differentiate between a number of alternative explanations of the slump, including the absence of bold and consistent fiscal stimulus, the limited room for expansionary monetary policy because of a liquidity trap, asset price deflation operating through the long-term problems caused by overinvestment, inadequate returns on saving and debt overhang, and disruption of financial intermediation.

The results indicate that all of these explanations have some validity. Fiscal policy has generated limited effects on output except in the wake of the September 1995 stimulus package, whose beneficial effects were rapidly reversed by an abrupt shift to fiscal contraction.

Figure 2.13. Decomposition of Components of Demand

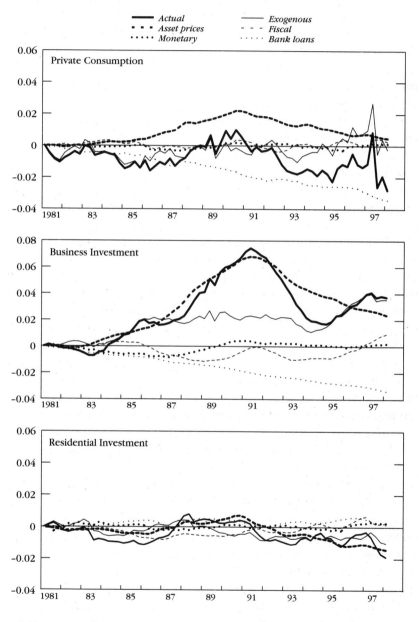

Source: IMF staff estimates.

Expansionary monetary policy is also found to have been effective in stimulating demand in late 1997 and 1998, but presumably reached close to its practical limit as short-term interest rates were cut to very low levels. Domestic asset price changes were an important factor behind the rise in the output gap over the bubble period and the subsequent decline. However, the important role assigned to land prices appears inconsistent with explanations that emphasize pure wealth effects as an explanation of the slump (changes in land prices have different effects on individuals depending on whether they own land or not), or with explanations that emphasize structural problems caused by declining rates of return on reproducible capital.

What the analysis reveals is the central role played by financial intermediation in magnifying the impact of asset prices on the economy. Increases in bank lending, operating both directly and through a self-reinforcing cycle with increases in land prices (the main source of collateral) and stock prices (an important component of bank capital), help explain much of the expansion in the output gap in the mid- to late-1980s. The reverse process operated with equal force over the contraction, as undercapitalized banks responded to falling asset prices and other balance sheet pressures by restraining lending to maintain capital adequacy standards.

The importance of banks both in overall lending and, in particular, in providing capital to smaller companies, which have failed in their usual role of leading the economy out of recession, provides an obvious mechanism through which domestic asset prices and bank lending could have disrupted activity. The central role played by financial intermediation in the slump also generates a compelling reason for the limited effectiveness of standard macroeconomic policies. If the corporate sector is limited in its ability to obtain funds, then this will blunt the impact of monetary policy (as such policy operates largely through the banking system) and of fiscal policy (as companies and individuals will be constrained in their ability to respond to government stimulus). Finally, it provides a ready explanation for the recession in 1997–98. Already undercapitalized banks responded to the prospect of tighter banking regulations in early 1998 (when "prompt corrective action" was introduced) by further cutting back on lending, exacerbating the weakness already generated by fiscal contraction and the Asia crisis, and sending the economy rapidly into the doldrums.

41

At the same time, the limitations of this exercise should be borne in mind. VAR analysis is a powerful tool, but it assumes that the underlying responses are linear and have not changed over time. Both assumptions could be questioned in the context of the type of slump currently experienced in Japan. Individuals could react differently to events depending on the state of the macroeconomy, with behavior at the tip of a cyclical upturn being rather different from that at the bottom of a downturn. Similarly, the impact of financial sector deregulation since 1980 may have altered the relationship between the corporate sector and the banking system.

More analysis, looking more deeply at the mechanisms through which the banking system might affect output, would be needed to support the results from this paper (see Chapter 7 for some subsequent work on this topic). However, the fact that these results appear robust across a number of different specifications provides evidence that banking system problems are indeed at the heart of the current weakness in activity.

## Appendix. Data Sources

The sources for the variables were as follows:

Output and components of demand: The National Income Accounts.

Direct government spending: The sum of real quarterly government consumption and public investment.

Taxes net of transfers: Nominal seasonally unadjusted quarterly general government deficit (defined from its components) less unadjusted direct government spending. As the series was not seasonally adjusted and tax policy normally occurs on an annual basis, the series used in the regressions was the four quarter moving average, first differences by subtracting the same value from the year before. Projected after 1997:Q1 due to lack of data.

The real interest rate: The gensaki rate less the inflation rate of the GDP deflator (adjusted for indirect tax changes) over the previous 4 quarters.

The real exchange rate: The IMF's multilateral real exchange rate calculated using data on unit labor costs across developing countries.

Real stock prices: Monthly averages of the Nikkei 225 index, divided by the GDP deflator.

Real land prices: The average value of land in the six major cities, divided by the GDP deflator. Interpolated from semiannual data.

Real loans: The sum of liabilities of the corporate sector and borrowing by the private sector, as measured by the flow of funds accounts, divided by the GDP deflator.

# References

Ando, Albert, 1998, "Demographic Dynamics and the Causes of the Japanese Recession" (unpublished: Philadelphia; University of Pennsylvania).

Bayoumi, Tamim, Christopher Towe, and Ichiro Oishi, 1998, "Fiscal Policy Issues," in *Japan: Selected Issues*, IMF Staff Country Report 98/113 (October) (Washington: International Monetary Fund).

Bernanke, Ben S., 1983, "Nonmonetary Effects of the Financial Crisis in the Propagation of the Great Depression," *American Economic Review*, Vol. 73 (June), pp. 257–71.

Bordo, Michael, Takatoshi Ito, and Tokuo Iwaisako, 1997, "Banking Crises and Monetary Policy: Japan in the 1990s and U.S. in the 1930s" (unpublished: University of Tsukuba).

Borio, Claudio, 1996, "Credit Characteristics and the Monetary Policy Transmission Mechanism in Fourteen Industrial Countries: Facts, Conjectures, and Some Econometric Evidence," in *Monetary Policy in a Converging Europe*, ed. by K. Alders, K. Koedijk, C. Kool, and C. Winder (Dordecht: Kluwer Academic Publishers).

Drees, Berkhard, and Ceyla Pazarbaşioğlu, 1998, *The Nordic Banking Crises: Pitfalls in Financial Liberalization?* IMF Occasional Paper No. 162 (Washington: International Monetary Fund).

Gordon, Robert, 1988, "Back to the Future: European Unemployment Today Viewed from America in 1939," *Brookings Papers on Economic Activity: 1*, Brookings Institution, pp. 271–304.

Hicks, John, 1937, "Mr. Keynes and the Classics: A Suggested Reinterpretation," *Econometrica*, Vol. 6, pp. 147–59.

Johansen, Soren, 1991, "Estimation and Hypothesis Testing of Cointegration Vectors in Gaussian Vector Autoregression Models," *Econometrica*, Vol. 59 (November), pp. 1551–80.

Keynes, John M., 1936, *The General Theory of Employment, Interest and Money* (London: Macmillan).

Krugman, Paul, 1998, "It's Baaack: Japan's Slump and the Return of the Liquidity Trap," *Brookings Papers on Economic Activity: 2*, Brookings Institution, pp. 137–205.

Kwon, Eunkyung, 1998, "Monetary Policy, Land Prices, and Collateral Effects on Economic Fluctuations: Evidence From Japan," *Journal of the Japanese and International Economies*, 12: pp. 175–203.

Lincoln, Edward, 1998, "Japan's Financial Problems," *Brookings Papers on Economic Activity: 2*, Brookings Institution, pp. 347–85.

Lipworth, Gabrielle, and Guy Meredith, 1998, "A Reexamination of Indicators of Monetary and Financial Conditions," in *Structural Change in Japan: Macroeconomic Impact and Policy Challenges*, ed. by B. Aghevli, T. Bayoumi and. G. Meredith (Washington: International Monetary Fund).

Ogawa, Kazuo, and Shin-ichi Kitasaka, 1998, "Bank Lending in Japan: Its Determinants and Macroeconomic Implications" (unpublished; Osaka: Osaka University).

Ogawa, K., S. Kitasaka, T. H. Yamaoka, and Y. Iwata, 1996, "Borrowing Constraints and the Role of Land Asset in Japanese Corporate Investment Decision," *Journal of the Japanese and International Economies*, Vol. 10 (June), pp. 122–49.

Ogawa, Kazuo, and Kazuyuki Suzuki, 1998, "Land Value and Corporate Investment: Evidence from Japanese Panel Data," *Journal of the Japanese and International Economies*, 12: pp. 132–49.

Posen, Adam, 1998, *Restoring Japan's Economic Growth* (Washington: Institute for International Economics).

Romer, Christina, 1992, "What Ended the Great Depression?" *Journal of Economic History*, Vol. 52, pp. 757–84.

Wescott, Robert, 1996, "Assessing the Risks of a Credit Squeeze Among Small and Medium-Sized Enterprises in Japan," in *Japan: Selected Issues*, IMF Staff Country Report No. 96/114 (Washington: International Monetary Fund).

# 3

# Identifying the Shocks: Japan's Economic Performance in the 1990s

*Ramana Ramaswamy and Christel Rendu*

The Japanese economy experienced its worst postwar recession in late 1997 and throughout 1998. Output contracted for five consecutive quarters before growth turned positive in the first quarter of 1999. The decline in activity followed a seven-year period in which the Japanese economy grew at an average of about 1½ percent a year. The tepid economic performance of recent years contrasts starkly with average growth of about 4 percent achieved during the 1980s. Japanese economic performance during the 1990s also fared unfavorably from an international perspective. Not only did output grow more slowly in Japan than in other major industrial countries, but the volatility of output in Japan rose during the 1990s, whereas it declined significantly in the other Group of Seven countries (Figure 3.1).

A visible sign of the economic crisis in Japan could be seen in the banking sector. Moreover, the failure of both equity and land prices to recover from the collapse in the early 1990s, and Moody's downgrading in November 1998 of Japan's sovereign debt in response to the rapidly rising fiscal deficits and public debt, further heightened the unease about economic conditions in Japan. A striking and somewhat novel aspect of the crisis in Japan was the limited range of options available for using traditional macroeconomic policy tools. With the Bank of Japan's overnight call rate close to zero during 1999, there was minimal further scope for providing support to the economy through a lowering of nominal short-term interest rates. Moreover, given the recent deterioration in public finances, and the rise in long-term bond yields, the scope for further fiscal stimulus is also seriously limited.

Figure 3.1. Growth and Volatility Comparisons

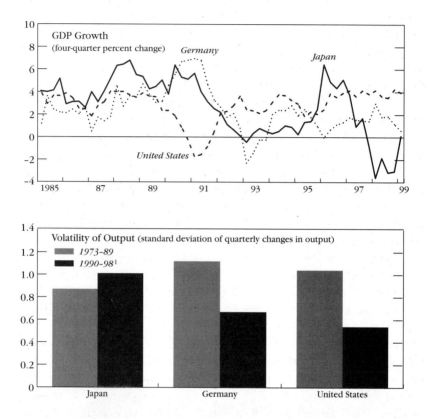

Sources: IMF, World Economic Outlook database; and IMF staff estimates.
[1]For Germany, data start in 1991:Q2 to exclude reunification effects.

How did Japan get saddled with problems of this magnitude? And what policy options are available for dealing with them? The focus of recent analyses, perhaps not surprisingly, has tended to be more on what should be done to get the Japanese economy back on track, than on providing a systematic analysis of what went wrong. The "policy literature" falls into three broad groups. One view, associated prominently with the recent work of Posen (1998), and with some adherents in international policy circles, argues the case for a substantial fiscal stimulus to revive the Japanese economy. This viewpoint attributes the relative ineffectiveness of past fiscal stimulus packages both to the temporary nature of many of the measures undertaken and to the adoption of programs—such as land purchases—that have had little impact on activity, rather than to the inappropriateness of fiscal policy as an effective tool for reviving the economy.

Krugman (1998) makes the case for the continuing relevance of monetary policy in Japan, despite an apparent liquidity trap—that is, the configuration of nominal interest rates close to zero, mild deflation, and a significant output gap. The liquidity trap, however, implies that monetary policy has to be conducted primarily through injecting liquidity rather than by targeting an interest rate. Thus, the Bank of Japan ought to expand the monetary base in a sustained way to increase inflation expectations and lower real interest rates. Krugman downplays the importance of solving the banking crisis as a precondition for getting the Japanese economy moving. He argues that the interplay of adverse selection and moral hazard would have bad banks lending more, not less.

In contrast, the credit-crunch viewpoint argues that recent reforms in the banking sector in Japan, such as the implementation of "prompt corrective action" rules, discourage banks in difficulties from lending indiscriminately. Some empirical evidence lends credence to the hypothesis of activity being dampened recently by a credit crunch.[1]

The above discussion suggests that there is no clear consensus on the policy measures needed for reviving the Japanese economy. This chapter aims not to make an explicit case for adopting one policy option over another, but focuses primarily on providing a systematic analysis of the factors leading up to the current conundrum in Japan. The reasons for the emphasis on what happened, rather than on what needs to be done now, are twofold. One follows from the obvious perspective that a better understanding of the recent past should help in making more reasoned choices among the different policy options. The other, as observed earlier, is driven by the relative paucity of econometric work on what went wrong in Japan in the 1990s. While some of the popular writings on recent developments in Japan have been perceptive, they have had a tendency to be either discursive or sweeping in their generalizations. It is not

---

[1]Bayoumi (in Chapter 2 of this volume) uses VAR estimations to provide evidence for the hypothesis that disruptions to bank lending have played an important role in explaining the recent weaknesses in activity.

easy, for instance, to test empirically the role played by structural factors such as lifetime employment practices, the nature of financial intermediation, or the pursuit of implicit industrial policies in dampening growth in the 1990s. It is, however, easier to test econometrically the validity of generally held beliefs regarding the role of macroeconomic factors in inducing the stagnation of output in the 1990s.

This chapter uses a vector autoregression (VAR) model, with structural identifying restrictions, to quantify the extent to which the growth slowdown in Japan during the 1990s was driven by shocks to the different expenditure components of real GDP. VAR estimations of this type can prove useful in providing techniques for quantifying existing intuitions about, for example, whether negative shocks to private investment were more important than negative shocks to private consumption in dampening activity in the 1990s. Moreover, the results of such estimations may motivate the questioning of existing priors—such as whether developments in international trade did play an important role—and also uncover new stylized facts that explain the slowdown in activity. Further, as discussed below, the VAR approach can be useful in providing benchmarks for evaluating the effectiveness of macro policies—that is, for providing a counterfactual scenario of whether the economy would have been better or worse off in the absence of the monetary and fiscal policies that were actually pursued.

The main conclusions of this chapter are:

- negative shocks to both residential and nonresidential private investment contributed importantly to the marked deceleration of output in the 1990s;
- despite the collapse of both equity and land prices in the 1990s, there has not been a large buildup of negative shocks to private consumption;
- significant negative shocks to public consumption, rather surprisingly, are also shown to have played a role in dampening activity in the 1990s—an explanation that figures prominently in the VAR estimations, but one that appears to have been neglected in most recent analyses of Japan;
- despite the strong appreciation of the yen during the first half of the 1990s, the external sector does not appear to have been a major drag on growth; and
- the VAR estimations do not provide supporting evidence for the counterfactual conjecture that activity would have been signifi-

cantly weaker in the absence of the expansionary shift in the stance of fiscal policy in the 1990s.

## Trends in the Main Economic Indicators

This section provides a brief overview of the trends in the main economic indicators in the 1990s as a precursor to the VAR estimations. A snapshot of aggregate demand developments—captured in Figure 3.2—reveals the following broad trends. The decline in private investment—both residential and nonresidential—was precipitous following the collapse in asset prices. After what proved to be a transient pickup in 1996, related in part to new opportunities created by deregulation, private investment declined sharply yet again. Public investment, which has served as the main ingredient of countercyclical fiscal policy in the 1990s, filled in to a considerable extent the slack left by private investment. Private consumption grew more slowly in the aftermath of the collapse of asset prices; significant declines in the level of private consumption have, however, been a more recent phenomenon, occurring mainly during 1997–98. The external sector's contribution to growth (both positive and negative) has been under 1 percentage point during the 1990s, except in 1997, when it contributed about 1½ percentage points to growth.

Despite the significant slowing of the Japanese economy in the 1990s, unemployment remained low until early 1998, and has increased sharply only recently. The average rate of unemployment between 1991–97 was less than 3 percent, just slightly higher than the average unemployment rate during the boom years of the 1980s. Unemployment increased sharply to a record high of 4.9 percent in June 1999, however, as many large firms that were the main practitioners of lifetime employment practices perceived the need to change existing labor market practices as part of efforts to restructure, and have been shedding labor. Consumer price inflation fell sharply in the immediate aftermath of the collapse in asset prices, but it has remained broadly flat thereafter.

## The VAR Model

A VAR essentially consists of any system of equations in which each variable in the system is determined by its own lagged values

49

**Figure 3.2. Japanese GDP at 1990 Prices, 1990–99**

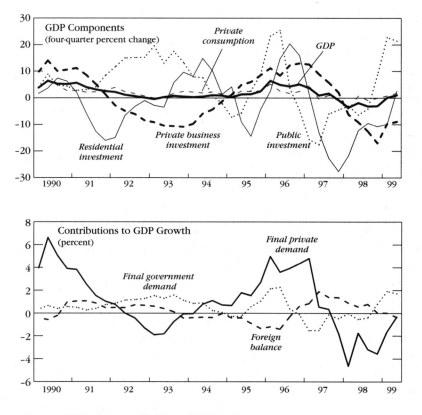

Sources: Nikkei Telecom; WEFA; and IMF staff estimates.

and the lags on all other variables of that system. The VAR approach is useful when the intention is to analyze a phenomenon without necessarily having any strong priors about competing explanations of it. The method allows the regularities found in the data to tell the story. Given that such an approach does not impose a prior theoretical structure on the data, however, it is important to combine the results coming out of the VAR estimations with explanations of why they should make intuitive sense. This paper attempts such a juxtaposition in discussing the types of shocks that the Japanese economy was subject to in the 1990s, and draws conclusions about the effectiveness of the policies pursued during this period.

**Table 3.1. Unit Root Tests**

| Variable | ADF | PP | Specification |
|---|---|---|---|
| Private consumption | −1.97 | −2.32 | c, t, 4 lags |
| Private nonresidential investment | −2.03 | −1.43 | c, t, 2 lags |
| Private residential investment | −2.00 | −2.24 | c, 4 lags |
| Exports | −3.30 | −3.03 | c, t, 4 lags |
| Imports | −3.00 | −1.78 | c, t, 3 lags |
| Public consumption | −1.99 | −1.80 | c, 2 lags |
| Public investment | −2.16 | −1.98 | c, t, 1 lag |
| Inventory ratio | −3.98* | −6.60** | c, t, 2 lags |
| Real household wealth | −0.81 | −0.94 | c, 2 lags |
| Fiscal balance ratio | −7.54** | −0.26 | c, t, 3 lags |
| Real interest rate | −2.91** | −5.65** | 4 lags |

Notes: ADF and PP tests. Specification mentions the best specification possible based on the residual properties (Q-statistic). C stands for constant, t for trend. ** (*) indicates that the unit root test is rejected at the 1% (5%) significance level.

The VAR model adopted for analyzing economic developments in the 1990s in Japan focuses on the different components of the national accounts, and is sequenced in two stages.[2] The first-stage, eight-variable VAR, is composed of private consumption, private nonresidential fixed investment, private residential fixed investment, public investment, public consumption, exports, imports, and inventories, all measured in constant 1990 prices. The data span the period 1973:Q1 to 1998:Q2. Unit root tests (Table 3.1) indicate that the levels of these variables are nonstationary. Accordingly, all variables except inventories are estimated in first difference logs.[3] Inventories

---

[2]The methodology adopted for the VAR estimations in this paper follows closely the approaches adopted for analyzing the 1990–91 recession in the United States, by Blanchard (1993), and the 1990–92 recession in the United Kingdom, by Catão and Ramaswamy (1996).

[3]We further test if the variables are cointegrated. The Johansen rank test reveals the presence of three cointegrating relationships. Based on this finding the natural modeling strategy may appear to be to estimate a vector error correction mechanism (VECM) with three cointegrating vectors. However, the problem with this strategy lies in assigning economic meaning to three long-run relationships in a large system based on purely statistical criteria. We therefore opt for a VAR in first differences as the more meaningful estimation strategy in this context. Note, moreover, that cointegration is of less importance when the focus is mainly on isolating shocks, and not on parameter estimation. Nevertheless, in order to check if the estimations carried out using first differences were robust, we estimated a VECM with three cointegrating vectors. The results indicate that the

are entered into the model as a ratio of GDP (and this ratio is stationary). GDP is derived as an auxiliary equation given that it is the sum of the components in the VAR. The system is estimated with the smallest number of lags necessary to obtain white-noise residuals in all equations of the system; in this case two lags were found to be sufficient. Using this criterion as a basis for choosing the optimal lag length makes sense in large systems where parsimony becomes an issue; moreover, the results were relatively stable when experimented with three and four lags.

The first-stage VAR is estimated to obtain an indication of what the residuals of each of the expenditure equations look like. The residuals of each of the equations of the VAR provide us with a potential benchmark for judging whether the behavior of a variable in any given period deviates markedly from the previous history of the system. For example, when a large residual is obtained for private consumption, it indicates a change in the pattern of private consumption expenditure that is neither explained by the past history of the pattern of private consumption expenditure nor by the history of changes in the other components of the VAR system.

The problem with focusing on the residuals of the VAR system is that they do not represent the "true" shocks to each of the expenditure components. VAR residuals, as is well known, are generally correlated across equations, because of their joint dependence on common underlying trends and also due to the direct contemporaneous dependence of the variables on each other. To get a measure of the uncorrelated shocks to each of the demand components—that is, to make a judgment about how much the behavior of any given variable has truly changed in relation to the performance that can be expected on the basis of past behavior—we need some identifying restrictions. We choose two identifying assumptions to orthogonalize the shocks.[4] First, we assume that within each quarter, the residuals of the VAR equations are related to each other only through their common dependence on activity. For example, we assumed that the residuals of

---

relative magnitude of the shocks to the different components of real GDP are much the same as those derived from the VAR in first differences, but the absolute magnitude of all the shocks are smaller when the VECM strategy is implemented.

[4]The two identifying assumptions adopted imply that there are 44 restrictions in total. Note that to identify the system at least 28 restrictions are needed.

the private consumption equation depend on private fixed investment residuals only through their common dependence on GDP. While this assumption is somewhat restrictive, it is not unduly so, since the feedback effects among these variables tend to take longer than one quarter to occur. The second identifying assumption is that public consumption and gross exports are contemporaneously exogenous, and hence can be used as instruments for GDP.[5]

By including these identifying restrictions in the first-stage VAR, we can purge the residuals of each of the expenditure components of shocks originating from the other expenditure components. For instance, one way of purging private consumption residuals of shocks originating from the other expenditure components is by regressing the residuals of the private consumption equation on the residuals of the auxiliary GDP equation. This cannot be accomplished directly, however, given the simultaneity bias arising from the first identifying restriction. Hence, we use the residuals of the public consumption and export equations in the VAR to create an instrument for GDP residuals. The residuals of the private consumption equation (or the residuals of the other expenditure components as the case may be) in turn are regressed on the instrument to attain a measure of the orthogonalized shocks. In order to be able to make relative comparisons, such as, for instance, the observation that shocks to private fixed investment in Japan have been larger than shocks to private consumption in the 1990s, we normalize the orthogonalized residuals by their respective standard deviations. The impact that the different shocks have on overall activity will of course be a function of the relative weights of the respective components of the national accounts system.

## Results of the First-Stage VAR

The results of the first-stage VAR, based on the national accounts expenditure variables, are reported in Table 3.2. These shocks are

---

[5]Block exogeneity tests do not reject the hypothesis that both public consumption and exports Granger-cause the rest of the macroeconomic system. The estimated chi-square test for the joint exclusion of public consumption and exports is 30.39, which is significant at the 1 percent level. Moreover, single equation tests carried out separately for each of the expenditure components are also consistent with the assumption of the exogeneity of public consumption and exports.

**Table 3.2. First-Stage VAR Shocks**

| | Private Consumption | Private Residential Investment | Private Nonresidential Investment | Public Investment | Trade Balance | Public Consumption | Inventories |
|---|---|---|---|---|---|---|---|
| 1990:Q2 | 0.05 | -0.28 | -1.05 | 0.80 | 0.43 | 0.53 | 1.60 |
| 1990:Q4 | -2.57 | -0.04 | -0.38 | 0.54 | 2.82 | 0.20 | 1.78 |
| 1991:Q2 | -2.47 | -1.67 | -1.44 | 2.13 | 2.90 | -1.44 | 2.11 |
| 1991:Q4 | -1.17 | -3.96 | -1.87 | 2.83 | 1.85 | -1.22 | 3.32 |
| 1992:Q2 | -0.67 | -4.18 | -3.28 | 3.96 | 2.60 | -4.25 | 2.31 |
| 1992:Q4 | -2.20 | -5.15 | -4.24 | 4.94 | 3.37 | -3.71 | 2.30 |
| 1993:Q2 | -2.12 | -6.02 | -6.10 | 5.34 | 3.70 | -5.01 | 3.24 |
| 1993:Q4 | -1.07 | -4.39 | -6.38 | 5.50 | 2.09 | -6.84 | 2.22 |
| 1994:Q2 | -1.70 | -3.56 | -5.14 | 4.31 | 2.54 | -7.24 | 1.61 |
| 1994:Q4 | -0.78 | -4.34 | -4.58 | 2.81 | 2.02 | -6.92 | 0.63 |
| 1995:Q2 | -1.57 | -5.33 | -1.04 | 1.89 | 1.01 | -5.87 | -0.57 |
| 1995:Q4 | -0.56 | -5.52 | -0.77 | 4.24 | -0.63 | -5.82 | -2.21 |
| 1996:Q2 | -3.33 | -5.23 | -2.54 | 7.06 | 0.47 | -6.33 | -1.63 |
| 1996:Q4 | -3.32 | -3.87 | -1.06 | 2.77 | 1.73 | -6.60 | -2.29 |
| 1997:Q2 | -2.01 | -5.94 | -0.05 | 2.19 | 2.53 | -7.18 | -5.36 |
| 1997:Q4 | -3.37 | -8.50 | 2.15 | 1.49 | 2.52 | -7.28 | -6.11 |
| 1998:Q2 | -1.52 | -7.26 | 0.07 | 0.93 | 1.79 | -8.69 | -8.33 |

Note: Each observation in the table represents the cumulative sum of the orthogonalized shocks from 1990:Q2, expressed as a ratio to the standard deviation of the respective shocks.

computed on the basis of the procedure outlined above. Each observation in the table represents the cumulative sum of shocks from the given starting date (and expressed as a ratio of the respective standard deviations). We chose 1990:Q2 as the benchmark for cumulating the shocks since it marks the period when equity prices began to fall in Japan. Choosing 1991:Q2, the period when property prices began to collapse, as an alternative starting point for cumulating the shocks does not qualitatively change the results. Since the tables report the cumulative shocks, a decline, for example, in the level of the positive shocks from one quarter to the next should be interpreted as a negative shock in that latter quarter. And a negative shock simply indicates that the value taken by any variable in a given period is less than what would be predicted on the basis of the past performance of that variable, and the past performance of every other variable in the VAR system.

A notable feature of the first-stage VAR results is that the cumulative buildup of negative shocks to private consumption in Japan has been relatively small during the 1990s. The negative shocks to private consumption that do appear in the immediate aftermath of the collapse of equity prices tend to dissipate toward the end of 1994. The negative shocks reappear in 1996 but are never very large thereafter.

There is, however, a large buildup of negative shocks to both private residential fixed investment and private nonresidential fixed investment by the end of 1993; in the case of the latter, they are almost six times larger than the negative shocks to private consumption at around this time. The negative shocks to residential investment tend to persist and become very large by the end of 1997. While negative shocks to nonresidential investment tend to dissipate from 1995 onward, this process is never very smooth, and sizable negative shocks reappear periodically during the interim.

The buildup of positive shocks to the trade balance up until the second quarter of 1993 reported in Table 3.2 suggests that the external sector in Japan did not act as a dampener on activity during this period, despite the significant appreciation of the exchange value of the yen. The dissipation of the positive shocks to the trade balance by end-1995, and the reappearance of mild positive shocks toward the end of 1997, appears, however, to be consistent with the continued appreciation of the yen until mid-1995, and its sharp depreciation thereafter.

There are large positive shocks to public investment in the 1990s. These correspond in their timing, as can be expected, with the implementation of the various fiscal stimulus packages that were weighted heavily in favor of public investment. Table 3.2 shows a buildup of very large negative shocks to public consumption by the second half of 1994. These negative shocks persist and become even larger by the second quarter of 1998. The potential dampening effects of trends in public consumption on activity in the 1990s have rarely been discussed in the literature. Are these particular results therefore just a quirk of the estimation process adopted, or is there an underlying significance to the large negative shocks to public consumption? This issue, as well as intuitive explanations for the observed pattern of shocks to the other expenditure components, is discussed below.

The absence of large negative shocks to private consumption does indeed pose something of a puzzle at first pass. The asset price collapse in Japan during the 1990s has been very sizable. Equity prices had fallen by about 60 percent from their peak by the middle of 1992, and have not recovered significantly since then. And land prices in the six largest Japanese cities fell by a similar magnitude during the course of the decade. These declines in asset prices in Japan were significantly greater than those observed, for example, in Sweden and the United Kingdom, which had themselves experienced sizable declines in asset prices in the early 1990s. Figure 3.3 illustrates the contrasting experiences among these countries rather clearly. The private savings ratio in Japan stayed relatively stable following the collapse in asset prices, whereas this ratio rose by almost 12 percentage points over the course of two years in Sweden, as private consumption was pruned drastically.

How then does one explain the relatively small negative shocks to private consumption that are derived from the VAR estimations? Firstly, households in Japan hold just about 5 percent of their total financial assets as equities, and furthermore, the proportion of listed equities held by the household sector has been declining ever since the mid-1980s.[6] Consequently, the impact of the boom-bust cycle

---

[6]See the various issues of the *Annual Securities Statistics* of the Tokyo Stock Exchange.

Figure 3.3. Selected Countries: Personal Savings

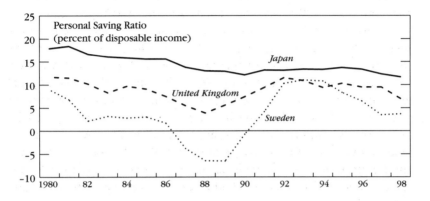

Source: IMF, World Economic Outlook database.

in equity prices on private consumption in Japan can be expected to be smaller than in countries where households are significant owners of equity.[7] Moreover, Japan did not experience any significant increase in unemployment up until the beginning of 1998. Consequently, households in Japan most likely did not experience the pressing need to increase precautionary savings that is normally associated with periods of rising unemployment, as had been observed in Sweden, for example.[8] A possible scenario is that, looking ahead, if unemployment does increase significantly, there is the likelihood of negative shocks to private consumption as precautionary factors start coming into play. The impact of changes in property prices on private consumption will, likewise, also be a function of the institutional features of the housing market. While home owners gain from rising property prices, non-home owners simultaneously face potential opportunity costs as possible future owners of property. Home ownership in the six largest Japanese

---

[7]It is interesting to note in this context that the impact of wealth effects arising from equity price movements on private consumption has been estimated to be relatively small even in the case of the United States. See, for instance, the discussions in Poterba and Samwick (1995), and Starr-McCluer (1998).

[8]See Carroll (1992) for a detailed discussion of issues pertaining to precautionary savings.

cities is roughly about 50 percent, a much lower percentage than in countries such as the United Kingdom and the United States. Consequently, the effects of the boom-bust cycle in property prices on private consumption are likely to be more muted in Japan than in countries where home ownership is proportionately larger. Other special features of the housing market in Japan, such as the asymmetry in the treatment of capital gains and inheritance taxes on property (landholdings provide a favorable tax shelter in the inheritance tax system, but are taxed heavily in the capital gains tax system), as well as the very high absolute levels of property prices, tend to render the housing market particularly illiquid, and dampen potential wealth effects.[9] Putting it all together, the relatively small negative shocks to private consumption derived from the VAR are indeed consistent with what could be expected given the specific institutional features of asset and labor markets in Japan.

The large negative shocks to both private nonresidential fixed investment, and private residential fixed investment fit in rather well with conjectures about the unwinding in the 1990s of the "overinvestment" of the latter half of the 1980s. The ratio of private gross fixed investment to GDP, for instance, increased by almost 5 percentage points to reach about 25 percent in 1990. Some of the investments undertaken during this period, spurred by a combination of rising asset prices (businesses in Japan own a significant chunk of the listed equities) and the lax lending policies of banks, were in projects that had low-returns and high risks. Figure 3.4 provides some stylized facts regarding trends in investment. The ratio of net business capital to potential output, for instance, increased sharply in relation to trend between 1987–91; despite the prolonged decline in the rate of private investment during the 1990s, this ratio is yet to revert fully back to trend. An alternative way of evaluating the investment story is in terms of the dynamic efficiency criterion of Abel and others (1989), which compares the relationship between additions to capital and the returns to it. The narrowing of the gap between capital income and the rate of investment in the latter half of

---

[9]For a more detailed discussion of these issues, see Ito (1992), and Nishimura and others (1998).

Figure 3.4. Business Capital-to-Output Ratio
and Efficiency of Investment

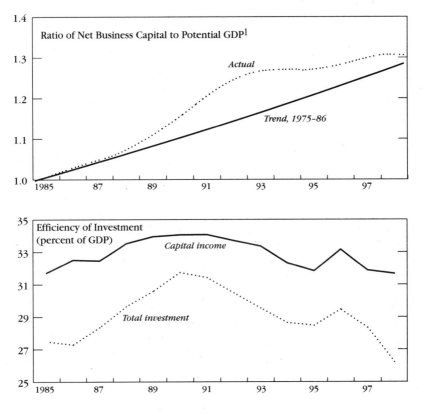

Sources: OECD; and Nikkei Telecom.
[1]Potential GDP is generated using a production function approach.

the 1980s, and its subsequent widening following the decline in the rate of investment in the 1980s, is again consistent with the hypothesis that the cost of the overinvestment (and declining returns to capital) in the latter half of the 1980s had to be its unwinding in the 1990s (Figure 3.4).

As noted earlier, the large negative shocks to public consumption pose something of a puzzle. However, a closer look at fiscal developments in Japan from a historical perspective provides a convincing story that is consistent with the results of the VAR estimations. The central government in Japan operated an implicit "golden rule"—fiscal deficits to be no higher than the value of public investment undertaken by the central government—up until 1975.[10] With the size of the fiscal deficits growing larger by the end of the 1970s, the central government abandoned the golden rule and funded deficits with both construction bonds (that is, bonds issued to finance investment projects undertaken by the central government) as well as deficit financing bonds (bonds issued to finance current expenditures). The golden rule was reinstated once again during the early 1990s, with only construction bonds being issued in this period. Consequently, there was an institutional bias in favor of public investment, and against public consumption, in the early 1990s. While deficit financing bonds began to be issued from 1993 onward, the fiscal stimulus packages during 1993–98 persisted with the emphasis on public investment.

A likely reason for the emphasis placed on public investment in the fiscal packages in Japan is that construction projects can be used as one-off stimulatory measures. In contrast, once a commitment has been made to increase public consumption, it is more difficult to reverse it at a later stage. Thus, when viewed solely as a tool of countercyclical fiscal policy, spending programs that focus on public investment provide governments with greater flexibility than ones that place emphasis on public consumption. A trend that appears to have gone relatively unnoticed in much recent analyses on Japan is that, as a consequence of the policy choices that were adopted in the fiscal arena, the average growth of public consumption in the 1990s declined significantly in relation to its trend growth between 1973–90, whereas public investment grew on average in the 1990s at about twice the pace of the previous period (Figure 3.5). Given that public consumption constitutes roughly the same share of overall output that public investment does, the impact of the negative shocks to public consumption is likely to have broadly offset the positive shocks to public investment in the 1990s.[11]

---

[10]For a more detailed discussion, see Bayoumi (1998) and Ishi (1996).

[11]The contribution of public consumption to growth in the 1990s was, on average, about half that of the contribution between 1973–90. In contrast, the contribution of public investment to growth in the 1990s was, on average, twice that of the contribution in the earlier period.

Figure 3.5. Public Consumption and Public Investment
*(Percent change)*

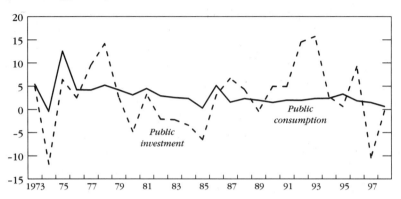

Sources: Nikkei Telecom; WEFA; and IMF staff estimates.

## The Second-Stage VAR

The first-stage VAR provides a useful framework for understanding the precise manner in which deviations in the pattern of expenditure components from past trends contributed to the dampening of activity in the 1990s. However, the changes in the behavior of economic agents during this period did not occur in a vacuum. Both monetary and fiscal policies were used actively in Japan during the 1990s to influence the course of economic developments. In the case of monetary policy, the official discount rate (ODR) was lowered from 6 percent in mid-1991 to about 1¾ percent by end-1993. As activity continued to be weak through 1994, the ODR was lowered sharply to ½ percent by end-1995, a level at which it has remained since then. The Bank of Japan eased monetary conditions further by lowering its operating target for the overnight call rate to 0.25 percent in September 1998, and to "as low as possible" in February 1999. In the case of fiscal policy, there has been at least one major stimulus package every year since 1992, except in 1997, when fiscal policy turned contractionary with the implementation of cuts in public works spending and the increase in the consumption tax.

How does one judge whether the monetary and fiscal policies pursued during this period were successful or not? The fact that economic activity continued to stagnate in the 1990s is not necessarily an indication of the failure of policies. The counterfactual scenario could clearly be one in which economic conditions in Japan would have been even more dismal had the expansionary monetary and fiscal policies not been undertaken. How then can such a counterfactual hypothesis be verified empirically? The VAR approach has both a limitation and an advantage for evaluating the counterfactual hypothesis about the effectiveness of policies. The main limitation is that one is attempting to draw structural inferences from what is, despite the identifying restrictions adopted, essentially a nonstructural exercise. The advantage of the VAR methodology, however, is that because of its focus on residuals (or shocks, as the case may be) it provides a convenient metric for estimating how the shocks would have evolved once monetary and fiscal policies are incorporated as part of an enlarged second-stage VAR.

How can monetary and fiscal policies be proxied in the case of Japan, and how do they enter into the second-stage VAR for evaluating the counterfactual scenario? We use a real interest rate, defined as the 3-month CD rate minus consumer price inflation, to proxy the effects of monetary policy.[12] Getting a proxy for fiscal policy turns out to be more complicated in the case of Japan. Both public investment and public consumption, which have been used to varying degrees as tools of fiscal policy, are already in the first-stage VAR. One way of getting an appropriate variable to represent the additional discretionary fiscal effects in a second-stage VAR would be to strip out both public investment and public consumption from the general government balance. To capture the effects of discretionary fiscal policy, we take the ratio of the "trend" of the adjusted general government balance to "trend" GDP.[13] (It should be noted that using the nonadjusted general government balance instead in the estimations does not change the results of the second-stage VAR qualitatively). The second-stage VAR also incorporates the net worth of the household sector as a ratio of GDP to capture the impact of potential wealth effects. Granger-causality tests indicate that the monetary, fiscal, and household wealth variables are block exogenous to the

---

[12]Using the GDP deflator rather than the consumer price inflation to calculate real interest rates does not make a difference to the results.

[13]The "trend" components of both the general government balance and GDP are calculated using the Hodrick-Prescott filter.

system and are accordingly entered as exogenous variables in the enlarged system.[14]

How do we evaluate the counterfactual scenario about the effectiveness of policies in terms of the pattern of shocks derived from the second-stage VAR? An intuitive way of trying to make sense of this question is to consider the baseline of a hypothetical scenario in which the slump in activity during a given period coincides with the implementation of contractionary monetary and fiscal policies. Negative shocks derived from a first-stage expenditure-based VAR should disappear, or at least decline significantly in the second-stage VAR, if the slump in activity was precipitated by the implementation of these contractionary policies. In the case of Japan, the scenario being considered is obviously the obverse. The slump in activity coincides in timing with a significant easing of monetary and fiscal policies. In order for the counterfactual hypothesis—that the slump in activity would have been even more severe in the absence of the expansionary monetary and fiscal policies pursued—to be true, the negative shocks in the first-stage VAR should become even more negative in the second-stage VAR. The intuition for using this metric as a test of the counterfactual is that, once past relationships between activity and policies are incorporated into the estimation process, the deviation of activity from historical relationships in the second-stage VAR should be more severe than it is in the first-stage VAR. Correspondingly, if the shocks in the second-stage VAR do not become more negative, or in fact become less negative, then these results are consistent with the hypothesis that the slump in activity would not have been much worse in the absence of the actual monetary and fiscal policies that were pursued.

Table 3.3 reports the results from estimations of the second-stage VAR. (The estimations stop in 1997:Q1 because of lags in the availability of data on the government's fiscal balance.) It can be seen that the shocks to private consumption in the second-stage VAR are not very different from those in the first-stage VAR. The fact that these results are consistent with the hypothesis that policies had lit-

---

[14]The estimated chi-square test for the joint exclusion of these variables is 131.48, which is significant at the 1 percent level. When these tests are overridden, and the policy variables are included as endogenous variables, the results of the second-stage VAR do not change much.

**Table 3.3.** Enlarged VAR Shocks
*(Deterministic variables: real interest rates, household wealth, fiscal balance)*

| | Private Consumption | Private Residential Investment | Private Non residential Investment | Public Investment | Trade Balance | Public Consumption | Inventories |
|---|---|---|---|---|---|---|---|
| 1990:Q2 | -0.08 | -0.21 | -1.35 | 0.27 | 0.53 | 0.39 | 1.72 |
| 1990:Q4 | -2.04 | 0.89 | -2.40 | 0.94 | 2.33 | 1.46 | 3.28 |
| 1991:Q2 | -2.25 | -1.07 | -3.32 | 1.56 | 2.97 | 0.22 | 3.62 |
| 1991:Q4 | -0.30 | -4.33 | -3.38 | 1.75 | 1.21 | 0.57 | 4.31 |
| 1992:Q2 | -0.53 | -4.97 | -3.81 | 1.25 | 3.10 | -1.98 | 2.65 |
| 1992:Q4 | -1.46 | -6.39 | -3.88 | 1.38 | 2.93 | -1.96 | 2.10 |
| 1993:Q2 | -1.15 | -8.30 | -4.86 | 1.15 | 3.34 | -4.14 | 2.20 |
| 1993:Q4 | -0.88 | -6.88 | -4.74 | 0.57 | 3.09 | -4.71 | 0.48 |
| 1994:Q2 | -1.25 | -5.54 | -4.15 | 0.19 | 3.37 | -4.55 | -0.06 |
| 1994:Q4 | -0.97 | -6.39 | -2.76 | -2.13 | 3.21 | -3.80 | -1.84 |
| 1995:Q2 | -1.87 | -7.27 | 1.42 | -4.00 | 1.74 | -2.70 | -4.03 |
| 1995:Q4 | -1.28 | -7.26 | 1.60 | -2.15 | 0.23 | -2.94 | -5.95 |
| 1996:Q2 | -3.77 | -6.69 | -1.22 | 1.25 | 0.86 | -3.27 | -4.60 |
| 1996:Q4 | -3.10 | -4.96 | 0.24 | -2.21 | 1.63 | -2.92 | -5.45 |
| 1997:Q1 | 1.22 | -5.85 | -1.14 | -1.74 | 0.85 | -2.63 | -4.93 |

Note: Each observation in the table represents the cumulative sum of the orthogonalized shocks from 1990:Q2, expressed as a ratio to the standard deviation of the respective shocks.

tle impact on private consumption during the 1990s should not come as much of a surprise. As argued previously, wealth effects in Japan are likely to have been small. And banks played only a limited role in extending consumer credit against collateral to households. Consequently, one would expect the response of private consumption to changes in monetary policy to be small, as borne out by the results of the second-stage VAR. The apparent failure of fiscal policy to stimulate private consumption can also be explained. As noted earlier, the fiscal stimulus packages were weighted heavily in favor of public works projects and measures to support land purchases. Moreover, the tax reductions incorporated in the fiscal packages have mostly tended to be temporary in duration, and ad hoc in conception, a combination that is unlikely to prove effective in stimulating private consumption.

It can also be seen from Table 3.3 that the shocks to private residential fixed investment do not change much until 1992:Q2 in the second-stage VAR when compared with the first-stage estimations, but then become visibly more negative thereafter. Shocks to private non-residential fixed investment, in contrast, become more negative until 1992:Q2, but then become less negative thereafter. This would imply that while private residential investment did respond positively to the fiscal stimulus packages, nonresidential investment did not. The fact that the shocks to private residential investment get more negative precisely during the period when the fiscal stimulus packages, with their emphasis on construction projects, land purchases, and subsidized loans for investments in residential property, are implemented in earnest argues in favor of a positive relationship between the stimulus packages and residential investment. In contrast, one would not expect, on a priori grounds, a strong relationship to exist between fiscal stimulus and nonresidential investment, particularly if the negative shocks to private nonresidential investment partly reflect the necessary unwinding in the 1990s of the overinvestment in the previous decade. These arguments find support in an experiment in which the fiscal policy variable is dropped from the enlarged VAR. As can be seen from Table 3.4, the shocks to private residential investment revert back to the levels of the first-stage VAR. In contrast, the shocks to private nonresidential investment become larger, suggesting that while such investment does not respond to fiscal stimulus, it does to changes in monetary policy.

**Table 3.4. Enlarged VAR Shocks**
*(Deterministic variables: real interest rates, household wealth)*

| | Private Consumption | Private Residential Investment | Private Nonresidential Investment | Public Investment | Trade Balance | Public Consumption | Inventories |
|---|---|---|---|---|---|---|---|
| 1990:Q2 | -0.01 | -0.39 | -1.06 | -0.00 | 0.82 | 0.54 | 1.89 |
| 1990:Q4 | -2.05 | 0.36 | -1.40 | 0.05 | 2.93 | 1.48 | 3.33 |
| 1991:Q2 | -2.21 | -1.44 | -2.78 | 1.08 | 3.45 | 0.33 | 3.85 |
| 1991:Q4 | 0.10 | -4.42 | -3.44 | 2.00 | 1.78 | 1.26 | 4.96 |
| 1992:Q2 | -0.11 | -4.69 | -4.79 | 2.11 | 3.30 | -1.24 | 3.33 |
| 1992:Q4 | -0.53 | -5.49 | -6.42 | 3.84 | 3.05 | -0.40 | 3.57 |
| 1993:Q2 | 0.07 | -6.98 | -8.56 | 4.55 | 3.33 | -2.06 | 4.20 |
| 1993:Q4 | 0.15 | -5.54 | -8.61 | 4.02 | 2.86 | -2.93 | 2.44 |
| 1994:Q2 | -0.48 | -4.45 | -7.34 | 2.96 | 3.09 | -3.25 | 1.51 |
| 1994:Q4 | -0.25 | -5.05 | -6.65 | 0.98 | 2.60 | -2.63 | 0.08 |
| 1995:Q2 | -1.12 | -5.67 | -3.00 | -0.24 | 0.86 | -1.49 | -1.61 |
| 1995:Q4 | -0.63 | -5.68 | -2.90 | 2.08 | -0.76 | -1.89 | -3.64 |
| 1996:Q2 | -3.27 | -5.51 | -5.06 | 5.27 | 0.13 | -2.46 | -2.48 |
| 1996:Q4 | -2.84 | -3.90 | -3.23 | 0.95 | 0.77 | -2.54 | -3.42 |
| 1997:Q1 | 1.52 | -5.04 | -4.10 | 0.95 | 0.33 | -2.10 | -3.19 |

Note: Each observation in the table represents the cumulative sum of orthogonalized shocks from 1990:Q2, expressed as a ratio to the standard deviation of the respective shocks.

The shocks to the trade balance are relatively unaffected in the second-stage VAR, as can reasonably be expected. And the shocks to both public investment and public consumption get smaller, reflecting their strong collinearity with the fiscal variable in the enlarged VAR.

Thus, while the results of the second-stage VAR are consistent with the conjecture that activity would not have been significantly weaker in the absence of the discretionary fiscal policies that were actually pursued in the 1990s, this does not necessarily constitute an argument about the ineffectiveness of policies in general in the Japanese context. Fiscal policy could conceivably have been more successful in stimulating the economy had it been implemented in a less *ad hoc* manner and concentrated more on measures that could have had a more direct and longer-lasting impact on activity.

## Conclusions

This chapter has provided a framework for identifying the driving forces of the slow growth in Japan during the 1990s. Large negative shocks to both private residential investment and private nonresidential investment have been shown to be the principal factors dampening activity during the 1990s. The negative shocks to private investment essentially reflected the unwinding in the 1990s of the overinvestment that took place in the latter half of the 1980s. Negative shocks to public consumption also contributed to the slowdown of activity. Despite the severe collapse of asset prices in the 1990s, negative shocks to private consumption proved to be relatively small, reflecting the low ownership of equities by households, and the absence of an urge to increase precautionary savings due to the low levels of unemployment in Japan. The external sector did not act as a major dampener on activity despite the significant appreciation of the yen in the first half of the 1990s.

The VAR estimations do not lend support to the counterfactual conjecture that activity would have been significantly weaker in the absence of the expansionary shift in the stance of fiscal policy in the 1990s. The relative ineffectiveness of fiscal policy identified by the VAR model is likely to reflect the shortcomings in the design and implementation of the stimulus measures—tax reductions tended to be temporary in duration and *ad hoc* in conception, and some of the spending measures had neither a direct nor long-lasting impact on activity.

## References

Abel, Andrew B., N. Gregory Mankiw, Lawrence H. Summers, and Richard J. Zeckhauser, 1989, "Assessing Dynamic Efficiency: Theory and Evidence," *Review of Economic Studies*, Vol. 56, pp. 1–20.

Bayoumi, Tamim, 1998, "The Japanese Fiscal System and Fiscal Transparency," in *Structural Change in Japan: Macroeconomic Impact and Policy Challenges*, ed. by Bijan B. Aghevli, Tamim Bayoumi, and Guy Meredith (Washington: International Monetary Fund).

Blanchard, Olivier, 1993, "What Caused the Last Recession? Consumption and the Recession of 1990–91," *American Economic Review, Papers and Proceedings*, May, pp. 270–74.

Carroll, Christopher D., 1992, "The Buffer-Stock Theory of Saving: Some Macroeconomic Evidence," *Brookings Papers on Economic Activity*, No. 2, pp. 61–157.

Catão, Luis, and Ramana Ramaswamy, 1996, "Recession and Recovery in the United Kingdom in the 1990s: Identifying the Shocks," *National Institute Economic Review*, July, pp. 97–107.

Ishi, Hiromitsu, 1996, "Budgets and the Budgetary Process in Japan," *Hitotsubashi Journal of Economics*, Vol. 37, No. 1, June.

Ito, Takatoshi, 1992, *The Japanese Economy* (Cambridge, Massachusetts: MIT Press).

Krugman, Paul, 1998, "Japan's Trap," ⟨http://web.mit.edu/Krugman/www/japtrap.html⟩.

Nishimura, K. A., Yamazaki, F., Idee, T., and Watanabe, T., 1998, "The Myth of Land in the Land of Many Myths: What Brought Japanese Land Prices Up so High in the 1980s and Made them Nose-Dive in the 1990s," paper presented at the NBER Japan Project, Tokyo, October.

Posen, Adam S., 1998, *Restoring Japan's Economic Growth*, Institute for International Economics, Washington, D.C., September.

Poterba, James M., and Andrew A. Samwick, 1995, "Stock Ownership Patterns, Stock Market Fluctuations, and Consumption," *Brookings Papers on Economic Activity*: 2, pp. 295–373, Brookings Institution.

Starr-McCluer, 1998, "Stock Market Wealth and Consumer Spending," Working Paper, Federal Reserve Board of Governors, Washington, D.C., April.

# 4

# Explaining the Slump in Japanese Business Investment

*Ramana Ramaswamy*

Business investment in Japan declined for five consecutive quarters through end-1998, with the decline for 1998 as a whole being about 11¼ percent. Despite the pickup in the first quarter of 1999, surveys of business investment intentions and monthly orders data point toward renewed declines later in the year. The decline in business investment was more precipitous than during any other episode in Japan's postwar history; even with the recent increase, business investment has declined by almost 20 percent between the first quarter of 1997 and the first quarter of 1999.

The sharp decline in the rate of business investment since the bursting of the asset price bubble in 1990–91 has included both cyclical as well as structural elements, though the latter appears to have been the dominant driving force. The share of business investment in GDP fell from about 20 percent in 1990 to about 16 percent in 1998—with a transient recovery in 1996 spurred in part by new opportunities created by deregulation (Figure 4.1).The contrast between trends in business investment in Japan and in the United States since 1990 is striking. The share of business investment in GDP has risen in the United States by approximately the same magnitude as it has fallen in Japan in the 1990s. Consequently, while the share of business investment in GDP in Japan was almost 11 percentage points higher than in the United States in 1991, by 1999 it was only about 4 percentage points higher.

While the share of aggregate business investment in GDP has declined significantly in the 1990s, the disaggregated trends across sec-

Figure 4.1. Trends in Japanese Investment

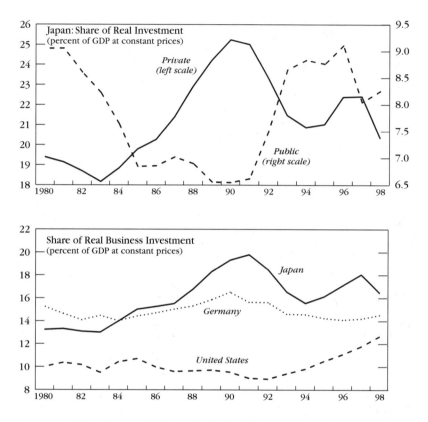

Sources: Nikkei Telecom; WEFA; and IMF, *World Economic Outlook.*

tors provide some interesting contrasts (Figure 4.2). The steepest declines in the rate of business investment in the 1990s occurred in
manufacturing and construction—sectors that had expanded most
closely in tandem with the buildup in asset prices in the latter half of
the 1980s. Investment declined sharply in the immediate aftermath of
the asset price collapse in the banking, insurance, and services sectors, but has picked up robustly since 1996. In both transportation
and communications, and electricity—sectors in which deregulation
initiatives have been prominent—the share of investment in output
continued to rise even after asset prices collapsed in the early 1990s.

70

Figure 4.2.  Sectoral Trends in Business Investment
*(Rates of investment, 1990 prices)*

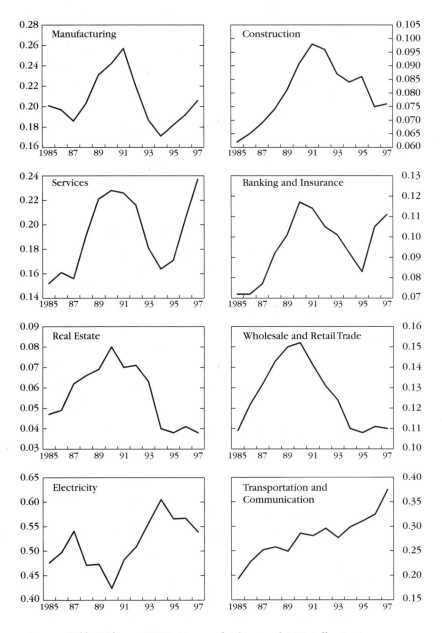

Sources: Nikkei Telecom; WEFA, Nomura database; and IMF staff estimates.

This chapter aims to explain the reasons for the steep decline in the rate of business investment in Japan in the 1990s. The analysis is carried out in two stages. The first discusses the various alternatives proposed to explain the decline in business investment in Japan. This is followed by econometric estimates of the determinants of aggregate business investment in Japan. The main conclusions emerging from the regression analysis are that structural factors have been a dominant force driving the slump in business investment in the 1990s. In particular, the unwinding of the capital stock overhang from the 1980s and the impact of the debt burden have played prominent roles. The decreasing effectiveness of the system of corporate governance provided the milieu in which firms incurred large debts in pursuit of rapid market expansion at the expense of profitability, a strategy that backfired when growth expectations declined. The collapse in equity prices in the 1990s also contributed to the slump in business investment. While the regression analysis does not assign a prominent role to cyclical factors in accounting for the slump in business investment, other evidence indicates that business investment was constrained by a credit crunch during 1997–98.

## Alternative Explanations of Business Investment

Some of the more prominent hypotheses put forward to explain the slump in business investment in Japan are that it constitutes the unwinding in the 1990s of the overinvestment in the latter half of the 1980s; that business investment was held back by the effects of an excessive buildup of debt; that the decline in business investment is related to a credit crunch arising from the interactions between the asset price collapse and an overextended banking system; and that the changing structure of the Japanese economy, including the trend decline in the growth of the labor force and deindustrialization, had a negative impact on business investment in the 1990s. This section discusses each of these hypotheses from the perspective of the relevant theoretical literature. This exercise provides guidance in selecting the specification used for estimating the aggregate business investment function in the following section.

## The Overinvestment Hypothesis

In order to make a convincing case that the decline in business investment in the 1990s was a response to overinvestment during the 1980s, it is necessary to nail down the answers to the following set of questions. How is overinvestment to be measured? And what were the conditions that allowed firms to overinvest?

While there is no standard way for measuring overinvestment, it can nevertheless be deduced in a number of ways. A rising capital-output ratio, for instance, could indicate a declining response of output to investment, and a potential case of overinvestment. Drawing inferences about overinvestment from trends in the capital-output ratio, however, has to be done with care—for instance, the increase in the capital-output ratio could reflect the rising capital intensity of production accompanying certain phases of economic development, and not the declining efficiency of investment. One way of overcoming the interpretation problems associated with measures of the capital-output ratio is to compare how the ratio of capital to output has changed over time in relation to its own trend.[1] Figure 4.3 shows that the ratio of net business capital to potential output in Japan increased sharply in relation to trend in the latter half of the 1980s. Despite the prolonged decline in the rate of investment in the 1990s, this ratio is yet to fully revert back to trend, suggesting that overinvestment did take place in the 1980s and is yet to be unwound fully.

An alternative criterion for measuring overinvestment is the dynamic efficiency test proposed by Abel and others (1989), which compares trends in gross investment with those in gross capital income. In the steady state, if investment exceeds capital income, then the economy is clearly overinvesting, as capital accumulation is absorbing more resources than all past accumulation is making available for consumption. In the case of Japan, the share of gross operating surplus in GDP was significantly higher than the rate of business investment in the mid-1980s, suggesting that the dynamic

---

[1]An upward trend in the real capital-output ratio (as has occurred in Japan) can also reflect the effects of a declining trend in the relative price of capital. For instance, with a Cobb-Douglas production function, capital income is a constant proportion of nominal output. Accordingly, if the relative price of capital falls, its real level will increase.

Figure 4.3. Indicators of Overinvestment

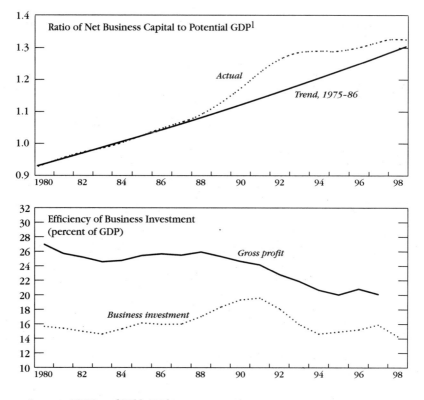

Sources: OECD; and Nikkei Telecom.
[1]Potential GDP is generated using a production function approach.

efficiency criterion was being satisfied easily. However, the gap between the share of gross operating surplus in GDP and the rate of
business investment narrowed sharply in the latter half of the 1980s,
and continued at the compressed levels into the 1990s despite the
sharp declines in the rate of business investment, suggesting a decline in the efficiency with which investment was being deployed
(see Figure 4.3). This experience is also consistent with the trend decline in corporate profitability (Figure 4.4). Thus, the trends in the relationship between capital income and business investment in Japan
also provide indirect evidence supportive of the overinvestment
hypothesis.

Figure 4.4. Corporate Profitability, 1980–98

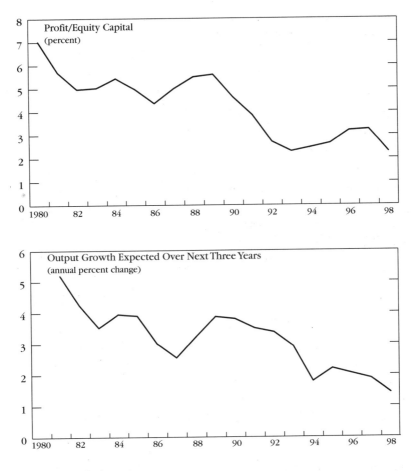

Source: Bank of Japan.

What were the driving forces behind the overinvestment in the latter half of the 1980s? During this period, high investment reflected a blend of exuberant expectations of growth and an easy access to finance, that in turn allowed growth expectations to be largely validated. Large firms, particularly those in manufacturing, invested heavily in equipment and buildings in this period by tapping into the buoyant equity market, and also by issuing convertible bonds. The booming stock market made both these sources of capital relatively cheap. Deprived to some extent of their traditional client base as a consequence of financial liberalization, banks turned to funding the investment plans of small and medium-sized firms, particularly those in the real estate sector, using overvalued collateral as the basis for such loans. The macroeconomic environment also abetted the high levels of borrowing. The official discount rate was halved in several steps to 2½ percent between end-1985 and early-1987, and then remained unchanged until mid-1989.

There were a number of reasons why the system of corporate governance in Japan failed to provide the necessary checks and balances against overinvestment. Despite some warning signals, both shareholders and banks may have been lulled by past successes into not constraining the corporate sector's strategy of attempting to expand market share. Moreover, at times shareholders were not fully aware of the true health of firms, masked as they were by nontransparent accounting practices. The "*keiretsu*" system, involving close relationships—including those of cross-share ownership—between banks and industrial groups, offered firms a relatively cheap source of funds and favored strategies of market expansion, given the minimal threat of being taken over in case profitability was adversely affected.[2] While banks could intervene when contractual obligations associated with routine payments of interest and principal were not met, they often tended in practice to bail out the firms in trouble rather than forcing them to restructure.[3] Japanese firms were therefore able to implement their market expansion strategies without being too constrained by considerations of profitability. The investment boom finally petered out when monetary policy was tightened sharply in 1989–90, and the asset price bubble collapsed thereafter, resulting in a drastic reduction in access to cheap sources of funds.

## The Debt Hypothesis

The high levels of indebtedness of Japanese firms has often been adduced as an important factor behind the slump in business invest-

---

[2]See Hoshi, Kashyap, and Scharfstein (1991) for a discussion of the Keiretsu system.

[3]See Chapter 9 by Levy.

Figure 4.5. Japanese Corporate Indebtedness, 1980–98

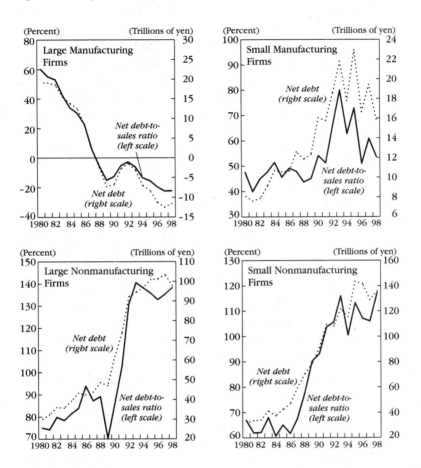

Source: Bank of Japan.

ment as it amplifies the vulnerability of firms to negative shocks. Figure 4.5 shows that the buildup in debt was substantial during the latter half of the 1980s for a significant part of the corporate sector, with the notable exception of large manufacturing firms that financed capital formation largely through retained earnings and the issue of equity. While the link between high indebtedness and vulnerability to negative shocks is intuitive, however, the relationship between debt and investment is a complex one from an analytical point of view.

The theoretical literature in this area indicates that there are both advantages as well as disadvantages to financing investment through debt, though, as discussed below, the Japanese experience appears to have been more one of being saddled with the disadvantages.

Early models of the relationship between debt and investment—for instance, the Modigliani-Miller theorem—concluded that the source of financing should not have an impact on the investment decisions of firms. The Modigliani-Miller theorem is, however, predicated on a series of restrictive assumptions regarding the nature of capital markets, and recent developments in the theory of asymmetric information and imperfect markets have shown that financial policies of the firm do have an impact on investment.[4]

Developments in the theory of asymmetric information led to a line of research where it was argued that financing investment through debt rather than equity could in principle have advantages for firms. The existence of debt contracts allows firms to tap into funds that may not otherwise be available. For instance, since lenders cannot in general observe and monitor fully the actions of firms, risk-averse creditors would prefer noncontingent contracts that assure them of a regular stream of earnings and legal rights to principal, rather than enter into contingent contracts entailed by equity ownership. Thus, other things being equal, the existence of debt contracts allows investment to be higher than it otherwise would be, by making it possible to tap into the funds of risk-averse agents. Firms can also in principle fund their investments more cheaply with debt than with equity under certain circumstances. In cases where the "equity premium" arises more on account of asymmetric information rather than the "true" riskiness of the investment projects, it is cheaper for the firm to obtain finance through debt rather than equity.[5] Also, as stressed by Jensen (1988) and Shleifer and Vishny (1988), another potential advantage of debt over equity is that it constrains firms with large cash flows, but low growth prospects, from diversifying into unconnected and wasteful projects because of the contractual obligation to set aside part of the cash flows for interest payments, and the potential threat of bankruptcy when contracts are violated.

---

[4]See, for instance, the discussion in Fazzari, Hubbard, and Peterson (1988).

[5]For more detailed discussions of these issues, see Bernanke and Campbell (1988).

While the asymmetric information literature argues that some debt is better than no debt, incurring high levels of debt can nullify its potential advantages. High levels of debt increase the sensitivity of the firm to adverse shocks, implying a higher probability of bankruptcy, and lowers the range of circumstances over which the firm can offer noncontingent contracts. Thus, debt financing will cease to be relatively cheaper than equity financing when a firm's debt levels are already high. High levels of debt also magnify the sensitivity of firms' net worth and equity values to negative aggregate shocks, thereby amplifying normal business cycle fluctuations. High debt has a particularly deleterious impact on activity during deflationary episodes, or more generally when inflation turns out to be lower than prior expectations, as the contract is fixed in nominal rather than real terms.

In the case of Japan, some of the potential advantages of debt financing for investment were negated, both on account of the high levels of debt that had been built up by the time a series of negative shocks hit the economy in the early 1990s, and by both inflation and growth thereafter being lower than were expected when many of the debt contracts were initially incurred. A sense of complacency based on past successes had undermined corporate governance, with firms continuing to expand production capacity despite declining profitability, and slippages in contractual obligations associated with debt tended at times to be tolerated. Moreover, given the weakened state of the banking system in the 1990s, banks that had provided much of the debt to the corporate sector were not in a position to exercise the necessary corporate oversight function—particularly by acting preemptively to deal with emergency problems—while insolvency law was not well suited to provide for corporate reorganization through the legal system.[6]

## The Credit Crunch and Asset Price Collapse Hypotheses

The bank lending channel usually tends to get treated separately in the literature from the asset price channel as a determinant of investment. The impact of equity price fluctuations on investment is generally incorporated into investment functions through some vari-

---

[6]See Chapter 9 by Levy.

ant of Tobin's Q—defined as the ratio of the market value of equity to the replacement value of physical capital. The bank lending channel—that is, the one linking bank loans and activity—is assumed to have an impact on investment that is independent of the effects of asset price fluctuations, because asymmetric information or institutional factors render bank loans as imperfect substitutes for either bonds or equities.[7]

In the case of Japan, however, the effects of the bank lending and asset price channels on investment have in practice been significantly intertwined. The fact that banks in Japan have counted part of their hidden capital gains on holdings of equity as bank capital implies that fluctuations in equity prices have a direct impact on bank capital, and therefore on their capacity to lend. Disruptions to bank lending, in turn, have the potential to have strong adverse effects on investment in Japan because of the important role played by banks in the process of financial intermediation.

The collapse of asset prices in the early 1990s precipitated the problems in the banking sector. Equity prices fell by about 60 percent between 1990–92, and, despite the pickup in early 1999, are still more than 50 percent below peak levels. Land prices began declining from 1991 onward, with the average price of land in the six largest Japanese cities in 1998 being only about 40 percent of the peak values in 1990. As noted above, one effect of the collapse in asset prices was to erode bank capital and, therefore, their capacity to lend. The decline in asset prices, at the same time, also eroded the collateral of firms, making it riskier for banks to expand lending, even in situations where bank capital was not a binding constraint. Assessing the role of the credit crunch in holding back business investment in Japan involves examining the effects of the interactions among deteriorating loan collateral, declining bank capital, and the nature of the regulatory environment on business investment.

Recent research has come up with mixed evidence regarding the role of the credit crunch in constraining investment. Bayoumi (in Chapter 2 of this book) argues that while a strict credit crunch did

---

[7]See, for instance, Bernanke and Gertler (1995) for a discussion of the analytical and empirical basis of the importance of the bank lending channel. Chapter 7 of this volume discusses financial intermediation and bank lending in the Japanese context in more detail.

not occur until 1997–98, part of the effects of the asset price collapse on investment in Japan was channeled through bank lending.[8] One reason for the absence of stronger evidence of a credit crunch in a period when bank capital was being eroded by the collapse in asset prices could be related to the forbearance provided by the prevailing regulatory environment on the expectation that economic conditions would soon improve. The regulatory environment in Japan underwent a major strengthening from 1997 onward in response to the deepening of the banking crisis, and the realization that the underlying problems were not just cyclical. With new regulations guiding the operations of the banking sector, banks responded to the erosion of capital by cutting back lending sharply. A study by Woo (1999), for instance, found that there was a positive and statistically significant correlation between bank capital and lending growth in 1997, contrary to the experience in earlier years when the deteriorating capital positions of the banks failed to be a binding constraint on their lending activities.

## The Changing Structure of the Japanese Economy Hypothesis

There are a number of strands to the relationship between the changing structure of the Japanese economy and business investment. One argument is that supply-side factors, such as the decline in the growth of the labor force in the 1990s, implied the need for a slower growth of capital stock in the steady state, and therefore warranted a downward transitional adjustment of investment in relation to GDP from previous levels (Figure 4.6).[9] A closely related argument is concerned more with the future—that projected trends of a declining labor force will imply a relatively slower growth of capital stock and potential output in the years ahead. In as much as these projected trends have already been factored into growth expectations, they could offer a potential supply-side explanation for the trend decline in the rate of business investment. Another supply-side argument is that the sharp decline in the share of manufacturing em-

---

[8]Sekine (1999), using panel data, finds that small firms were credit constrained during the first half of the 1990s.

[9]See Prescott (1999) for a discussion of the supply-side explanation of the investment decline in Japan.

Figure 4.6. Labor Market Trends in Japan

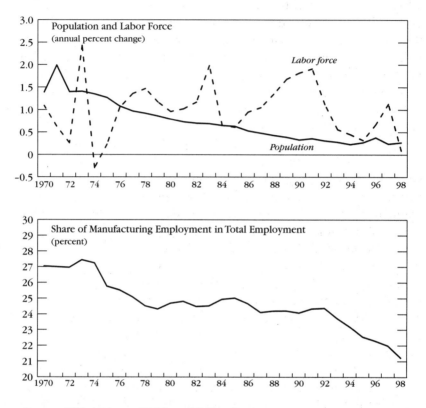

Sources: Nikkei Telecom; WEFA; and IMF staff estimates.

ployment associated with the rapid pace of deindustrialization in the 1990s, and the growing importance of the service sector, imply a lower steady state capital-labor ratio; the slump in business investment in the 1990s can be interpreted in part as the transitional adjustment to a lower equilibrium capital-labor ratio.

While the decline in the trend growth of the labor force may have been one of the factors contributing to the slump in business investment, it appears unlikely to have been a major determinant. While the growth of the labor force did decline in the 1990s, this decline was not very pronounced—it grew on average at about 0.8 percent between 1990–98, compared with 1.2 percent between 1980–90, be-

cause slower population growth was partly offset by a rising participation rate. The decline in hours worked in the 1990s was sharper
when compared with the previous decade; nevertheless, the difference, on average, was under 1 percentage point a year. In order for
the labor supply explanation to hold, it is necessary to explain why
a decline in the growth of the labor force, or of hours worked, of this
magnitude ought to have led to a substantial slump in business investment in the 1990s.

The link between deindustrialization and the slump in business investment may have been a more important one for Japan in recent
years than that between trends in the labor force and investment. All
advanced economies have experienced a gradual trend decline in the
share of manufacturing employment since about the early 1970s, driven in major part by the relatively faster growth of productivity in
manufacturing.[10] While Japan experienced a slower pace of deindustrialization until the early 1990s, its share of manufacturing employment declined sharply by about 3 percentage points to 21 percent between 1994–98—that is, it declined by about the same
magnitude in the last 4 years as it did in the prior 20 years. The recent decline in the share of manufacturing employment in Japan was
also relatively steep when compared with the pace of deindustrialization over any 4–5 year span in other industrial countries. Since
manufacturing is relatively more capital intensive, the recent changes
in the structure of Japanese employment may have accounted in part
for the slump in business investment as part of the transition toward
a lower capital-labor ratio.

## Econometric Estimation

There has been, in general, less of a consensus over the appropriate econometric strategy for estimating aggregate investment
functions than has been the case with some other macro relationships, in part due to the analytical controversies over the determinants of business investment. The empirical strategy adopted in this

---

[10]For a more detailed analysis of deindustrialization, see Rowthorn and Ramaswamy (1997 and 1999).

chapter is an eclectic one, combining both the neoclassical and Keynesian approaches to estimating investment functions, and is influenced by the issues that are particularly important to Japan, as discussed above.

The main purpose of the econometric estimation is to identify the extent to which business investment in Japan has been influenced by "structural" factors such as debt and capital stock overhangs, and the asset price collapse, as opposed to "cyclical" factors such as changes in output, interest rates, and credit. The general form of the proposed specification is:

$$I/Y = f(\Delta Y,\ K/Y,\ D/S,\ \Delta C,\ \Pi,\ Q,\ P_k/P,\ \rho/w,\ \Delta r,\ T)$$

where $I$ is real business investment; $Y$ is real output; $K$ is real business capital stock; $D/S$ is the ratio of debt to sales; $C$ is credit; $\Pi$ is profitability; $Q$ is Tobin's Q (the ratio of the value of equity to the value of physical capital); $P_k/P$ is the relative price of capital; $\rho/w$ is the ratio of the cost of capital to the cost of labor; $r$ is the real interest rate; and $T$ is a time trend.

While economic theory broadly influences the choice of variables for the general specification of the investment function, the specific choice of the functional form adopted was based on pragmatic considerations as well. For instance, when it comes to choosing between incorporating the cost of capital or relative factor rentals in the specification, the choice of variable was based on the one that "fits" better, despite the fact that using the cost of capital instead of relative factor rentals in the econometric specification implies that only one of the first order conditions for profit maximization is utilized.

The debt ratio and credit are also used as explanatory variables, under the hypothesis that financial policies do matter for business investment, and that firms are liquidity constrained. However, given the complex nature of the theoretical relationship between debt and business investment that was discussed earlier, the debt ratio is divided by expected growth to get a measure of overindebtedness ($D^*$). The rationale for this choice is that it is debt in excess of growth expectations rather than debt itself that should have a negative impact on business investment. The capital output ratio is used as an explanatory variable to capture the effects of the capital stock overhang on the rate of business investment. The specification incorporates Tobin's Q to capture the impact of equity price movements on

84

business investment. The changes in output, credit, and the interest rate are incorporated, as noted earlier, to capture the impact of cyclical effects on the rate of investment. For the empirical specification, profitability is defined as the ratio of recurring profits to sales. A trend term is included to proxy other structural influences on business investment.

There is a statistical conundrum in estimating aggregate investment functions for Japan in the post–oil shock period. Aggregate time series data for a number of variables exhibit significant changes in trend, reflecting the fact that there was an asset price bubble and the overheating of the economy in the latter half of the 1980s, followed by a collapse of asset prices and a prolonged period of stagnation of activity in the 1990s and, more recently, a severe recession. Consequently, time series data on variables such as the first differences of output and credit, as well as the rates of investment and profits, which can generally be expected on *a priori* grounds to be stationary, appear to be nonstationary over the sample period when formal tests are conducted.

One way to approach the econometric estimations is to adopt a purely statistical approach—that is, any variable that tests indicate to be nonstationary is differenced one stage further. However, while adopting such an approach would satisfy statistical criteria, it has the problem of ignoring potentially important levels of relationships. Moreover, differencing variables such as output and credit twice over is not useful for drawing meaningful economic inferences about the determinants of business investment. Consequently, the approach adopted in this chapter is to estimate the investment function in its economically meaningful form. This implies the inclusion of apparently nonstationary variables in the estimated equation. The regressions provide stationary residuals, however, indicating that the estimates are consistent.

Table 4.1 summarizes the results from estimating the preferred specification. Quarterly data are used, spanning the period from 1981 to end-1998. The dependent variable is the rate of business investment—defined as the ratio of real business investment to real output lagged one period (to take account of endogeneity issues). The estimated equation closely follows the general specification outlined above, except for using the change in the real interest rate (defined as the 3-month CD rate minus the 12-month change in the CPI) in-

### Table 4.1. OLS Estimates of Business Investment[1]
*(Dependent variable is ratio of business-investment to lagged GDP)*

| Regressor | Coefficient | Standard Error | T-Ratio [Prob] |
|---|---|---|---|
| CONSTANT | 0.3859 | 0.0693 | 5.5677[.000] |
| $\Delta Y$ | 0.2479E-6 | 0.2448E-6 | 1.0123[.315] |
| K/Y (−1) | −0.2091 | 0.0462 | −4.5230[.000] |
| D* (−1) | −0.0029 | 0.6134E-3 | −4.7946[.000] |
| $\Delta C$ | −0.0563 | 0.0649 | −0.8665[.390] |
| $\Delta r$ (−1) | −0.0016 | 0.8299E-3 | −1.8729[.066] |
| $\pi$ (−1) | −0.4054 | 0.3119 | −1.2997[.199] |
| Q (−1) | 53.6388 | 17.2666 | 3.1065[.003] |
| TREND | 0.0025 | 0.2765E-3 | 8.9418[.000] |

| | | | |
|---|---|---|---|
| R-squared | 0.9013 | R-bar-squared | 0.8883 |
| S.E. of regression | 0.0069 | F-stat.  F( 8, 61) | 69.6022[.000] |
| Mean of dependent variable | 0.1636 | S.D. of dependent variable | 0.0207 |
| Residual sum of squares | 0.0029 | Equation log-likelihood | 253.6422 |
| Akaike Info. criterion | 244.6422 | Shwarz Bayesian criterion | 234.5240 |
| DW-statistic | 0.5933 | | |

| Augmented Dickey-Fuller Tests of the Residual | | | | |
|---|---|---|---|---|
| | DF | ADF (1) | ADF (2) | ADF (3) | ADF (4) |
| Test statistic[2] | −3.3319 | −3.0960 | −2.6056 | −2.5812 | −2.9943 |

Note: The sample period is 1981:Q2 to 1998:Q3 for the main regression and 1982:Q3 to 1998:Q3 for the augmented Dickey-Fuller tests.
[1]OLS—Ordinary Least Squares.
[2]The 95 percent critical value for the augmented Dickey-Fuller statistic is −2.9062.

stead of the change in the relative factor rentals as one of the dynamic factors. The relative price of capital is dropped in the preferred specification, as the coefficient is wrongly signed in regressions that included it.

The coefficients for both the capital output ratio and the adjusted debt ratio are negative, and the estimates highly statistically significant in both cases. Thus, the regression results provide empirical support to the intuition that the debt burden and the capital stock overhang have had an important influence in explaining the collapse of business investment in the 1990s. The coefficient of Tobin's Q is positive and the estimate is statistically significant at the 5 percent level, suggesting that the decline in business investment was also driven by the collapse in equity prices. The finding of a strong positive relationship between business investment and Tobin's Q is not surprising given that large firms had financed a substantial part of their capital expenditures by issuing equity, and much of the listed equities are held by the corporate sector rather than by households.[11] The coefficient for the profit rate is wrongly signed but is not statistically significant, implying that there is no well-defined relationship between business investment and profitability, and is consistent with assessments that Japanese firms followed a market expansion strategy without paying due heed to profitability considerations. The time trend is positive and highly statistically significant, as might be expected given the rising capital-output ratio. The estimated relationships remain stable when changes are made either to the lag structure of the explanatory variables, to the estimation period, or when specific dynamic factors are excluded from the regressions.

The regression results indicate that none of the cyclical factors— the change in output, the change in credit, and the change in the real interest rate—has a statistically significant relationship with business investment. The cyclical factors are not statistically significant even when the regression is estimated with the level of business investment as the dependent variable rather than the ratio of business investment to lagged GDP as the dependent variable. The absence of a statistically significant relationship between credit and business investment appears at first sight puzzling, particularly given the severity of the recent banking crisis. However, the anecdotal evidence points toward a credit-crunch only between end-1997 and end-1998, as the regulatory system was tightened and the system of "prompt corrective action" went into operation. Consequently, a regression estimated on aggregate data spanning the period 1980–98 may find it difficult to capture this particular episode of the credit crunch.

## Conclusions

Business investment has declined steeply in the 1990s in Japan, and—as this Chapter has argued—the slump has been driven primarily by structural factors—the unwinding of the capital stock over-

---

[11]The collapse of equity prices in Japan in 1990 was accompanied by a significant increase in volatility. Estimations with a bivariate VAR (not reported here for the sake of brevity) indicate that the increase in volatility had a negative impact on business investment. Thus, the dampening effect of the asset price collapse on business investment was likely amplified by the increased volatility.

hang from the 1980s and the impact of the debt burden. Slippages in corporate governance provided the milieu in which firms incurred large debts and embarked on a strategy of market expansion. The collapse in equity prices in the 1990s also contributed to the slump in investment, both by making equity financing costly and by reducing the net worth of the corporate sector.

# References

Abel, Andre, B., N. Gregory Mankiw, Lawrence H. Summers, and Richard J. Zeckhauser, 1989, "Assessing Dynamic Efficiency: Theory and Evidence," *Review of Economic Studies,* Vol. 56, pp. 1–20.

Bernanke, Ben S., and John Y. Cambell, 1988, "Is there a Corporate Debt Crisis," *Brookings Papers on Economic Activity:* 1, Brookings Institution.

Bernanke, Ben S., and Mark Gertler, 1995, "Inside the Black Box: The Credit Channel of Monetary Policy Transmission," *Journal of Economic Perspectives,* (Fall), pp. 27–48.

Fazzari, Steven M., Glenn Hubbard, and Bruce Peterson, 1988, "Financing Constraints and Corporate Investment," *Brookings Papers on Economic Activity:* 1, Brookings Institution.

Hoshi, Takeo, Anil Kashayp, and David Scharfstein, 1991, "Corporate Structure, Liquidity, and Investment: Evidence from Japanese Industrial Groups," *Quarterly Journal of Economics,* Vol. 106, (February), pp. 33–60.

Jensen, Michael, C., 1988, "Takeovers: Their Causes and Consequences," *Journal of Economic Perspectives,* Vol. 2, (Winter), pp. 21–48.

Prescott, Edward, C., 1999, "Some Observations on the Great Depression," *Federal Reserve Bank of Minneapolis Quarterly Review,* Vol. 23:1 (Winter).

Rowthorn, Robert E., and Ramana Ramaswamy, 1997, "Deindustrialization: Causes and Implications," *Staff Studies for the World Economic Outlook* (Washington: International Monetary Fund).

———, 1999, "Growth, Trade and Deindustrialization," *IMF Staff Papers,* Vol. 46, March (Washington: International Monetary Fund).

Sekine, Toshitaka, 1999 "Firm Investment and Balance-Sheet Problems in Japan," IMF Working Paper 99/111 (Washington: International Monetary Fund).

Shleifer, Andrei, and Vishny, Robert W., 1988, "Value Maximization and the Acquisition Process," *Journal of Economic Perspectives,* 2:1 (Winter), pp. 7–20.

Woo, David, 1999, "In Search of Capital Crunch: Supply Factors Behind the Credit Slowdown in Japan," IMF Working Paper 99/3 (Washington: International Monetary Fund).

# 5

# Where Are We Going? The Output Gap and Potential Growth

*Tamim Bayoumi*

Estimating potential output is a basic tool in macroeconomics. The growth of potential provides an indicator of the likely evolution of activity over the next few years, while the output gap is central to making policy recommendations on short-term demand management.[1] The marked contrast between the sparkling performance of the United States economy in the 1990s and the mediocre growth of much of continental Europe and Japan has brought renewed attention to the issue of how best to estimate potential growth and output. In particular, the assessment of how much of Japan's recent slowdown represents cycle factors versus a slowdown in the growth of potential output is clearly crucial to deciding on the appropriate policy response. If the slowdown is largely cyclical, the solution is to raise aggregate demand, while if more fundamental forces are at work, structural issues should be given greater prominence.

Broadly speaking, there are two methods of estimating the output gap and growth in potential. In the first, the output gap is based on some direct measure of spare capacity, and potential is derived residually—for example, using the Okun coefficient to calculate the gap

---

[1]Both the IMF and the OECD provide estimates of the level of potential output for developed economies in their macroeconomic forecasting exercises across member countries. A discussion of the methodology used in the IMF is provided in De Masi (1997) (see also Adams, Fenton and Larsen, 1987). We follow the usual convention in defining potential output as the level of output that leaves inflation unchanged.

as a function of the unemployment rate. Alternatively, the level of potential output can be calculated directly, either using trends or structural approaches, such as combining factor inputs through an assumed production function, with the gap being derived residually. In the remainder of this chapter, the former methodology will be referred to as the "demand-side" approach and the latter as the "supply-side" approach. Some researchers have combined these methods using simultaneous equation methods, thereby producing a joint estimate of the two concepts. Examples of such an integrated approach include the simultaneous equation system proposed by Adams and Coe (1990) or the structural vector autoregression method suggested by Blanchard and Quah (1989).[2]

All of these calculations work best when structural change is relatively limited, as this minimizes the uncertainties associated with measuring the intensity of factor inputs (for example, the natural rate of unemployment). Unfortunately, the 1990s have been a period of particularly significant underlying changes in the Japanese economy, associated with a switch from growth based on capital accumulation and catch-up to greater attention to profitability and innovation. It is an unfortunate fact of life that at the very moment when an estimate of the output gap is most useful, its calculation is also at its most uncertain. To assess these underlying uncertainties, this chapter compares the results from a range of alternative approaches to estimating the output gap and rate of increase in potential output.

Another issue is the degree to which temporary constraints on the supply of output should be reflected in potential, such as the impact of weather on agricultural output or financial intermediation problems on output more generally. In particular, in the case of Japan, should supply constraints associated with financial intermediation problems caused by banking strains (see Chapter 2) be reflected in potential output?[3] Recalling that potential output represents the level of output

---

[2]This approach is not considered here, largely because I suggest a structural explanation for any divergence between the two approaches. For similar models to that used by Adams and Coe for the United States, see Coe and Krueger (1990) for the (then) Federal Republic of Germany and Citrin (1991) for Japan. The Blanchard and Quah approach has been applied to Japan by Prasad (1995).

[3]Clearly, such banking strains are also likely to reduce aggregate demand, thus causing a widening output gap as well as lower potential output. A survey of the overall output costs of banking crises is contained in IMF (1998), Chapter IV.

at which inflation remains stable (that is, the output equivalent of nonaccelerating inflation rate of unemployment, or the NAIRU), it can be argued that such constraints should be included when the purpose of the exercise is to assess the appropriate stance of demand-management policies—provided they are likely to continue for the period over which changes to aggregate demand are likely to operate. These rigidities affect macroeconomic conditions, and hence the appropriate stance of current policies, while the future relaxation of these constraints can be incorporated in the future growth rate of the potential output of the economy. Demand-side estimates may, in these circumstances, provide a more accurate measure of the short-term movements of potential output, with supply-side approaches being more relevant for assessing medium-term conditions.

## Demand-Side Estimates of the Output Gap

In this section, the output gap is estimated using a series of measures of slack in the economy, namely the unemployment rate, the ratio of job seekers to job offers, capacity utilization, a combination of all of these measures, and an inverted Phillips curve. In all cases, the underlying methodology is similar, involving regressing the logarithm of real GDP on the chosen measure(s) of the output gap, a time trend, a time trend to the power one-half, and a time trend to the power one-third:

$$\log(y_t) = \alpha + \beta X_t + \gamma_1 t + \gamma_2 t^{(1/2)} + \gamma_3 t^{(1/3)} + \varepsilon_t \qquad (5.1)$$

where $y_t$ is real output, $X_t$ represents the measure(s) of demand pressures, $t$ is a time trend, $\varepsilon_t$ is an error term, and other Greek letters are estimated coefficients.[4] Such a regression assumes that the indicators of slack are contemporaneous with the cycle. This is reasonable for many measures, although unemployment is often thought to be a

---

[4]The time trend terms are included so as to provide an initial way of detrending output. It is well known that any function can be approximated by a Taylor expansion of the higher powers of $t$. However, in this case, the terms in the expression become progressively more explosive. As visual inspection and economic intuition both point to a slowing of the rate of growth of output in Japan over time, the trend was modeled using successively lower powers of time. Such an expansion would appear to be capable of approximating any concave time series, although I do not know of any formal proof of this proposition.

lagging indicator of the cycle, implying that it will tend to measure past values of the output gap.

Equation (5.1) can be used to provide a direct estimate of the output gap, together with a residually estimated level of potential output:

$$\log(1 + y_t^{gap}) = \log(y_t/y_t^{pot}) = \beta X_t \tag{5.2}$$

$$\log(y_t^{pot}) = \log(y_t) - \beta X_t = \alpha + \gamma_1 t + \gamma_2 t^{(1/2)} + \gamma_3 t^{(1/3)} + \varepsilon_t \tag{5.3}$$

where $y_t^{gap}$ is the output gap and $y_t^{pot}$ is the level of potential output. The crucial assumption made is that the error term reflects movements in potential output, not changes in the output gap. This is clearly a strong assumption, but appears reasonable given the desire to use estimates of economic slack to infer the output gap. In practice, to reduce the level of noise in the potential output series, the path may be calculated using some sort of averaging technique. For example, in the calculations reported below, the growth rate of potential is estimated as a moving average over four year periods.

As noted earlier, a Phillips curve can be inverted to provide a specification of this type. Starting from a standard linear Phillips curve:

$$\pi_t = \alpha + \beta_1 \pi_{t-4} + \beta_2(\pi_t^m - \pi_t) + \beta_3 \log(y_t) + \gamma_1 t$$

$$+ \gamma_2 t^{(1/2)} + \gamma_3 t^{(1/3)} + \varepsilon_t \tag{5.4}$$

where $\pi_t$ is the four-quarter rate of core inflation and $\pi_t^m$ is the rate of inflation of imported goods. The term in lagged inflation can be thought of as representing the impact of both past inflation and expectations of future inflation, while the time trends again serve to initially detrend real GDP.[5] To turn equation (5.4) into the form of equation (5.1) simply requires moving the term in the log of output to the right-hand side. In addition, nonlinearities in the Phillips curve can be incorporated by adding a term in the square of the output gap (i.e., $((\pi_t - \alpha - \beta_1 \pi_{t-4} - \beta_2(\pi_t^m - \pi_t))/\beta_3)^2)$ to the specification.

Table 5.1 reports the results of the demand-side regressions, estimated from the first quarter of 1975 to end-1998 for the measures of economic slack and the beginning of 1982 to end-1998 for the Phillips

---

[5]Future expectations of inflation were not included in the estimation by instrumenting future actuals, as they often are in Phillips curve analysis, as this would have truncated the sample period and hence reduced its value for current analysis.

## Table 5.1. Demand-Side Regressions of the Output Gap

| | Unemployment Rate | Vacancy Ratio | Capacity Utilization | Combined Estimate | Linear Phillips Curve | Nonlinear Phillips Curve |
|---|---|---|---|---|---|---|
| Unemployment rate | −0.07 (11.9)** | | | −0.03 (4.4)** | | |
| Ratio of job sectors to job offers | | 0.10 (16.3)** | | (0.09) (7.3)** | | |
| Capacity utilization rate | | | 0.33 (6.5)** | 0.00 (1.3) | | |
| Core inflation | | | | | 1.70 (5.7)** | 1.70 (5.6)** |
| Fourth lag of core inflation | | | | | −0.67 (1.9) | −0.67 (1.8) |
| Imported inflation differential | | | | | 0.01 (0.6) | 0.01 (0.5) |
| Square of output gap | | | | | | −0.24 (0.0) |
| Time trend | −0.01 (4.2)** | −0.00 (0.9) | −0.01 (3.2)** | 0.00 (0.1) | −0.14 (4.6)** | −0.14 (4.5)** |
| Time trend to the power one–half | 0.65 (6.6)** | 0.18 (2.0)* | 0.76 (5.8)** | 0.23 (2.6)* | 8.27 (4.2)** | 8.26 (4.1)** |
| Time trend to the power one–third | −1.18 (6.0) | −0.27 (1.6) | −1.45 (5.6)** | 0.36 (2.0)* | −17.65 (4.0)** | −17.63 (3.9)** |
| Adjusted $R^2$ | 0.995 | 0.997 | 0.992 | 0.998 | 0.992 | 0.992 |
| DW | 1.05 | 0.37 | 0.17 | 0.76 | 0.74 | 0.74 |

Source: IMF staff calculations.

Notes: The sample period is 1975:Q1–1998:Q4 for the non–Phillips curves and 1982:Q1–1998:Q4 for the Phillips curves. T-statistics are reported in parentheses, with one and two asterisks reflecting significance at the 5 and 1 percent level, respectively.

curves.[6,7] The coefficients on the first three estimates of economic slack (the unemployment rate, vacancy ratio, and capacity utilization

---

[6]The year 1975 was chosen as the starting date for most regressions so as to provide a long sample period without allowing the extraordinary growth rates during the golden years of the 1960s and early 1970s to dominate the sample. The more recent starting date for the Phillips curve regressions reflects the fact that inflation stabilized in Japan in the early 1980s having been quite variable through the 1970s. Given that inflation expectations presumably also stabilized in the early 1980s, a later starting period is likely to give better estimates, particularly in the absence of a term representing inflation expectations.

[7]Vacancies, capital utilization, and inflation were included in levels, while the unemployment gap was calculated as the difference between actual unemploy-

**Table 5.2. Demand-Side Estimates of the Output Gap and Potential Output Growth**
*(Percent)*

| | Unemployment Rate | Vacancy Ratio | Capacity Utilization | Combined Regression | Phillips Curve | Range |
|---|---|---|---|---|---|---|
| **Estimated output gap** | | | | | | |
| **1998** | **–3.6** | **–2.5** | **–2.9** | **–3.0** | **–1.8** | **–3.6 to –1.8** |
| 1991 | 3.3 | 6.7 | 2.5 | 6.4 | 1.9 | 1.9 to 6.7 |
| **Estimated potential output growth[1]** | | | | | | |
| **1998** | **2.2** | **1.5** | **1.4** | **1.8** | **1.5** | **1.4 to 2.2** |
| 1991 | 3.5 | 3.1 | 4.4 | 3.0 | 4.1 | 3.0 to 4.4 |
| **Estimated change 1991–98** | | | | | | |
| Output gap | –6.9 | –9.2 | –5.4 | –9.4 | –3.7 | –9.4 to –3.7 |
| Potential output[1] | –1.3 | –1.6 | –3.0 | –1.1 | –2.6 | –3.0 to –1.1 |

Source: IMF Staff calculations.
[1]Potential output growth is defined as the annualized growth rate over the last four years.

rate) are all highly significant, although, when the three measures are combined into a single regression, the coefficient on capacity utilization (which has the lowest *t*-statistic in the individual regressions) is no longer significant. In the case of the linear Phillips curve, the coefficients are all correctly signed, but only that on the current core inflation rate is significant at conventional levels. When the nonlinear term in the output gap is included in the Phillips curve it is insignificant and has almost no impact on the regression results. All of the regressions show evidence of autocorrelation in the residuals, presumably reflecting correlated changes in the path of potential output.

Table 5.2 and Figure 5.1 report the resulting estimates of the output gap and the implied annualized rate of growth of potential output (calculated as a moving average over the previous four years). The results for the nonlinear Phillips curve are not reported as they were virtually identical to the linear version. The estimates of the 1998 output gap fall into a fairly narrow range, varying between –3.6 and –1.8 percentage points of GDP, while the output gap is estimated to have been substantially positive in 1991, at the height of the bub-

---

ment and the natural rate. The natural rate in turn was estimated using a Hodrick-Prescott filter (with a smoothing coefficient of 40,000). The interpretation of smoothing coefficients is discussed further below.

Figure 5.1. Demand-Side Estimates of the Output Gap

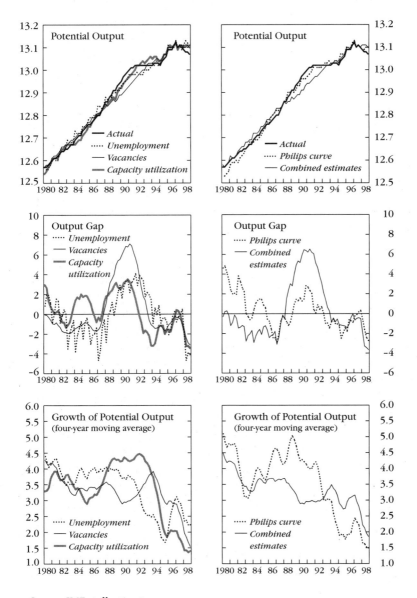

Source: IMF staff estimates.

ble. The estimates for the rate of growth of potential output in 1998 vary within the relatively limited range of 1.4–2.2 percent, well below values for earlier in the 1980s and early 1990s.[8] In terms of the contributing factors to the slowdown in activity through the 1990s, the output gap is estimated to have fallen between 3.7 and 9.4 percentage points of GDP between 1991 and 1998, while the rate of growth of potential output is estimated to have been reduced by between 1.1 and 3.0 percent per annum, implying that the slowdown in growth during the 1990s reflects both a marked swing in the output gap and a significant slowing of the growth of potential output.

## Time-Series Estimates of Potential Output

The main alternative approach to estimating the output gap involves directly estimating potential output, then calculating the output gap residually. The easiest way of doing this is to assume that potential output follows a univariate time series process associated with the path of real GDP. Estimating from the first quarter of 1975, three approaches of this type were considered, regressing output on a split time trend (with the split occurring in the first quarter of 1990), regressing the logarithm of output on the power sequence of time trends already discussed in the preceding section (that is, time, time to the power one-half, and time to the power one-third), and using a Hodrick-Prescott (HP) filter. As results from an HP filter depend upon the smoothing parameter chosen, the results from two possible values (14,400 and 40,000) are reported.[9]

---

[8]This is unlikely to simply reflect short-term cyclical factors, as the revival of output in 1995 and 1996 is included in the calculation for 1998 due to the four-year lag used to calculate the growth of potential output.

[9]See Hodrick and Prescott (1981) and Laxton and others (1998) Box 7 pages 30–31 for a description of the properties of the Hodrick Prescott filter. Briefly, the HP filter minimizes a weighted average of the square of deviations from the trend and the square of changes in the underlying trend, with the smoothing parameter providing the weight to be put on deviations from the trend. The higher the smoothing parameter, therefore, the less the trend will vary with movements in the underlying variable. A smoothing parameter of 40,000, for example, uses a relative weight on deviations of the trend of 200 (the square root of 40,000), loosely implying that a 0.05 percent movement in the trend from one quarter to another is given the same weight as a 10 percent deviation from the trend.

Table 5.3. Supply-Side Estimates of the Output Gap and Potential
Growth Using Univariate Trends
*(Percent)*

| | Split Time Trend | Power Sequence | Hodrick-Prescott Filter | | Range |
|---|---|---|---|---|---|
| | | | 40,000 | 14,400 | |
| Estimated output gap | | | | | |
| **1998** | **−3.7** | **−4.7** | **−4.8** | **−3.5** | **−4.8 to −3.5** |
| 1991 | 3.9 | 5.2 | 4.7 | 3.7 | 3.7 to 5.2 |
| Estimated potential output growth[1] | | | | | |
| **1998** | **2.1** | **2.3** | **2.2** | **1.8** | **1.8 to 2.3** |
| 1991 | 3.3 | 3.1 | 3.3 | 3.5 | 3.1 to 3.5 |
| Estimated change 1991–98 | | | | | |
| Output gap | −7.6 | −9.9 | −9.5 | −7.2 | −9.9 to −7.2 |
| Potential output[1] | −1.2 | −0.8 | −1.2 | −1.7 | −1.7 to −0.8 |

Source: IMF staff calculations.
[1]Potential output growth is defined as the annualized growth rate over the last four years.

The results from the estimation, shown in Table 5.3 and Figure 5.2, again show that the estimates of the output gap in 1998 cluster in a relatively narrow range.[10] What is striking about this range, however, is that it does not correspond to that found in the earlier demand-side estimates. Compared to the equivalent figures in Table 5.2, the estimates of the 1998 output gap are universally larger (3½–4¾ percentage points of GDP as opposed to 1¾–3½ percentage points) and the estimated rate of growth of potential also tends to be larger. In short, univariate techniques generate significantly higher estimates of the current growth of potential output, and hence the output gap, than do direct measures of economic slack.

Further, comparing Tables 5.2 and 5.3, we find that this pattern—that the demand-side estimates of the output gap are smaller (in absolute value) than the supply-side estimates—does not hold true for 1991. Hence, the divergence between the demand- and supply-side estimates of the output gap appears to be a recent phenomenon, consistent with it being associated with short-term supply constraints, plausibly associated with financial system difficul-

---

[10]The two Hodrick-Prescott filters provide the upper and lower estimates of the output gap, illustrating the sensitivity of this filter to the assumed smoothing parameter.

Figure 5.2. Trend Estimates of Potential Output

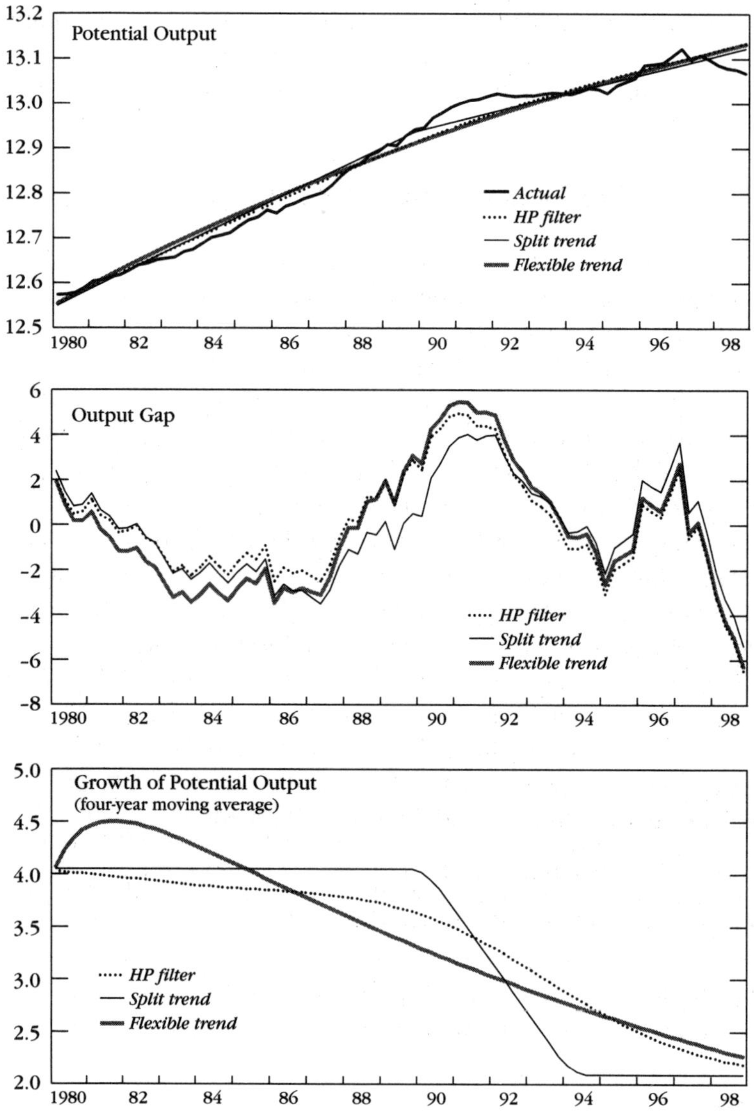

Source: IMF staff estimates.
Note: HP refers to Hodrick-Prescott filter.

ties.[11] Comparing the midpoints of the ranges of estimated output gaps using the two techniques implies that temporary supply constraints may have reduced potential output by 1–2 percentage points of GDP in 1998, with corresponding potential gains from relieving such constraints, although this is clearly a very rough calculation.

## Production Function Approaches

A more sophisticated method of directly estimating the level of potential output is to use a production function. This approach, which is currently used by the Japan desk as well as most other Group of Seven desks in the IMF, postulates an underlying production function, and proceeds to estimate potential output based on suitably adjusted inputs of labor, capital, and an assumed level of technological progress.[12] In addition to being highly flexible, a major advantage of a production function approach is that it links the evolution of potential output to inputs of labor and capital. Given the need for the IMF staff to integrate estimates of potential output into an overall assessment of past and future trends in the Japanese economy, this link is very useful, particularly in the context of assessing the likely future evolution of the economy, and argues powerfully for maintaining this framework even if it is unlikely to identify temporary supply constraints associated with banking weakness.

In the case of Japan, a Cobb-Douglas production function is assumed, so that potential output can be calculated as:

$$\log(y_t^{pot}) = \alpha + \beta\log(h_t^{pot}) + (1 - \beta)\log(k_t^{pot}) + TFP_t \qquad (5.5)$$

where $h_t^{pot}$ and $k_t^{pot}$ are the level of labor hours and capital, respectively, that can be employed without creating inflationary pressure, $TFP_t$ is the level of technological progress, $\beta$ is the share of labor income in GDP, and $\alpha$ is a scaling factor. While conceptually straight-

---

[11]Comparison of Figures 5.1 and 5.2 shows that this divergence is true for 1996, the peak of the cycle prior to the current recession. Demand-side estimates of the output gap show the economy barely reaching potential in 1996, while supply-side estimates have the economy clearly above potential.

[12]De Masi (1997) describes approaches used within the IMF to calculate potential output.

forward, implementing this approach requires a number of judgments, which are best illustrated by reference to the approach currently taken by the Japan desk:

- *Hours worked.* This is the product of the trend labor force, average hours worked, and (one minus) the natural rate of unemployment. Each of the components needs to be adjusted for the cycle (as the discouraged worker effect is quite strong in Japan, the labor force is cyclical). This is accomplished using a Hodrick-Prescott filter with a relatively high smoothing parameter (40,000) to minimize the impact of cyclical fluctuations on the trend. Even so, until recently these estimates of the natural rate of unemployment and hours worked were adjusted judgmentally as they were still considered to be likely to be affected by the current cycle.

- *Capital stock.* As capital is a stock series with limited cyclical variation, the actual level is used rather than a cyclically adjusted estimate. The IMF staff calculate their own capital stock series based on the permanent inventory method with a fixed rate of depreciation. By contrast, the official series assumes that additional investment is fully productive for a fixed number of years and is then eliminated, the so-called "one-horse shay" approach. The disadvantage of the official series is that, because the capital stock does not depreciate steadily over time, the current estimate of capital continues to include large amounts of the investment generated during the bubble period of the late 1980s. Another issue is that there is a widespread perception that much of the investment during the bubble years was not productive, as shown by the large amounts of bad debt in the banking system, and hence that the measured capital stock may overstate the productive capital stock.[13]

- *Trend productivity.* This is estimated from actual productivity using a Hodrick-Prescott filter, and again until recently was adjusted judgmentally.

---

[13]Another way of looking at this is that the Cobb-Douglas production function assumes that capital has a marginal return that is fixed over time. To the extent that overinvestment has depressed the marginal rate of return below its long-term level, the production function overestimates the potential level of output.

Table 5.4. Supply-Side Estimates of the Output Gap and Potential
Growth Using a Production Function
*(Percent)*

|  | Previous Estimate | Eliminating All Judgmental Adjustments | Using Official Capital Stock | Adjusting Capital for Scrapping | Range | Current Estimate |
|---|---|---|---|---|---|---|
| Estimated output gap |  |  |  |  |  |  |
| **1998** | **−5.7** | **−3.6** | **−4.0** | **−3.5** | **−5.7 to −3.5** | **−4.1** |
| 1991 | 3.0 | 3.6 | 4.1 | 3.3 | 3.0 to 4.1 | 3.5 |
| Estimated potential output growth[1] |  |  |  |  |  |  |
| **1998** | **2.1** | **1.7** | **1.9** | **1.7** | **1.7 to 2.1** | **1.9** |
| 1991 | 3.9 | 3.9 | 3.7 | 3.9 | 3.7 to 3.9 | 3.8 |
| Estimated change 1991–98 |  |  |  |  |  |  |
| Output gap | −8.7 | −7.2 | −8.1 | −6.8 | −8.7 to −6.8 | −7.6 |
| Potential output[1] | −1.9 | −2.1 | −1.8 | −2.1 | −2.1 to −1.8 | −1.9 |

Sources: IMF staff estimates.
[1]Potential output growth is defined as the annualized growth rate over the last four years.

To investigate the importance of alternative assumptions, Table 5.4
shows a number of calculations using the production function approach. Previous desk estimates of the output gap, using a range of
judgmental adjustments, are shown first, followed by the results implied by removing all such adjustments. From this new baseline, the
effect of reestimating the model using two alternative capital stock
series are then reported, namely replacing the IMF staff's capital
stock estimate with the official capital stock series and reducing the
staff's estimate of the business capital stock by ¥3 trillion per quarter
since the first quarter of 1990 (for a cumulated total of ¥99 trillion, or
20 percent of GDP), the approximate value of the aggregate bad
loans in the banking system, in order to approximate the impact of
accelerated scrapping of misallocated investments made during the
bubble period. The final calculation removes the judgmental adjustments to productivity and the natural rate of unemployment, but retains some adjustments to average hours worked—and represents the
series currently used by the IMF Japan desk.[14]

---

[14]While average hours worked fell rapidly over the 1990s, this largely associated with legislated changes in working hours rather than a long-term downward
trend.

The results from this exercise are reported in Table 5.4 and Figure 5.3. When the judgmental adjustments applied by the staff are excluded, the estimated output gap for 1998 falls by over one-third, from 5.7 percentage points of GDP to 3.6 percentage points, and the rate of growth of potential output is reduced from 2.1 percent to 1.7 percent. These results approximately span the range of values produced by univariate supply-side estimates, but are larger than their demand-side equivalents.[15] Switching to the official capital stock series raises both the output gap and potential output growth, while assuming a higher rate of scrapping has little impact on the estimates despite the size of the adjustment. These differences largely reflect the fact that significant short-term changes in behavior, such as judgmental adjustments, tend to be incorporated into the output gap while gradual changes in trends, such as the gradual reduction in the capital stock assumed to be caused by scrapping, is largely offset by changes in estimated trend growth in total factor productivity.

The IMF staff's current estimate of potential output, which removes most of the judgmental adjustments to the inputs, produces a 1998 output gap of 4.1 percent, at the lower end of the "supply-side" estimates of the output gap but above the results using "demand-side" techniques, and a current rate of growth of potential output of 1.9 percent.

To further examine the evolution of the IMF staff's estimate of potential output over time, Table 5.5 reports the growth of potential over successive four year periods starting in 1987, 1991, 1995 and 1999, and decomposes the growth into its component parts, for both the current estimate of potential output and the earlier estimate incorporating a wider range of judgmental adjustments. The current series shows the growth in potential falling by almost 1 percent every 4 years, from 3.7 percent in the late 1980s to a projected value of 1.1 percent between 1999 and 2002. The main contributor to this decline is a fall in the growth of capital inputs, followed by lower trend growth in the labor force (particularly over 1999–2002). Trend growth in total factor productivity is also estimated to have declined modestly (by about ⅓ percent over the full period), while a marked

---

[15]Approximately equal reductions in the output gap in 1998 come from taking out the judgmental adjustments to productivity and labor inputs.

## Figure 5.3. Production Function Estimates of Potential Output

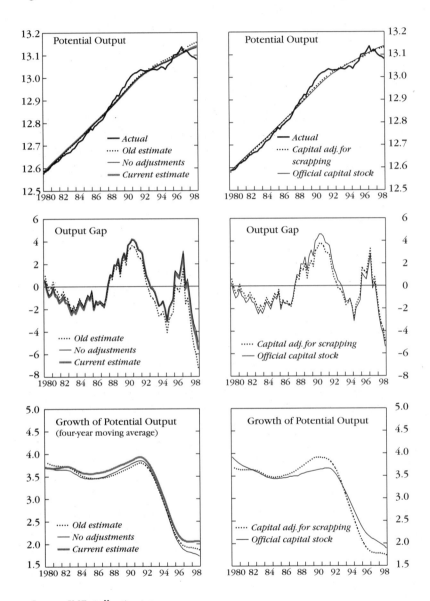

Source: IMF staff estimates.

Table 5.5. Decomposing the Growth of Potential Output Over Time
*(Annualized percentage change)*

|  | 1987–90 | 1991–94 | 1995–98 | 1999–2002 |
|---|---|---|---|---|
| Potential output | | | | |
| **Current** | **3.74** | **2.74** | **1.87** | **1.09** |
| Previous | 3.88 | 2.86 | 2.07 | 1.20 |
| Difference | –0.14 | –0.12 | –0.20 | –0.11 |
| *Of which:* | | | | |
| Labor force | | | | |
| **Current** | **0.76** | **0.62** | **0.46** | **0.08** |
| Previous | 0.76 | 0.67 | 0.56 | 0.09 |
| Difference | — | –0.05 | –0.10 | –0.01 |
| Average hours | | | | |
| **Current** | **–0.40** | **–0.56** | **–0.52** | **–0.35** |
| Previous | –0.40 | –0.56 | –0.49 | –0.18 |
| Difference | — | — | –0.03 | –0.17 |
| Capital stock | | | | |
| **Current** | **2.19** | **1.68** | **1.06** | **0.52** |
| Previous | 2.19 | 1.68 | 1.06 | 0.32 |
| Difference | — | — | — | –0.20 |
| Total factor productivity | | | | |
| **Current** | **1.15** | **1.01** | **0.90** | **0.81** |
| Previous | 1.30 | 1.08 | 0.94 | 0.91 |
| Difference | 0.15 | 0.07 | 0.04 | 0.10 |

Source: IMF staff calculations.

decline in trend hours largely associated with a legislated reduction in the work week also lowered potential growth over the period to 1998. The current estimate of the growth rate of potential is consistently between 0.1 and 0.2 percent per annum below the old estimates, reflecting lower estimated trend productivity and trend labor inputs.

The calculations can also be used to assess the reasons for the decline in the growth of output over the 1990s. If the estimated rate of growth of potential seen over the late 1980s period had been maintained between 1991 and 1998, potential output would have been over 10 percent higher at the end of the period. By comparison, between 1991 and 1998 the output gap is estimated to have changed by 8½ percentage points of potential, implying that long-term supply trends have a slight preponderance in explaining the slowdown in output compared to demand factors or more temporary constraints on supply.

# Conclusions

This chapter has examined the output gap and potential output growth in Japan using a number of different techniques, focusing on the results from demand indicators and estimates of potential output based on smoothing techniques or a production function. The results within each type of estimate were relatively consistent. However, estimates using demand indicators generally give smaller estimates of the output gap and growth of potential than do supply indicators in 1998, although not in 1991, consistent with the view that demand-side indicators may reflect short-term constraints on potential output while supply-side estimates provide a better assessment of the medium-term situation. Highly stylized calculations imply that such constraints could currently be lowering potential output by a percentage point or two. As a result, demand-side indicators tend to put more weight on a slowdown in potential in explaining the mediocre performance in the 1990s than do direct estimates of potential, although all approaches found both effects to be important.

In many respects, however, the divergences in estimates across different techniques were relatively small given the uncertainties illustrated by the wide range of views on both the outlook and appropriate policies in Japan. Most estimates of the output gap fell within the 2½–4½ percentage point range, and most estimates of potential growth were within 1½–2¼ percent. The staff's current estimates of the growth of potential output (1.9 percent) and the output gap (4.1 percentage points) are within these ranges, although above the midpoints in both cases, reflecting the fact that the methodology is not designed to identify short-term supply constraints. Overall, while the flexibility and analytical transparency of the production function makes it a particularly attractive approach, it may be useful to augment production function estimates with the results from alternative approaches. This is particularly true at times such as the present, when the level of uncertainty about the underlying output gap is large, especially in the light of the possible impact of financial system strains, while the importance of the output gap in policy assessment is high.

Looking to the future, an obvious way of extending this analysis is to incorporate direct indicators of the supply-side, such as unionization, demographics, replacement ratios and employers contributions to social security into the estimation. Such an extension could provide a more nuanced explanation for recent movements in potential output and the natural rate of unemployment than the univariate techniques used here.

# References

Adams, Charles, and David T. Coe, 1990, "A Systems Approach to Estimating the Natural Rate of Unemployment and Potential Output for the United States," *IMF Staff Papers* Vol. 37 pp. 232–93.

Adams, Charles, Paul R. Fenton, and Flemming Larsen, 1987, "Potential Output in Major Industrial Countries," in *Staff Studies for the World Economic Outlook* World Economic and Financial Surveys (Washington: International Monetary Fund).

Blanchard, Olivier, and Danny Quah, 1989, "The Dynamic Effects of Aggregate Demand and Aggregate Supply Disturbances," *American Economic Review* Vol. 79 pp. 655–73.

Citrin, Daniel, 1991, "Potential Output and the Natural Rate of Unemployment: Recent History and Medium Term Prospects," unpublished manuscript, International Monetary Fund.

Coe, David T., and Thomas Krueger, 1990, "Wage Determination, the Natural Rate of Unemployment, and Potential Output," ed. by Leslie Lipschitz and Donogh McDonald, *German Unification: Economic Issues* IMF Occasional Paper No. 75 (Washington: International Monetary Fund).

De Masi, Paula R., 1997, "IMF Estimates of Potential Output: Theory and Practice," in *Staff Studies for the World Economic Outlook* World Economic and Financial Surveys (Washington: International Monetary Fund).

Hodrick, Robert J. and Edward C. Prescott, 1981, "Post-War U.S. Business Cycles: An Empirical Investigation," Carnegie-Mellon University Discussion Paper, No. 451.

International Monetary Fund, 1998, *World Economic Outlook,* (Washington: International Monetary Fund), May.

Laxton, Douglas, Peter Isard, Hamid Faruqee, Eswar Prasad, and Bart Turtelboom, 1998, *MULTIMOD Mark III: The Core Dynamic and Steady-State Models* IMF Occasional Paper No. 164 (Washington: International Monetary Fund).

Prasad, Eswar, 1995, "Trends and Cycles in the Japanese Economy", (unpublished manuscript, International Monetary Fund).

# 6

## Too Much of a Good Thing?
## The Effectiveness of Fiscal Stimulus

*Martin Mühleisen*

In response to the prolonged economic downturn, the Japanese government adopted an expansionary fiscal policy stance for most of the 1990s. With a brief interruption in 1997, when growth temporarily improved, the general government's fiscal position (excluding social security) steadily deteriorated from balance in FY1990 to an estimated deficit of 8 percent of GDP in FY1998. In particular, the government tried to revive activity through a series of stimulus packages between 1992 and 1995, and again through substantive packages in 1998 and 1999 (Table 6.1). These packages have involved significant "headline" figures (often above 2 percent of GDP), capped by a ¥24 trillion package (5 percent of GDP) in November 1998.

However, doubts have been raised over the amount of real economic stimulus provided by the government (e.g., Posen, 1998). The demand impact of the stimulus packages has largely been limited to the so-called "real water" measures (items that lead directly to government expenditure and thus boost economic activity), such as public works spending and tax cuts. Significant portions of the stimulus packages' headline amounts, however, have consisted of financial measures—such as loans provided to government financial institutions (GFIs) by the Fiscal Investment and Loan Program (FILP)—which have not directly led to higher aggregate demand as long as the economy was not severely credit-constrained. For example, the November 1998 package included ¥8 trillion in public investment

**Table 6.1. Japanese Stimulus Packages**
(Trillions of yen)

| | Sep.–86 | May–87 | Aug.–92 | Apr.–93 | Sep.–93 | Feb.–94 | Apr.–95 | Sep.–95 | Apr.–98 | Nov.–98 |
|---|---|---|---|---|---|---|---|---|---|---|
| Tax reductions | ... | 1.0 | ... | 0.2 | ... | 5.9 | 5.4 | ... | 4.6 | 6.0 |
| Public investment | 2.0 | 3.7 | 6.3 | 7.6 | 2.0 | 3.7 | ... | 8.0 | 7.7 | 7.2 |
| Public works | 2.0 | 3.7 | 6.3 | 7.6 | 2.0 | 3.7 | ... | 5.6 | 3.1 | 4.8 |
| Central government (incl. joint projects) | 1.2 | 2.9 | 3.5 | 4.1 | 1.5 | 1.9 | ... | 4.6 | 1.6 | 4.8 |
| Independent local government projects | 0.8 | 0.8 | 2.8 | 3.5 | 0.5 | 1.8 | ... | 1.0 | 1.5 | ... |
| Earthquake relief and disaster prevention | ... | ... | ... | ... | ... | ... | 5.1 | 1.9 | 1.0 | 0.6 |
| Environment, science and technology | ... | ... | ... | ... | ... | ... | 0.3 | 0.4 | 2.6 | 1.8 |
| Welfare, health care, and education | ... | ... | ... | ... | ... | ... | ... | ... | 1.0 | ... |
| Real water measures | 2.0 | 4.7 | 6.3 | 7.7 | 2.0 | 9.6 | 5.4 | 8.0 | 12.3 | 13.2 |
| Spending vouchers | ... | ... | ... | ... | ... | ... | ... | ... | ... | 0.7 |
| Land acquisition[1] | 0.3 | 0.6 | 1.6 | 1.2 | 0.3 | 2.8 | ... | 3.2 | 2.3 | 0.9 |
| Lending by Housing Loan Corporation | 0.7 | 0.7 | 0.8 | 1.8 | 2.9 | 1.2 | ... | 0.5 | ... | 1.2 |
| Lending by other public financial institutions | 0.6 | ... | 2.1 | 2.4 | 0.8 | 1.7 | 1.5 | 2.5 | 2.1 | 7.9 |
| Small and medium-sized enterprises | 0.1 | ... | 1.2 | 1.9 | 0.8 | 1.4 | 1.4 | 1.3 | 2.0 | 0.0 |
| Employment measures | ... | ... | ... | 0.0 | ... | 0.0 | ... | 0.0 | 0.1 | 1.0 |
| Other | 0.5 | ... | 0.9 | 0.5 | ... | 0.3 | 0.1 | 1.2 | ... | 6.9 |
| Total package | 3.6 | 6.0 | 10.7 | 13.2 | 5.9 | 15.3 | 7.0 | 14.2 | 16.7 | 23.9 |
| *Memorandum items:* | | | | | | | | | | |
| Total package (percent of GDP) | 1.1 | 1.7 | 2.3 | 2.8 | 1.2 | 3.2 | 1.4 | 2.9 | 3.4 | 4.9 |
| Real water measures (percent of total) | 54.0 | 78.3 | 58.4 | 58.6 | 32.9 | 62.8 | 77.9 | 55.9 | 73.9 | 55.2 |

Source: Data provided by the authorities.
[1]Partly based on IMF staff estimates.

and ¥6 trillion in tax cuts (later raised to ¥9 trillion) as real water components, while financial measures accounted for about ¥8 trillion (Box 6.1).[1]

The size and composition of public works measures have also attracted criticism. Public works measures constituted the bulk of most stimulus programs. However, budgetary allocations for public works projects were frequently below the amounts announced in the packages because these included a significant portion for land purchases (15 percent or more). In addition, a recent study by Ishii and Wada (1998) suggested that the actual increase of public works between 1992 and 1996 fell ¥10 trillion (2 percent of GDP) short of the amount contained in the stimulus packages, mainly as a consequence of poor implementation at the local government level. Questions have also been raised over whether diminishing returns to scale from public construction projects (owing to a weak project selection process, cost overruns, and a bias toward projects in rural areas) may have contributed to declining fiscal multipliers (Bayoumi, Towe, and Oishi, 1998).

A breakdown of the shift in the general government's structural balance indeed shows a surprisingly small role played by public investment in recent years.[2] While the general government's structural balance fell from a 2½ percent of GDP surplus in 1990 to a deficit of 3½ percent of GDP in 1998, the increase in public investment only contributed 1 percentage point to that decline (Figure 6.1). A more significant factor was the decline in (structural) tax revenue of more than 4 percent of GDP between 1990 and 1998.

How can the large increase in the fiscal deficit be reconciled with questions about the effectiveness of fiscal stimulus measures, and what has been the role of public investment and tax cuts? Deciding on the true level of economic stimulus provided by the government

---

[1]Recent financial measures may have had larger effects. For example, small and medium-sized enterprises (SMEs) were reported to suffer from insufficient access to bank credit in 1998, and the subsequent extension of public loan guarantees for SME borrowing (outside any stimulus program) has led to a substantial increase in SME investment.

[2]The structural balance is defined as the fiscal balance under a closed output gap. By eliminating the effects of cyclical swings on the fiscal position, the structural balance is a widely used measure for the fiscal policy stance.

## Box 6.1. Stimulus Programs, the Budget Process, and the Implementation of Public Works

Fiscal operations in Japan are conducted through complex institutional arrangements, the focal point of which is the central government's General Account, which receives almost all national tax and bond revenues. There are also 38 Special Accounts, largely under the control of individual ministries, which are partly cofinanced by borrowing, e.g., from the Fiscal Investment and Loan Program (FILP). Local governments comprise 47 prefectures and 3,200 municipalities, whose fiscal operations (especially taxation and borrowing) are to a substantial extent controlled by the central government. The FILP provides loans for government financial institutions (GFIs) and other public agencies. Although not formally part of general government, it operates under the authority of the Ministry of Finance, and its investment plan is often referred to as the "second budget."

Stimulus programs typically affect all layers of the public sector. Real water measures (tax cuts and public works) are implemented through supplementary budgets and, in some cases, initial budgets for the following fiscal year. Past stimulus programs have also contained substantial measures to be carried out by GFIs and other public sector agencies. For example, the November 1998 package took several steps to counteract credit shortages, including through capital injections and funds for GFIs worth ¥5.9 trillion (intended to promote additional loans and loan guarantees of up to ¥27 trillion), an extension of the ceiling for loans by the Housing Loan Corporation (at a cost of ¥1.2 trillion), and additional export credits for Asia (¥1 trillion). Although these measures have been partly financed by the central government budget, they have been implemented to a substantial extent through the FILP, drawing on deposits from public savings and pension schemes in the Trust Fund Bureau, and requiring no additional government borrowing.

The stimulus packages have relied on the substantial participation of local governments. Although stimulus packages are decided at the central government level, local authorities share in the revenue losses for most tax categories, and carry out the bulk of public works projects. The central government implements some public works on its own, but most of the investment projects have consisted of either jointly financed projects (with roughly equal shares) or projects carried out under the sole responsibilities of local governments. Local authorities have received additional financial support from the central government and the FILP but, recognizing the difficult financial situation of many local governments, the latest stimulus package in November 1998 no longer contained any provisions for fully self-financed local government public works.

The timing of the public works measures is difficult to predict. A typical stimulus program requires some 3–6 months between the date of announcement and commencement of the related construction projects. As for the central government, the coordination process required to pass a supplementary budget takes about a month, followed by one more month during which orders and contracts are completed. Another month typically passes before construction starts. The process for local governments depends on the passage of supplementary budgets in local councils that may be delayed, depending on the prevailing local political situation. In the case of large construction projects (exceeding ¥500 billion), progress is delayed further by adherence to WTO government procurement regulations (which require an interval of 40 days for the bidding process).

Official statistics do not provide a comprehensive picture on the progress of implementation. Survey-based construction indicators (on orders and public works starts) published by the Ministry of Construction are available 4–6 weeks after the end of a calendar month. These data cover up to 50 percent of GDP-based public investment and precede preliminary national income data with a short lead of at most one quarter. However, information provided by the indicators does not correspond to the fiscal accounts, comprehensive information for which is only available after 12 months from the end of the fiscal year, owing largely to a delay in consolidating the accounts of local authorities.

At the time of writing, the following data were available to evaluate the impact of stimulus packages: (i) Monthly information for central government accounts through May 1999; (ii) preliminary national income accounts for the first quarter of 1999; (iii) full national income accounts (including general government) for FY1997; and (iv) central and local government settlement data for FY1997.

Figure 6.1. Components of General Government
Structural Balance, 1980–98

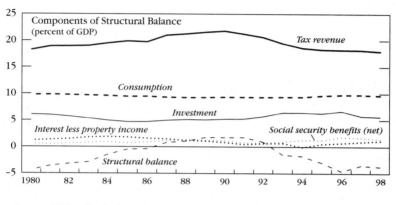

Source: IMF staff calculations.

is clearly important for future policy analysis. This chapter seeks to address these questions by focusing on the following issues:[3]

- The limited rise in public investment. The first section of the chapter explores why the increase in public investment has been relatively small in recent years, compared to the prominent role of public works in the stimulus packages.
- Why was there a sharp drop in tax revenue? The revenue decline went well beyond the scope of the government's tax cuts in recent years. As laid out in the second section, this has reflected a sharp unexplained fall in tax elasticity in the early 1990s.

This chapter also addresses the question why Japan has had to rely to a relatively large extent on discretionary policy measures. The generally low cyclical variability of unemployment and social welfare benefits in Japan imply a low level of automatic stabilizers in Japan compared to other major industrial countries. Without active policy

---

[3]An analysis of the impact of fiscal policy on activity, which is beyond the scope of this paper, is contained in Lipworth and Meredith (1998) and in the chapters by Bayoumi and Ramaswamy and Rendu in this book. Lipworth and Meredith estimated a multiplier of public expenditure of 1–1¼, while VAR approaches employed by the other authors yielded an estimate about half the size.

measures, such limited automatic stabilizers would have constrained the fiscal support to the economy. The third section thus analyzes the extent to which stimulus measures have been used to offset the relative lack of automatic stabilizers in Japan.

The limited transparency of the Japanese fiscal system hampers much of the following analysis. Japanese fiscal accounts offer only a partial picture of government finance operations, mainly because of insufficient account consolidation across various layers of government (see Box 6.1). In particular, detailed consolidated accounts for the general government are only provided in the context of the National Income Accounts. These data become available electronically with a lag of 9 months from the end of the fiscal year, owing to difficulties in compiling the accounts of some 3,300 local authorities that carry out the bulk of public expenditure, and many details are further delayed. As a result, most of this paper focuses on stimulus measures that took place before 1998.

## Stimulus Packages and Public Investment

All of the stimulus packages in the last ten years have included significant additional public works spending. Public works (typically consisting of infrastructure-related construction projects) have traditionally played an important role in Japan, partly reflecting the infrastructure needs of an expanding economy and partly for political reasons (Schlesinger, 1997). They have been seen as an instrument to quickly boost aggregate demand, given the swift impact of a rise in public orders on employment and incomes in the construction sector.[4]

Consequently, overall public investment has seen a sizable increase in recent years.[5] The share of public investment in GDP rose from 6½ percent in fiscal year 1990 to 8¾ percent in 1995 (see Fig-

---

[4]Japan's construction sector accounts for 10 percent of total employment, compared to an average of 6–7 percent in other major industrial countries.

[5]Public works spending accounts for roughly three-quarters of general government investment. Fiscal data on public works spending are not fully available on a timely basis, but national income accounts provide an early estimate for the demand impact of the stimulus packages.

Figure 6.2. Japanese Public Investment
*(Percent of GDP)*

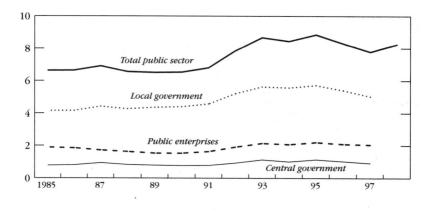

ure 6.2), with particularly strong increases in some of the years with large stimulus packages. For example, in fiscal years 1992 and 1993, the government implemented four successive packages with a combined worth of ¥20 trillion in public works, leading to record investment increases in both years. Similarly, a ¥6 trillion package in 1995 provided a strong boost to investment in that year. Investment fell in 1996 and 1997 as stimulus measures were phased out, but rose again strongly in the wake of the 1998 packages.

Nevertheless, investment seems to have risen by much less than might have been expected from the stimulus measures. As shown in Figure 6.3, the nominal increase in public investment (on a national accounts basis) has indeed been much smaller than the public works components of the stimulus packages.[6] The increase in public investment in 1993, for example, was only around ¥4 trillion (panel A), or less than a third of the packages' public works measures in that year (panel C). Similarly, the investment increase in 1995 was about ¥3 trillion, compared to public works measures worth ¥6 trillion.

What has caused these disappointing results? There appear to be three main factors behind the comparatively small investment in-

---

[6]For ease of comparison, the scales in panels A–C of Figure 6.3 have been kept the same, so that an investment change of, say, ¥10 trillion is identical in all three panels.

Figure 6.3.  Changes in Public Investment [1]
*(Trillions of yen)*

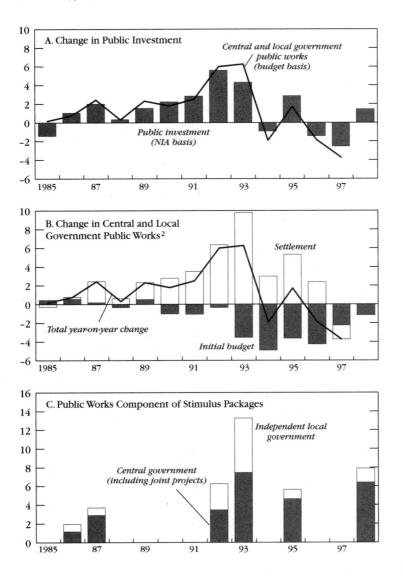

Sources: National income accounts (A); central government general account
budget (A,B); White Book on Local Government Finance (A,B); and data provided by
the Ministry of Finance (C).
Note: NIA = National Income Accounts.
[1]Fiscal year basis (April-March).
[2]Contains double-counted expenditure items.

crease, namely the contractionary nature of initial budgets throughout the 1990s, financial difficulties at the local government level, and shortfalls in the implementation of the stimulus measures.

## Contractionary Initial Budgets

Stimulus packages have served in part to offset expenditure cuts in initial budget plans. Reflecting the government's determination to maintain fiscal discipline, initial budgets were typically contractionary throughout the 1990s, containing substantial expenditure cuts compared to actual spending levels of the previous year. The restrictive stance is reflected by the fact that initial budgets are planned (and reported) with reference to the previous year's initial budget, rather than the higher level of spending implied by supplementary budgets. Although a useful device for maintaining budget discipline, this mechanism obscures the level of contraction frequently implied by initial budgets. In many years, the fiscal stance switched to contraction early in the fiscal year before expansionary stimulus packages were enacted in response to worsening economic conditions.

This process is illustrated for the sum of central and local government public works expenditure in Panel B in Figure 6.3.[7] The dark bars—the difference between initial budget plans and actual expenditure in the previous year—reflect the contractionary nature of initial budgets, which provided for expenditure cuts of around ¥4 trillion (0.8 percent of GDP) per year between 1993 and 1996. Actual spending, however, increased in most of these years as supplementary budgets more than offset cuts planned in the initial bud-

---

[7]The figure shows the breakdown of changes in public works spending into two components:

$$(PW_t - PW_{t-1}) = (IB_t - PW_{t-1}) + (PW_t - IB_t)$$

where $PW$ is actual public works spending (budget settlement basis), and $IB$ the allocation for public works in the initial budget. For the purpose of this chart, budgetary spending by central and local governments has simply been added up, ignoring double-counted items (some 20 percent of total; see below). Time series data for consolidated general government spending have only been available on a settlement basis and do not allow for the breakdown shown in this chart.

**Figure 6.4. Public Works Spending of Central and Local Government**[1]
*(Trillions of yen)*

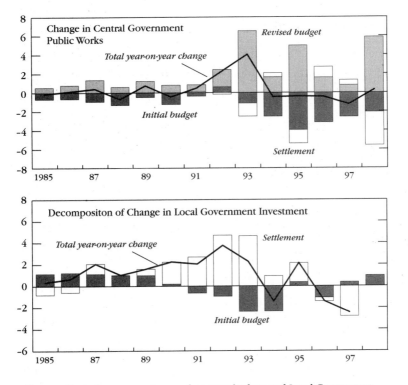

Sources: Central government general account budget; and Local Government Finance White Book.

[1]Fiscal year (April–March). Central government data for 1998 based on information provided in the budget documents.

gets. This is reflected in the chart, where the difference between initial budgets and final outcomes (indicated by white bars) roughly corresponds to the public works components of the stimulus packages.

Data for the central government alone allow a closer analysis of changes in actual public works spending (Figure 6.4). The availability of the central government's revised budget data facilitates a more detailed breakdown of changes in public works expenditure (the data do not exist for local governments as a whole). It holds that:

117

$$(PW_t - PW_{t-1}) = (IB_t - PW_{t-1}) + (RB_t - IB_t) + (PW_t - RB_t)$$

where $RB$ is the allocation for public works in the revised budget. The second term on the right hand side shows the change in the public works budget due to supplementary budgets, while the third term identifies expenditure shortfalls or overruns. The chart shows that central government projects are more or less fully implemented, and that the implementation occurs relatively fast. Central government funds for public works projects are generally spent in the budget year and small expenditure shortfalls (such as in 1993 and 1995) have been made up by additional expenditures in the following year.[8]

## Financial Difficulties of Local Governments

A second important factor explaining the muted impact of stimulus measures on public investment relates to the role of local governments. During the 1990s, the central government has assigned roughly two-thirds of the increased public works spending to local authorities (without providing a commensurate increase in funding). As a result, local government investment rose by more than ¥2 trillion per year in the early 1990s, with most of the increase accounted for by midyear supplementary budgets implementing the central government's stimulus packages (see Figure 6.4). The large stimulus programs of 1995, however, did not lead to a corresponding increase in local public works, and these have also dropped sharply in 1996 and 1997, consistent with the observations by Ishii and Wada (1998).

The capacity of some local authorities to expand public investment has been affected by their increasingly precarious financial situation. As tax revenues have been stagnant due to weak activity, particularly in larger urban prefectures that rely heavily on corporate tax payments, the continued rise in public investment has increasingly been financed through local bond issues. The amount of outstanding local government bonds shot up from 12 percent of GDP in 1990 to 22 percent of GDP by the end of fiscal year 1997, and some local au-

---

[8]A larger expenditure shortfall expected for FY1998 owes to the announcement of the package late in the fiscal year.

thorities have been on the verge of being put under direct administrative rule by the central government.[9]

As a result, more recent stimulus packages have served to offset an underlying decline in local government investment. For example, indications are that independent public works (which account for 60 percent of all local public works) were reduced on a large scale in 1999, more than offsetting increases in projects co-financed by the central government. FY1999 budget data for 25 prefectures showed a decline in locally funded public works by 16 percent compared to FY1998 initial budgets. Although public works funded by the central government increased by 5 percent, overall local public works were still projected to drop by 11 percent (Okue, 1999). Similarly, a Nikkei survey of 670 municipal governments found that cuts in self-financed investment projects were used to offset rising burdens in other areas.

## Implementation of Stimulus Measures

The extent to which stimulus packages have directly added to overall investment demand is difficult to estimate. Besides possible offsets through cuts in central or local expenditure elsewhere, some of the funds provided by the stimulus packages may have been allocated for use by public enterprises or have remained unused. However, the limited availability of relevant data makes it difficult to assess exactly how much of the government's stimulus plans have effectively translated into additional spending.

One approach is to relate spending in excess of initial budget plans to the size of the stimulus measures (Ishii and Wada, 1998). For example, using fiscal data available for the central and local governments, a crude implementation ratio can be calculated by comparing excess public works spending (over initial budgets) to the amount of public works in that year's stimulus packages. To account for some possible delay in the execution of projects, any budgetary over-

---

[9]The central government is required to intervene in local government finances if debt or deficit-related thresholds are exceeded. Bond issuance restrictions come into effect once the ratio of interest payments to revenues exceeds 20 percent. Moreover, prefectures fall under the financial restructuring authority of the central government if an adjusted deficit measure exceeds 5 percent of budgetary expenditures (20 percent for municipalities).

shooting of expenditure over and above revised budget estimates in the following year is added to excess spending of the current year. An implementation ratio below unity reflects either unspent supplementary budget funds or offsetting cuts in investment expenditure elsewhere.[10]

The calculation is complicated by two data-related issues. First, parts of the stimulus programs have been carried out by public enterprises, for which the concept of initial and supplementary budgets does not apply. However, changes in investment by public enterprises have largely mirrored central government investment, and have not been of a dimension that would fundamentally change the results of this exercise. Second, central and local government expenditure data contain double-counted items (essentially equal to the central government's contribution to jointly financed investment projects). Based on a comparison with national accounts data, the overlap is estimated to be around 20 percent, but the calculations also allow for a smaller or larger percentage.[11]

Based on this rough estimate, project implementation appears to have improved through the 1990s. Table 6.2 contains a range of estimates for the implementation ratio, depending on the assumed amount of double-counting between central and local government public works spending. Using the central case of a 20 percent expenditure overlap (Case II), as much as 90 percent of the stimulus packages' public works measures translated into additional demand in 1995 (the latest year for which data was available), compared to only around 60–70 percent in earlier years. While this most likely reflects the more urgent need for public stimulus given the depth of recession in the early 1990s, it is possible that the ratio again declined in 1998 as financial constraints on local governments began to bite.

---

[10]This measure does not allow for stimulus measures being implemented through initial budgets in subsequent years. However, the degree to which such measures were "additional" can be questioned, given that initial budgets were largely contractionary in recent years.

[11]An estimate for the overlap is obtained by adding central and local government expenditure (excluding social security and tax transfers) as reported in the respective fiscal accounts, and comparing this sum to general government expenditure (excluding social security) from the national income accounts.

## Table 6.2. Implementation of Public Work Projects
*(Billions of yen unless otherwise noted)*

|  | 1986 | 1987 | 1992 | 1993 | 1995 | 1998[1] |
|---|---|---|---|---|---|---|
| 1. Public works components of stimulus packages |  |  |  |  |  |  |
| Central government (incl. joint) | 1,155 | 2,898 | 3,450 | 7,458 | 4,630 | 6,400 |
| Independent local government | 800 | 800 | 2,800 | 5,800 | 1,000 | 1,500 |
| Total (A) | 1,955 | 3,698 | 6,250 | 13,258 | 5,630 | 7,900 |
| (In percent of GDP) | (0.6) | (1.0) | (1.3) | (2.8) | (1.2) | (1.6) |
| 2. Actual public works expenditure less initial budget allocation[2] |  |  |  |  |  |  |
| Central government | 780 | 1,304 | 1,647 | 5,594 | 4,678 | 5,870 |
| Local government | −573 | 943 | 4,706 | 5,570 | 1,765 | . . . |
| Combined central and local government public works expenditure (B) |  |  |  |  |  |  |
| Case I: 10 percent overlap | 186 | 2,022 | 5,718 | 10,048 | 5,799 | . . . |
| Case II: 20 percent overlap | 165 | 1,798 | 5,083 | 8,932 | 5,155 | . . . |
| Case III: 30 percent overlap | 145 | 1,573 | 4,447 | 7,815 | 4,510 | . . . |
| 3. Effective implementation ratio (B/A, in percent) |  |  |  |  |  |  |
| Case I: | 9.5 | 54.7 | 91.5 | 75.8 | 103.0 | . . . |
| Case II: | 8.4 | 48.6 | 81.3 | 67.4 | 91.6 | . . . |
| Case III: | 7.4 | 42.5 | 71.2 | 58.9 | 80.1 | . . . |

Sources: Data provided by the Japanese authorities; and IMF staff estimates.

[1]Staff estimate for actual public works expenditure. Note that the November 1998 package included public works worth Y1.4 trillion for inclusion in the initial budget for 1999.

[2]Including excess spending (over revised budget estimates) in following fiscal year.

# The Decline in Tax Revenue

The rising budget deficit in the 1990s has reflected a strong drop in tax revenue, particularly in the immediate post-bubble years. General government tax revenue dropped from a peak of 22 percent of GDP in FY1990 to 18 percent of GDP in FY1994, a level from which it has not yet recovered (Figure 6.5). The revenue fall was mainly seen in taxes collected by the central government (which are partly shared with local governments), while own-tax revenues of local authorities remained relatively steady at 7 percent of GDP. In the following paragraphs, the focus is thus on the main components of central government revenue.

Tax revenue losses were partly caused by a series of tax cuts since 1994, although the government's shift to fiscal consolidation in 1997

Figure 6.5. General Government Tax Revenue Developments

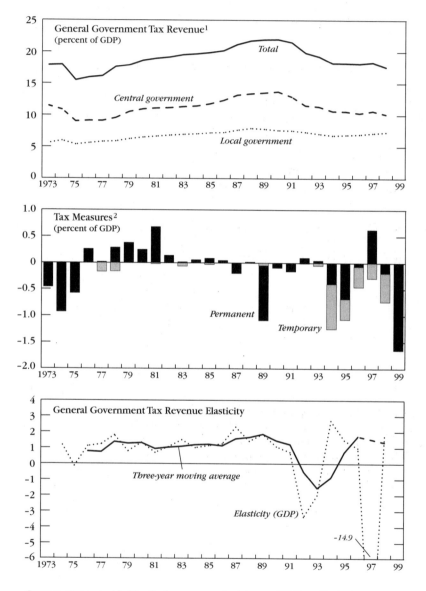

Sources: Data provided by the Japanese authorities; and IMF staff calculations.
[1]Data for 1997 (local government only), 1998, and 1999 are based on projections by the Japanese authorities.
[2]Tax measures only relate to taxes collected by the central government.

offset much of the earlier measures. Following the collapse of the bubble, the government's initial strategy was to support the economy through public works projects, and tax policy instruments were not used in a substantial way before early 1994. Since then, steps taken by the government included the following:

- A temporary tax cut of ¥6 trillion (1¼ percent of GDP) was announced in FY1994, consisting mainly of a 20 percent reduction in personal income tax payments across the board (affecting both the central and local government level). In the following year, a more substantial tax reform package included an upward shift in income tax brackets that resulted in permanent tax relief of ¥3½ trillion, which was to be offset from FY1997 by an increase in the consumption tax rate from 3 to 5 percent. In addition, the government granted a temporary income tax rebate of ¥2 trillion, which was also maintained in FY1996.

- In FY1997, the combination of the consumption tax rate hike with the expiration of temporary tax cuts resulted in an effective increase in the tax burden of about ¥6 trillion—roughly equal to the tax reductions implemented three years earlier.

- Personal income tax reductions resumed, however, as the economy entered into recession in late 1997. Personal income tax rebates granted in FY1998 amounted to around ¥4 trillion, of which ¥1 trillion was retroactive to taxes paid in FY1997. These temporary measures were replaced by permanent tax cuts in FY1999, effected through the lowering of the top marginal tax rate from 65 percent to 50 percent, and proportional reductions in other income tax brackets.

- The government also took steps to reduce corporate taxation. In particular, two rate cuts in FY1998 and FY1999—partly offset by base-broadening measures—brought the corporate tax rate down to 40 percent from 50 percent in 1990 (to which it had already been reduced from 55 percent during the late 1980s).

Indications are, however, that tax policy measures have played only a secondary role in the revenue drop. The cumulative revenue impact of tax measures remained limited. Between 1994 and 1998, permanent tax measures accounted for a cumulative reduction in revenues of ¾ percent of GDP, while temporary measures led to losses of about ¼ percent of GDP each year (see Figure 6.5). Overall, tax cuts accounted for only a 1 percent of GDP decline in revenue by

---

Box 6.2. Tax Elasticity

Tax elasticity measures how tax revenue would respond to changes in economic growth under an unchanged tax system. Most industrial economies have elastic tax systems (defined as elasticity being greater than one), where tax revenue grows at a higher rate than GDP even in the absence of tax policy measures. This reflects the influence of a variety of factors, including increases in the number of taxpayers, bracket creep, and improvements in tax administration.

To define elasticity, first consider the concept of tax buoyancy, to which the elasticity concept is closely related. Buoyancy compares the change in overall tax revenue to the change in the tax base (nominal GDP for the most part of this study):

$$Buoyancy = \frac{\Delta T/T_{-1}}{\Delta Base/Base_{-1}}.$$

However, part of the change in revenue may be due to tax policy measures taken by the government. For example, if it is estimated by the Tax Bureau that a tax rate increase yields an additional revenue of $M$ in the current year, adjusted tax revenue would equal $T^a = T - M$, and tax elasticity would be defined as:

$$Elasticity = \frac{\Delta T^a/T_{-1}}{\Delta Base/Base_{-1}} = \frac{(\Delta T - M)/T_{-1}}{\Delta Base/Base_{-1}}.$$

---

1998, compared to a much larger overall revenue decline of 4½ percent of GDP. Moreover, the revenue losses were largely concentrated in the period 1990–94, that is before the government embarked on its policy of tax cuts. This suggests that changes in tax revenue elasticity have played a major role in recent revenue developments.

## Trends in Tax Elasticity

The decline in tax revenue has indeed been associated with a fall in tax elasticity during years with a sharp slowdown in growth:[12]

---

[12]A discussion of the concept of tax elasticity and its application to Japanese fiscal data, including measurement problems, is contained in Box 6.2 and in the Appendix.

Table 6.3. GDP Growth, Tax Revenues, and Tax Elasticities
*(Average in percent)*

|  | 1976–85 | 1986–90 | 1991–94 | 1995–98 (excl. 1997) |
|---|---|---|---|---|
| Nominal GDP growth | 7.9 | 6.2 | 2.2 | 0.8 |
| General government tax revenue growth | 10.6 | 8.4 | –2.4 | –0.4 |
| **Elasticity** | **1.2** | **1.6** | **–0.5** | **1.3** |

Source: IMF staff calculations.

- During the late 1970s and early 1980s, tax elasticity was relatively constant around an average of 1¼, before rising to 1¾ between 1986 and 1990, the peak years of the asset price bubble (Table 6.3).
- As the economy entered into recession in the aftermath of the bubble years, tax elasticity also fell and became negative in 1991–94. Severe income and wealth losses appear to have had a depressing effect on tax collections (see below).
- In the mid-1990s, tax elasticity levels briefly recovered before dropping to an unprecedented low in the recession year of 1997 (although measurement problems associated with the revenue impact of the consumption tax hike are likely to exaggerate the dimension of the drop in that particular year).[13] However, elasticity appears to have again returned to more normal levels in 1998 and—if 1997 is excluded—has been close to its historic average in recent years.

An analysis of individual central government tax categories provides further details on elasticity developments. Despite obvious advantages of using GDP as a broad measure for the overall tax base, individual revenue components are more closely related to narrower macroeconomic aggregates (such as corporate tax revenue to corporate profits, etc.). Therefore, while tax elasticity of a revenue component may remain constant relative to a narrow base, a decline in that base relative to GDP could result in a drop in elasticity vis-à-vis GDP.[14] Alternative

---

[13]Moreover, nominal GDP growth in 1997 was close to zero, inflating the absolute value of the elasticity measure.

[14]If $\eta_{T,Base}$ is the elasticity of tax revenue relative to a particular tax base, it holds that $\eta_{T,GDP} = \eta_{T,Base} \cdot \eta_{Base,GDP}$.

tax bases have therefore been used to analyze individual revenue components.

In the case of corporate taxes, elasticity has been partly driven by the rise and fall of profits in connection with the asset price bubble.[15] As shown in Figure 6.6, corporate tax elasticity vis-à-vis profits was practically constant in recent years. The swings in elasticity relative to GDP are largely explained by profit developments. Having soared in the late 1980s, corporate profits fell by almost half between 1989 and 1993. As a result, corporate tax revenue—one quarter of total tax revenue—fell sharply in the early 1990s, but recovered between 1994 and 1996 when profits rebounded. However, corporate tax elasticity vis-à-vis profits has been below unity in recent years, contributing to a decline in the effective corporate tax rate from 50 percent in 1990 to 42 percent in 1997. It is still unclear to what extent this inelasticity reflects temporary factors (such as loss carry-forwards) that had yet to be unwound.

Reasons for the elasticity decline in other tax categories have been less evident. Indications are, however, that tax revenues have been affected particularly by a sharp slowdown in growth:

- Personal income tax elasticity dropped sharply in 1992 and 1997. Personal income remained broadly unchanged in relation to GDP (at around 70 percent), and tax elasticity relative to personal income therefore shows similar fluctuations to the elasticity relative to GDP (see Figure 6.6). Possible reasons for the weakening of the revenue collections in a recession are income cuts resulting in significantly lower tax claims due to a highly progressive tax system with high tax thresholds, deductions of real estate and financial asset losses, and increased noncompliance and slackening collection efforts.[16]
- Similarly, indirect tax elasticity has not been significantly affected by the choice of a particular tax base. Indirect tax elasticity has generally been more volatile, however, than the elasticity of other tax categories, and the impact of the 1992

---

[15]Corporate profits are taken from the Financial Statements of Incorporated Enterprises, published by the Ministry of Finance.

[16]An econometric analysis of tax income found a significant impact of land prices (and somewhat less of stock prices) on revenue. However, the effect was too small to fully account for the elasticity decline.

Figure 6.6. Elasticity of Central Government Tax Revenue
Components Using Alternative Tax Bases[1]

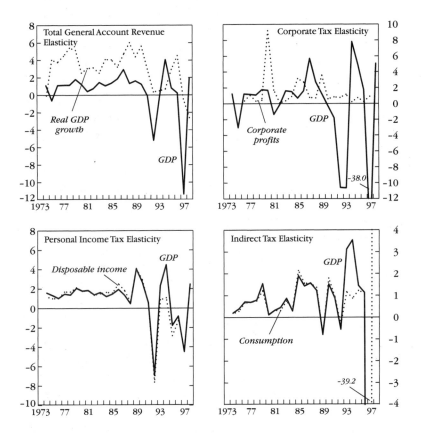

Sources: Japanese authorities (including fiscal estimates for 1998); and IMF staff
calculations.
[1]Except for total revenue, all charts show elasticity computed using GDP and an
alternative tax base.

recession has thus been of a lesser order than on the income tax
side. As for the exceptional elasticity drop in 1997, this may well
reflect difficulties in estimating the revenue impact of the consumption tax hike, given the sensitivity of the elasticity estimate
to that particular variable.

The relative impact of tax cuts and elasticity changes on tax revenue is highlighted by means of two tax revenue simulations:

- *Unchanged tax policies*: On the assumption that there were no tax measures by the government since 1990, tax revenue has been simulated on the basis of actual GDP growth and actual tax elasticities.
- *Unchanged tax policies and elasticities*: Assuming that tax elasticity would have remained at its average level for the 1970s and 1980s (around 1¼), tax revenue has been simulated on the basis of actual GDP growth.

The results illustrate that the effects of tax cuts were small, and that the tax increase in 1997 offset a large part of earlier reductions (Figure 6.7). By 1996, the cumulative impact of tax cuts on general government revenue accounted for 1½ percent of GDP, compared to an elasticity-related loss of around 3 percentage points (relative to what revenue would have been under pre-bubble elasticities). However, earlier tax cuts were substantially offset by fiscal tightening in 1997, including through the consumption tax increase that alone yielded revenue gains of about ½ percent of GDP. The 1998 tax measures led to a partial reversal of that stance with the result that, between 1990 and 1998, tax measures accounted for slightly more than 1 percentage point in an overall revenue loss of 5 percent of GDP.

## The Role of Discretionary Policies

Macroeconomic analysis of fiscal policy is frequently based on a decomposition of the fiscal deficit into a structural and a cyclical component. Movement in the structural balance is generally associated with discretionary fiscal policy measures, while the impact of automatic stabilizers (movements in the deficit reflecting cyclical fluctuations in economic activity) is given less prominence. As shown in Figure 6.8, movements in both the actual and structural fiscal balance and the output gap have been closely correlated in Japan in recent years. Compared to other major industrial countries, however, changes in the cyclical component appear to have been relatively small, particularly if compared to countries such as Canada, Germany, and the United Kingdom.

In Japan, the large deterioration in the structural deficit over the 1990s in part substituted for the relative lack of automatic stabilizers.

Figure 6.7. Relative Impact of Tax Measures
*(Percent of GDP)*

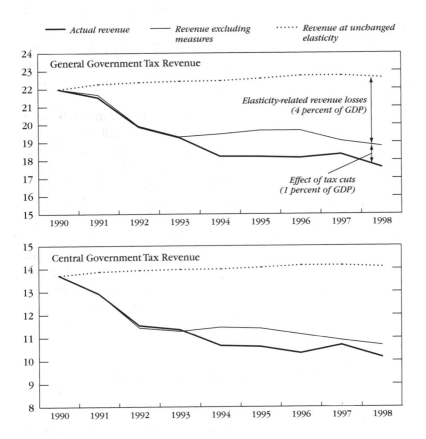

Sources: Japanese authorities; and IMF staff calculations.

Given the smaller impact of the economic cycle on the deficit, the need to use discretionary measures to adjust the fiscal stance puts greater weight on active fiscal policy management and results in a less smooth adjustment process:

- Compared to automatic stabilizers, discretionary policies suffer from implementation lags caused by procedural delays, and are more affected by forecast errors.
- In Japan, the perceived need to quickly return to fiscal balance in the face of increasing public debt levels may have con-

## Figure 6.8. G7 Countries Fiscal Balance and Output Gap

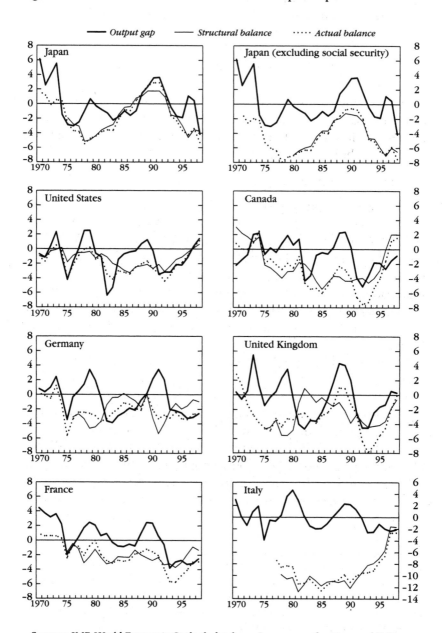

Sources: IMF, World Economic Outlook database; Japanese authorities; and IMF staff estimates.

tributed to an asymmetric reaction to economic shocks. Compared to automatic stabilizers, discretionary policies may have tightened early in the recovery, but loosened late in a downturn. The experience of 1997, when a sharp fiscal contraction contributed to the economic downturn, may have been a case in point.

An econometric approach has been used to quantify differences in automatic stabilizers across G-7 countries.[17] The regressions relate the change in the structural and cyclical balance in each country to changes in the output gap:

$$\Delta Balance = \beta_0 \Delta Output\ gap + \beta_1 \Delta Output\ gap_{-1} + \varepsilon.$$

The lagged output gap is included to reflect lags in the collection of taxes. The sample period was 1970–1997, with data taken from the IMF's databank. There is an element of circularity in this exercise, as the IMF's estimate of the structural deficit is derived from the estimated output gap. To help check the robustness of the results, the regressions were repeated using OECD estimates for the output gap (drawn from the Organization for Economic Cooperation and Development's analytical database) and IMF estimates of the structural balance.

The results of the estimation can be summarized as follows (Table 6.4):

- Japan has the lowest automatic stabilizers among the major industrial countries. An increase in the output gap of one percentage point translates into an increase of the cyclical deficit of about a third of 1 percent of GDP (even less when social security is excluded). This is only about half of the deficit response in countries with strong automatic stabilizers, for example, the U.K.[18] Other countries with relatively small automatic stabilizers

---

[17]Automatic stabilizers would *a priori* be expected to play a lesser role in Japan than in other countries. While Japanese tax elasticities have on average been comparable to that of other industrial economies, the low level and cyclical variation of both registered unemployment and social welfare benefits would imply that business cycle fluctuations have less direct implications for public spending than in many other countries.

[18]The estimated adjustment coefficients for the U.K. are similar to those obtained by Virley and Hurst (1995).

**Table 6.4. Comparison of Automatic Stabilizers Across G-7 Countries**

| | Data Source | Responsiveness of Automatic Stabilizer to Output Gap[1] | | | Responsiveness of Structural Balance to Output Gap[2] | | | Sum |
|---|---|---|---|---|---|---|---|---|
| | | Same year | One-year lag | Total | Same year | One-year lag | Total | |
| Japan | WEO | .32* | .00 | .32 | .44* | .04 | .48[3] | .80 |
| | OECD | .35* | .02 | .37 | .34 | .04 | .38[3] | .75 |
| Japan (excl. Social Security) | WEO | .23* | −.00 | .23 | .44* | −.00 | .44[3] | .67 |
| Canada | WEO | .56* | .07* | .63 | .05 | .01 | .06 | .69 |
| | OECD | .46* | .02 | .48 | .10 | −.03 | .07 | .55 |
| France | WEO | .56* | .03* | .59 | −.23 | .14 | −.09 | .50 |
| | OECD | .46* | .04* | .50 | −.01 | .06 | .05 | .55 |
| Germany | WEO | .55* | .05* | .60 | −.52* | −.19 | −.71 | −.11 |
| | OECD | .32* | .04 | .36 | .03 | −.08 | −.05 | .31 |
| Italy | WEO | .42* | −.04 | .38 | −.06 | −.29 | −.35 | .03 |
| | OECD | .28* | −.12 | .16 | .28* | −.19* | .09 | .25 |
| United Kingdom | WEO | .34* | .44* | .77 | −.08 | −.19 | −.27 | .50 |
| | OECD | .44* | .13 | .57 | −.13 | .55* | .42 | .99 |
| United States | WEO | .36* | .05* | .41 | .11* | .06 | .17 | .58 |
| | OECD | .32* | .05* | .37 | .16* | .11 | .27 | .64 |

Source: IMF staff calculations, based on World Economic Outlook and OECD Analytical Database.

[1]Based on OLS regressions of the change in the cyclical deficit (the difference between the actual and the structural deficit ratio) on the change in the output gap (using observations from 1970 to 1997). A star indicates significance at the 5 percent level. First row results are derived from WEO data, second row results are based on OECD data.

[2]Based on OLS regressions of the change in the structural deficit on the change in the output gap (using observations from 1970 to 1997). Star indicates significance at the 10 percent level.

[3]Coefficients are based on a restricted sample from 1983–95.

include the U.S. (with similarly low social benefit levels) and Italy, where high deficit and debt levels may have prompted the suppression of automatic stabilizers (Buti, Franco, and Orgena 1997).

- By contrast, Japan's structural balance has adjusted strongly to fluctuations in the business cycle in the past two decades. Historically, a change of 1 percentage point in the output gap has translated into an increase in the structural deficit of around half a percent of GDP, compared to a fifth of 1 percent or less in most other G-7 economies.

- Overall, Japan's fiscal stance has been strongly countercyclical. By adding up the coefficients of both equations, the estimates measure the overall responsiveness of fiscal policy to changes in the economic cycle. With the exception of the U.K., Japan's fiscal position has reacted more strongly (by a margin of 20–30 basis points) to changes in the output gap than that of other economies.

- The use of OECD output gap estimates produces some reduction in estimated automatic stabilizers but, in most cases, larger responses to the output gap. However, the differences are not large, and hence endogeneity does not appear to significantly bias the overall result.

## Comparison with Other Major Economies

The econometric results have been used to simulate a deficit path for Japan by applying other countries' reaction functions to Japanese output data. In the upper panel of Figure 6.9, average coefficients from other G-7 countries have been used to simulate both cyclical and structural deficit components for Japan, yielding a simulated overall fiscal balance. Since the model has been estimated in differences, the simulations are based on a dynamic method—with each year's outcome depending on the previous year's outcome—starting in 1981, when the actual and structural deficits were roughly equal. The simulation equation is:

$$Balance = Balance_{-1} + \hat{\beta}_0 \Delta Gap + \hat{\beta}_1 \Delta Gap_{-1} + \hat{\varepsilon}$$

with the $\beta$'s representing the average coefficients estimated for other G-7 economies, and residuals from the original Japan equation reflecting past exogenous shocks.

The simulations illustrate the difference between Japan and other industrial economies:

- Japan's fiscal system achieved a larger fiscal surplus during the bubble years than would have been true of other large economies in comparable circumstances (at the peak, the difference amounted to 1½ percent of GDP), and the deficit also reacted more sharply to the economic downturn through 1996. This has

133

Figure 6.9. Simulation of Structural Balance:
Comparison with Major G-7 Economies

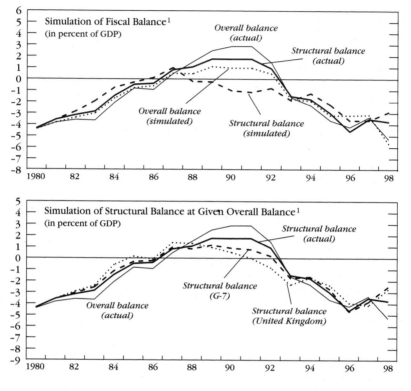

Source: IMF staff calculations.
[1]Using average of regression coefficients for G-7 economies (excluding Japan).

been achieved by large changes in the structural balance, which declined by 6½ percent of GDP between 1990 and 1996, compared to about 2½ percent of GDP using G-7 coefficients.

- The impact of the automatic stabilizers is illustrated in the lower panel of Figure 6.9, where structural balances were calculated by subtracting *simulated* automatic stabilizers from Japan's *actual* fiscal balance. By that measure, the turnaround in the structural balance between 1990 and 1996 implied by average G-7 coefficients would have been around 5½ percent of GDP, or 1 percentage point less than what actually occurred.

**Table 6.5.** Change in General Japan's Government Structural Balance, 1990–98
*(Percent of potential GDP)*

|  | 1990–96 | 1996–98 | 1990–98 |
|---|---|---|---|
| Overall balance (excluding social security) | −5.9 | 0.0 | −5.9 |
|   Stimulus measures | −2.5 | 0.8 | −1.7 |
|     Tax measures | −1.5 | 0.4 | −1.1 |
|     Public investment (−) | −1.0 | 0.4 | −0.6 |
|   Tax elasticity decline | −2.3 | −0.8 | −3.1 |
|   Other | −1.1 | 0.0 | −1.1 |
| *Memorandum items* (in percent of GDP): |  |  |  |
| Change in actual balance (excluding social security) | −6.6 | −1.7 | −8.3 |
|   *Of which:* |  |  |  |
|     Change in cyclical balance | −0.7 | −1.7 | −2.4 |

Source: IMF staff calculations.

- The adjustment implied by coefficients for the U.K.—which has the largest automatic stabilizers among the major economies—is still smaller at 4½ percentage points. Such a difference reflects a significant portion of the impact of the stimulus packages, which raised the deficit by about 2½ percent of GDP over the same period (Table 6.5). The path using U.K. data also illustrates that Japan's large fiscal easing in 1993 might have come earlier and could have been less sharp if automatic stabilizers had played a larger role. Similarly, the deficit reduction in 1997 and subsequent expansion would have been achieved by automatic stabilizers alone.

## Conclusion

This chapter has identified the major components contributing to fiscal expansion in Japan in recent years. Contrary to the notion that fiscal policy has mainly been driven by the government's various stimulus packages over the past years, a large drop in tax revenue elasticity in the early 1990s has been identified as the major force behind the widening of the structural deficit (see Table 6.5). Public works spending and tax cuts played an important role in subsequent years, yet their contribution to fiscal expansion was comparatively small.

The large stimulus packages of the past decade have partly been necessitated by the small size of automatic stabilizers in the Japanese economy. However, discretionary policies tend to adjust less efficiently to cyclical swings in the economy than automatic stabilizers, and the relatively larger need for discretionary measures has contributed to two adverse developments in Japan's budgetary process:

- Given a potentially large room for discretionary measures, the budgetary system has evolved toward a structure that seeks to protect fiscal policy from an expansionary bias, resulting in a cycle of contractionary initial budgets, followed by expansionary supplementary budgets in midyear. This structure has contributed to uncertainty and limited the effectiveness of fiscal policy measures.
- The same motive has also led to an overreliance on public works spending (which generally have low rates of return), as well as temporary tax cuts whose impact on demand is likely to have been limited.[19]

As economic activity recovers, a major concern for fiscal policy relates to the timing of renewed fiscal consolidation. Indeed, with Japan's fiscal position adjusting less to changes in the business cycle than in other countries, comparatively large improvements in the structural balance will be needed to achieve fiscal adjustment. The results of this chapter suggest, however, that discretionary polices would need to continue mirroring the gradual workings of automatic stabilizers during the anticipated upswing, as they did during the recession years of the past.

## Appendix. Calculating Tax Elasticities

### Choosing a base

The choice of a macroeconomic tax base constitutes the first step in calculating tax elasticities. The actual tax base (total taxable in-

---

[19]The impact of permanent tax cuts on consumer spending has been found to be about three times the size as that of temporary cuts (Watanabe and others. 1998).

comes) is not easily available in historical form and is also not commonly projected in economic models. However, the actual base is often closely related to a macroeconomic aggregate, such as GDP, personal income, or corporate profits. For this chapter, the aggregate that produced the smallest variation in tax elasticity was chosen as tax base (for example, GDP for total tax revenue, personal disposable income (before tax) for personal income tax, etc.). In the following, "tax base" refers to this macroeconomic aggregate.

## Basic definitions

Define tax revenue in year 0 by $T_0 = t_0 B_0$, with $t$ being the effective tax collection rate and $B$ the tax base. The budget revenue estimate for year 1 is given by

$$T_1^* = t_1^* B_1^* = t_0 B_1^* + \Delta t_1^* B_1^*. \tag{1}$$

where * denotes budget estimates. The first term of the right hand side is tax revenue at unchanged rates (given a projected rate of base growth). The second term is the expected revenue impact of tax policy measures, defined as $M = \Delta t_1^* B_1^*$, i.e., the change in the collection rate resulting from policy measures, times the new base. Estimates for $M$ are contained in Japanese budget documents.

This information can be used to compute tax elasticities and construct a time series for econometric analysis. Define tax revenue elasticity as

$$\eta = \frac{(T_1 - M - T_0)/T_0}{(B_1 - B_0)/B_0} = \frac{(\Delta T_1 - M)/T_0}{\Delta B_1/B_0} \tag{2}$$

where $T_1 - M$ is the part of tax revenue that is unaffected by tax changes. Unfortunately, however, this formula gives only an approximation for the true elasticity because $M$ is just an estimate for the budgetary impact of tax measures. The actual impact cannot be calculated for lack of observable data. This is illustrated by a breakdown of the deviation between actual and budgeted tax revenue:

$$T_1 - T_1^* = t_1(B_1 - B_1^*) + (t_1 - t_1^*)B_1^*. \tag{3}$$

The right-hand side decomposes the forecast error into an unanticipated change in the tax base and a deviation of the effective tax collection rate from its budget projection. The discrepancy in the tax collection rate reflects both under- or overestimation of the revenue impact of tax policy measures on the collection rate and unforeseen changes in tax elasticity. Without further information, the impact of both effects cannot be disentangled.

If the base projection in the budget is close to the final outcome (i.e., $B_1^*$ is approximately equal to $B_1$), $M$ is likely to be a good approximation and the elasticity can be calculated reasonably well. Therefore, the quality of elasticity calculations is closely linked to the quality of base projections and revenue forecasts in the budget.

### Possible sources for measurement error

Elasticity calculations for Japan are complicated by two shortcomings of Japanese fiscal data. First, estimates for the revenue impact of tax measures are on an appropriations basis, and may date back several years. For example, the estimate for the revenue impact of the consumption tax increase in 1997 dates from 1994, when the decision on tax increase was made, and may thus be based on inaccurate macroeconomic assumptions.

Second, estimates for general government tax elasticity are hampered by the lack of aggregate information on independent local government tax measures. The central government produces estimates for the impact of changes in shared taxes on local government revenue, but these taxes account for only a third of total local government tax revenue. Since fluctuations in local revenue have been small compared to central revenue, the impact of this lack of information may be limited, and has been ignored for the purpose of this paper. For the same reason, however, calculations for individual tax categories have been restricted to central government revenue only.

### Constructing adjusted time series

To calculate tax elasticities over a period of time, actual revenue data need to be converted into a series that shows what the revenues would have been had there been no changes in the tax system. One method would be to apply current tax rates to the bases of earlier years, thus simulating a revenue series that corresponds to the current tax structure. However, this method imposes heavy data requirements, including detailed information on the distribution of the base by brackets or rate categories (Chand, 1975).

A more readily useable procedure requires only information on the revenue impact of tax measures. The current year (year 0) is set as the reference year. In the most simple case, tax revenues of previous years are adjusted according to:

$$T^a_{-i} = T_{-i} \prod_{j=0}^{i-1} \frac{T_{-j}}{T_{-j} - M_{-j}}. \tag{4}$$

While this remains a practical way of obtaining adjusted time series, the disadvantages of this method are clear. Forecasting errors contained in $M$ accumulate over time and the proportional adjustment is a rather crude way of taking changes in the tax system into account. These shortcomings should be kept in mind when analyzing the results.

In the case of Japan, the method is slightly more complex because the authorities provide two estimates for the revenue impact of tax measures—a first-year impact and a full-year impact. The full-year impact refers to the hypothetical revenue gain or loss that would result if the tax measure would apply to the full fiscal year, whereas the first-year impact takes the timing of measures into account to estimate the actual revenue impact. Moreover, the authorities have also introduced temporary tax measures that need to be subtracted from tax revenue before calculating elasticities.

Again setting the current year as the reference year 0, define $\overline{M}_i$ as the first-year impact of a tax change becoming effective in year $i$. With $M_i$ denoting the full-year impact, adjusted tax revenue is defined as:

$$T^a_0 = (T_0 + M_0 - \overline{M}_0),$$

$$T^a_{-i} = (T_{-i} + M_{-i} - \overline{M}_{-i}) \prod_{j=0}^{i-1} \frac{T_{-j} + M_{-j} - \overline{M}_{-j}}{T_{-j} - \overline{M}_{-j}} \quad (i = 1, \ldots, n) \tag{5}$$

where $T_i$ denotes revenue net of temporary measures. Table 6.6 provides the data and calculations for the general government tax revenue elasticity.

**Table 6.6. Central Government Tax Revenues (General Account)[1]**
(Billions of yen, unless otherwise noted)

| | 1973 | 1974 | 1975 | 1976 | 1977 | 1978 | 1979 | 1980 | 1981 | 1982 | 1983 | 1984 | 1985 |
|---|---|---|---|---|---|---|---|---|---|---|---|---|---|
| Gross tax revenue | 13,366 | 15,036 | 13,753 | 15,658 | 17,333 | 19,953 | 23,730 | 26,869 | 28,952 | 30,511 | 32,358 | 34,908 | 38,199 |
| Temporary measures | 0 | 0 | 0 | 0 | -300 | -300 | 0 | 0 | -48 | 0 | -150 | 0 | -84 |
| Gross revenue, excl. temporary measures | 13,366 | 15,036 | 13,753 | 15,658 | 17,633 | 20,253 | 23,730 | 26,869 | 29,001 | 30,511 | 32,508 | 34,908 | 38,283 |
| First-year impact of measures | -336 | -1,002 | -205 | 189 | -185 | 348 | 441 | 326 | 1,383 | 308 | 7 | 43 | 289 |
| Revenue before measures | 13,701 | 16,038 | 13,958 | 15,469 | 17,818 | 19,905 | 23,289 | 26,543 | 27,618 | 30,203 | 32,501 | 34,865 | 37,994 |
| Full-year impact of measures | -378 | -1,115 | -372 | 383 | 81 | 463 | 634 | 367 | 1,531 | 308 | 7 | 157 | 187 |
| Full-year revenue equivalent | 13,323 | 14,923 | 13,586 | 15,852 | 17,899 | 20,368 | 23,923 | 26,910 | 29,149 | 30,511 | 32,508 | 35,022 | 38,181 |
| Adjusted revenue (Base = 1997) | 13,543 | 16,303 | 15,249 | 17,362 | 19,516 | 21,703 | 24,815 | 27,533 | 28,257 | 29,280 | 31,190 | 33,451 | 36,289 |
| | | | | | | | *(In percent)* | | | | | | |
| Growth of gross tax revenue | ... | 12.5 | -8.5 | 13.9 | 10.7 | 15.1 | 18.9 | 13.2 | 7.8 | 5.4 | 6.1 | 7.9 | 9.4 |
| Growth of adjusted tax revenue | ... | 20.4 | -6.5 | 13.9 | 12.4 | 11.2 | 14.3 | 11.0 | 2.6 | 3.6 | 6.5 | 7.3 | 8.5 |
| Nominal GDP growth | ... | 18.6 | 10.2 | 12.5 | 10.9 | 9.8 | 8.0 | 8.9 | 6.3 | 4.9 | 4.5 | 6.8 | 6.2 |
| Tax buoyancy | ... | 0.7 | -0.8 | 1.1 | 1.0 | 1.5 | 2.4 | 1.5 | 1.2 | 1.1 | 1.3 | 1.2 | 1.5 |
| Tax elasticity | ... | 1.1 | -0.6 | 1.1 | 1.1 | 1.1 | 1.8 | 1.2 | 0.4 | 0.7 | 1.5 | 1.1 | 1.4 |

Table 6.6 (concluded)

| | 1986 | 1987 | 1988 | 1989 | 1990 | 1991 | 1992 | 1993 | 1994 | 1995 | 1996 | 1997 | 1998 |
|---|---|---|---|---|---|---|---|---|---|---|---|---|---|
| Gross tax revenue | 41,877 | 46,798 | 50,827 | 54,922 | 60,106 | 59,820 | 54,445 | 54,126 | 51,030 | 51,931 | 52,060 | 53,941 | 50,165 |
| Temporary measures | 0 | 0 | 0 | –50 | 0 | 0 | –28 | –225 | –3,843 | –1,376 | –1,405 | –979 | –1,827 |
| Gross revenue, excl. temporary measures | 41,877 | 46,798 | 50,827 | 54,972 | 60,106 | 59,820 | 54,473 | 54,351 | 54,873 | 53,307 | 53,465 | 54,920 | 51,992 |
| First-year impact of measures | 318 | –599 | –234 | –1,939 | –282 | –3 | 537 | 79 | –443 | –2,399 | –210 | 2,534 | –633 |
| Revenue before measures | 41,559 | 47,397 | 51,061 | 56,911 | 60,388 | 59,823 | 53,936 | 54,272 | 55,316 | 55,706 | 53,675 | 52,386 | 52,625 |
| Full-year impact of measures | 131 | –599 | 65 | –1,958 | –306 | –4 | 473 | –9 | –562 | –2,388 | –170 | 2,481 | –385 |
| Full-year revenue equivalent | 41,690 | 46,798 | 51,126 | 54,953 | 60,082 | 59,819 | 54,409 | 54,263 | 54,754 | 53,318 | 53,505 | 54,867 | 52,240 |
| Adjusted revenue (Base = 1997) | 39,500 | 44,907 | 48,997 | 54,542 | 59,936 | 59,678 | 53,809 | 53,674 | 54,715 | 55,666 | 56,039 | 54,867 | 52,625 |
| *(In percent)* | | | | | | | | | | | | | |
| Growth of gross tax revenue | 9.6 | 11.8 | 8.6 | 8.1 | 9.4 | –0.5 | –9.0 | –0.6 | –5.7 | 1.8 | 0.2 | 3.6 | –7.0 |
| Growth of adjusted tax revenue | 8.8 | 13.7 | 9.1 | 11.3 | 9.9 | –0.4 | –9.8 | –0.3 | 1.9 | 1.7 | 0.7 | –2.1 | –4.1 |
| Nominal GDP growth | 4.7 | 4.7 | 6.8 | 7.0 | 8.0 | 5.6 | 1.9 | 1.0 | 0.5 | 2.2 | 3.0 | 0.2 | –2.1 |
| Tax buoyancy | 2.0 | 2.5 | 1.3 | 1.2 | 1.2 | –0.1 | –4.7 | –0.6 | –12.0 | 0.8 | 0.1 | 19.6 | 3.3 |
| Tax elasticity | 1.9 | 2.9 | 1.3 | 1.6 | 1.2 | –0.1 | –5.2 | –0.2 | 4.1 | 0.8 | 0.2 | –11.4 | 1.9 |

Source: Data provided by the Japanese authorities; and IMF staff calculations.
[1] Fiscal year (April–March).

# References

Bayoumi, T., 1998, "The Japanese Fiscal System and Fiscal Transparency," in B.B. Aghevli, T. Bayoumi, and G. Meredith (eds.), *Structural Change in Japan: Macroeconomic Impact and Policy Challenges* (Washington: International Monetary Fund).

Bayoumi, T., C. Towe, and I. Oishi, 1998, "Fiscal Policy Issues," in *Japan—Selected Issues,* IMF Staff Country Report No. 98/113 (Washington: International Monetary Fund).

Buti, M., D. Franco, and H. Ongena, 1997, *Budgetary Policies During Recession: Retrospective Application of the "Stability and Growth Pact" to the Post-War Period,* Commission of the European Communities, Economic Papers No. 121.

Chand, S.K., 1975, "Some Procedures for Forecasting Tax Revenue in Developing Countries," International Monetary Fund, Fiscal Affairs Department, Departmental Memorandum 75/91.

Ishii, H., and E. Wada, 1998, *Local Government Spending: Solving the Mystery of Japanese Fiscal Packages,* Institute for International Economics, Working Paper 98–5.

Lipworth, G., and G. Meredith, 1998, "A Reexamination of Indicators of Monetary and Financial Conditions," in B.B. Aghevli, T. Bayoumi, and G. Meredith (eds.), *Structural Change in Japan: Macroeconomic Impact and Policy Challenges* (Washington: International Monetary Fund).

Okue, K., 1999, "Filling the Vacuum: Japan Policy Monitor," Dresdner Kleinwort Benson Research Paper, Tokyo (April).

Posen, A., 1998, *Restoring Japan's Economic Growth* (Washington: Institute for International Economics).

Schlesinger, J. M., 1997, *Shadow Shoguns: The Rise and Fall of Japan's Postwar Political Machine* (New York: Simon & Schuster).

Virley, S., and M. Hurst, 1995, *Public Finances and the Cycle,* Treasury Occasional Paper No. 4 (London: H.M. Treasury).

Watanabe, K., T. Watanabe, and T. Watanabe, 1998, *Tax Policy and Consumer Spending: Evidence from Japanese Fiscal Experiments,* unpublished manuscript, Bank of Japan.

# 7

# Monetary Policy Transmission in Japan

*James Morsink and Tamim Bayoumi*

How monetary policy affects real activity is always a subject of lively interest to economists. Many channels have been identified, including interest rates, the exchange rate, inflationary expectations (higher expected inflation lowers the real interest rate), bank lending, balance sheet effects, and wealth effects, but there is little agreement on either their precise workings or their relative importance (see Mishkin, 1995).

When an economy is in a recession, monetary policy and the channels of monetary transmission receive particular scrutiny. In the case of Japan, two further factors make understanding the transmission mechanism especially important. First, the Bank of Japan has steadily lowered the overnight call rate—the operating target for monetary policy—to "as low as possible" (which turns out to be 0.03 percent given transactions costs). With monetary policy bumping up against the nominal floor on interest rates, and attention shifting to a possible role for quantitative easing, examining the monetary transmission mechanism may provide some insight into the effectiveness of policies in this unusual environment.

Second, the 1990s slump in activity was accompanied by a banking crisis. A growing body of research focuses on the bank lending channel of the monetary transmission mechanism (see Bernanke and Gertler, 1995, and Kashyap and Stein, 1997). Banks are seen as playing an important independent role in overcoming information problems and other frictions in credit markets, so that some borrowers (small firms, for example) cannot readily find substitutes for bank financing. As a result, changes to banks' ability to lend—either reflecting monetary policy developments or other changes to bank capital and funding—are transmitted to bank-dependent borrowers. As banks play a large role in Japan's financial intermediation, the bank lending channel may be of particular significance as a conduit for monetary policy and, given the problems being experienced by the banking sector, as an independent source of real disturbances.[1]

This chapter uses vector autoregressions (VARs) to examine the monetary transmission mechanism in Japan. This methodology—set out below—allows us to place minimal restrictions on how monetary shocks affect the economy, which—given the lack of consensus about the workings of the monetary transmission mechanism—is a distinct advantage. In addition, this approach recognizes explicitly the simultaneity between monetary policy and macroeconomic developments, that is, the dependence of monetary policy on other economic variables as well as the dependence of economic variables on monetary policy. Our strategy is first to estimate a basic monetary model with standard variables and then to extend the model to focus on the role of various factors—banks, securities markets, and components of private demand—in the monetary transmission mechanism.[2]

The empirical results indicate that both monetary policy and banks' balance sheets are important sources of shocks, that banks play a crucial role in transmitting monetary shocks to economic activity, that corporations and households have not been able to substitute borrowing from other sources for a shortfall in bank borrowing, and that business investment is especially sensitive to monetary shocks. We conclude that policy measures to strengthen banks are a prerequisite to restoring the effectiveness of the monetary transmission mechanism.

---

[1]Two different views of the banking crisis are contained in the literature. Krugman (1998) argues that bank weakness has had little impact on the effectiveness of monetary policy as impaired banks tend to lend too much, not too little. By contrast, Bayoumi, in Chapter 2 of this book, finds that the negative shocks to bank lending, either autonomous or caused by falling asset prices, have provided a major deflationary impetus over the 1990s.

[2]A more detailed discussion of the econometric methodology and empirical results is contained in Morsink and Bayoumi (1999).

# Methodology

Our basic model includes economic activity, prices, interest rates, and broad money.[3] Our measure of economic activity is real private demand (real GDP minus total government spending), because public sector demand is driven primarily by fiscal policy, which is assumed to be exogenous. We express private demand as a ratio to potential output for two reasons: our focus is the impact of monetary events on the cyclical behavior of real private demand; and this variable is (in principle) stationary, which allows the model to be estimated in levels, in line with the U.S. literature. We use the IMF's measure of potential output, which is based on a Cobb-Douglas production function (as discussed in Chapter 5). The price level is given by the natural logarithm of the consumer price index, while real broad money (M2+CDs) is divided by potential output, so that responses can be easily converted into policy multipliers.[4]

Our measure of the stance of monetary policy in Japan is the uncollateralized overnight call rate, the current operating target of policy. Although both the instruments and operating objectives of the Bank of Japan have evolved over time, mostly reflecting the development of financial markets, several authors have noted that monetary policy has consistently laid a strong emphasis on short-term interest rates.

The VAR is identified in the standard manner, using a Choleski decomposition with the ordering being private demand, prices, the overnight call rate, and broad money.[5] The ordering determines the level of exogeneity of the variables, so current shocks to activity are assumed independent of current shocks to all the other variables in

---

[3]The inclusion of the exchange rate yielded unstable and often perverse results, such as a positive and significant output response to an exchange rate appreciation. The omission of such a variable for Japan is in line with the empirical literature on monetary policy in the United States, which is another large, advanced economy that is not very open.

[4]The data sources are provided in the data annex. Real output and broad money are measured as ratios to potential output, prices are in logarithms, and the nominal interest rate is a ratio, so a change of 0.01 represents a 1 percentage point change in the relevant variable.

[5]This identification scheme is common in the empirical literature on monetary policy, though other approaches have also been used.

the system, while current shocks to money are assumed to be affected by current shocks to all other variables. This ordering was chosen on the basis of the speed with which the variables respond to shocks, with output assumed to be the least responsive, followed by prices, then short rates, and finally broad money.[6] In addition to a constant term and a time trend, the VAR also includes two dummy variables aimed at capturing the short-term shifting of demand seen in the quarter before and the quarter after the introduction of the consumption tax in April 1989 and its increase in April 1997, with each variable designed so that the impacts sum to zero over time. The VAR is estimated with quarterly, seasonally adjusted data from 1980Q1 to 1998Q3 using two lags—the results are similar when we change the ordering of the variables (for example, interest rate, money, output, and prices), start the estimation a few years earlier or later, or use different lags.

We extended the VAR in a number of different directions to examine alternative aspects of the monetary transmission mechanism. To analyze the sensitivity of different components of private demand to monetary shocks, we split private demand into its main components: private consumption, business investment, housing investment, and net exports. For each component (say, private consumption), we estimated a VAR with the following ordering: total private demand minus the demand component of interest, the demand component of interest, prices, the overnight call rate, and broad money.

To investigate the role of financial intermediation in the monetary transmission mechanism, we extended the basic VAR by including the main components of private sector funding. Specifically, we added loans received by corporations and individuals from the public sector (that is, from government financial institutions), loans from private financial institutions (essentially bank loans), and money raised in securities markets. The ordering is public loans, funds from securities, then bank loans, reflecting our assumption that private in-

---

[6]Given the planning processes involved in setting output and prices, these variables are assumed to react slowly. The monetary authorities are assumed to set the call rate with some information about the contemporaneous behavior of output and prices, but without a full picture of the behavior of quickly changing financial variables. In the extended VARs, decisions about lending and borrowing are assumed to reflect all current information.

stitutions—such as banks and securities markets—generally respond more quickly to requests for funding than government financial institutions (the results are similar for different orderings).

Next, to further examine the role of banks in the monetary transmission mechanism, we have incorporated the two main components of bank assets: loans and holdings of securities. Securities holdings are ordered last, reflecting the relative ease with which they can be adjusted. If, as we suspect, shocks to bank assets turn out to be important in causing output variations, how should we think about them, as distinct from interest rate and money shocks? One possibility, suggested by the literature on the credit crunch, is that loan shocks reflect changes in banks' capital strength (see Ito and Sasaki, 1998, and Woo, 1999). For example, an unexpected improvement in bank strength might cause banks to extend more loans. To test this hypothesis, we add a market-based indicator of bank strength—bank stock prices relative to overall stock prices—to the bank credit VAR.[7]

Finally, we estimate a single VAR that we feel captures the key elements of the monetary transmission mechanism. As business investment turns out to be much more sensitive to monetary shocks than other components of private demand, we run the VAR with private demand split into business investment and the remainder. We then include the other basic variables—prices, overnight call rate, and broad money. As our investigation of the transmission channel from the perspectives of both borrowers (private sector funding) and lenders (bank assets) revealed the important role played by bank loans, we include this variable.

# Results

## Basic Monetary Model

The basic model, which includes private demand, prices, interest rates, and money, provides three important results relevant to the

---

[7]The stock price index for the banking sector from the Tokyo Stock Exchange is available starting in 1983, truncating the sample period. The variable is normalized to unity over the sample period, so that changes have the interpretation of percentage deviations. This variable was ordered last in the VAR, given that market prices generally respond quickly to all types of shocks.

monetary transmission mechanism: interest rate shocks have significant effects on real private demand, consistent with an important role for monetary policy; broad money shocks also have significant effects on output, even though interest rates are included in the model, consistent with the idea that nonpolicy monetary shocks are also important in determining economic activity; and base money shocks have no significant impact on output.

The results from the basic model are illustrated through the model's impulse response functions reported in Figure 7.1. An unexpected rise in short-term interest rates causes a statistically significant decline in private demand, which bottoms out after 8–10 quarters. The implied multiplier for the interest rate is minus 0.6, calculated as the ratio of the fall in output (0.3 percent) to a typical interest rate shock (0.5 percent).[8] A broad money shock causes a significant increase in private demand, with a ¥100 increase in broad money raising real private demand by ¥80. The fact that a money shock has a large impact on economic activity, even when the interest rate is included as a separate variable in the VAR, is consistent with the idea that the interest rate channel alone does not fully account for the sources and transmission of monetary shocks in Japan.

Interest rates rise in response to price shocks, but are relatively insensitive to private demand shocks, consistent with the Bank of Japan's emphasis on price stability. The positive interest rate response to broad money innovations is somewhat counterintuitive— we might expect declining interest rates to accompany an expansion of liquidity. One possible explanation is that money shocks are indicative of future inflation, consistent with the price level's positive response to money shocks.

Thus far, we have assumed that monetary policy acts only through interest rates, not through the quantity of high-powered money ("quantitative easing"). To address the issue of whether base money is also important for aggregate demand when interest rates are

---

[8]This multiplier is similar to that obtained in Chapter 2 by Bayoumi, who uses a VAR methodology with a different set of variables, although only about half of that obtained by Lipworth and Meredith (1998), who use the Japan block of the IMF's MULTIMOD model, and at the lower end of the range of estimates from large econometric models presented by Krugman (1998).

**Figure 7.1. Impulse Response Functions for the Basic Model**
*(Responses to 1 standard deviation (SD) innovations)*

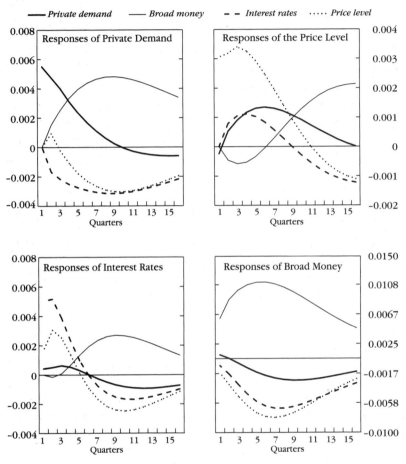

Source: IMF staff calculations.

held constant, we added base money to the basic model.[9] The impulse response of real demand to base money is small and insignificant—a typical money base shock raises real demand by less

---

[9]The equation for base money is ordered second to last (before broad money but after the short-term interest rate to account for the impact of interest rate changes on base money). The results are similar if base money is ordered last.

than 0.1 percent. In addition, adding base money has no perceptible impact on either the size or significance of the response of aggregate demand to broad money. This suggests that, at least in normal circumstances, quantitative easing may have only limited effects on activity.

## Components of Private Demand

The first experiment we conduct is to examine which components of real private demand are most affected by monetary policy. This is accomplished by rerunning the basic model with real private demand split between the particular component being examined and the remainder of private demand (ordered first to avoid spurious correlations).[10] For business investment, for example, the VAR involves private demand less business investment, business investment, prices, the overnight call rate, and broad money.

Figure 7.2 shows the response of the individual demand components to a change in interest rates and a change in broad money. The results indicate that monetary policy operates on the real economy largely through its impact on business investment. A typical innovation in the overnight call rate changes business investment by over 0.2 percentage points of potential output after 2½ years, compared to 0.1 percentage points for household spending (the sum of consumption and residential investment) and a negligible effect on net exports. The importance of business investment is consistent with the view that the bank lending channel dominates the monetary transmission mechanism in Japan, as such investment is largely funded out of bank lending, at least at the margin. Similar results are also found with regard to broad money.

## Private Sector Funding

The second extension to the basic model involves adding the main components of private sector funding: bank loans to corporations and households (hereafter simply called bank loans), loans from government financial institutions to these same sectors (henceforth, pub-

---

[10]The components of private demand are consumption, business investment, residential investment, exports, and imports.

**Figure 7.2. Components of Private Demand**
*(Responses to 1 SD innovations)*

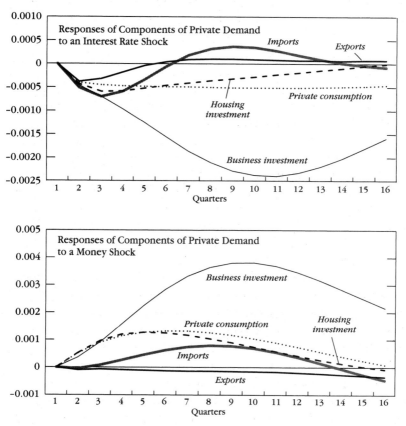

Source: IMF staff calculations.

lic loans), and funds raised by corporations through securities markets.[11] So the VAR comprises (in order) private demand, prices, the overnight call rate, broad money, public loans, funds from securities markets, and bank loans. The addition of these private sector funding variables has almost no impact on the responses within the basic

---

[11]These data come from the flow of funds accounts. The securities markets series aggregates funds from bonds, corporate paper, and equities.

Figure 7.3.  Responses of Private Demand to Funding Shocks

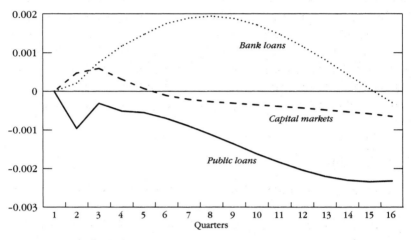

Source: IMF staff calculations.

model, with one important exception, namely that the impact of the overnight rate on demand becomes insignificant. As this is the main transmission channel for monetary policy in the model, this result would be important if it turned out to be robust. Further investigation indicates that this result is reversed, however, when the series measuring funds raised in securities markets is eliminated from the VAR. As this variable has very little impact on the rest of the model, and this is the only case in which our monetary VARs produce an insignificant interest rate response on output, we view this effect as a statistical aberration.

Turning to the results for the three funding variables, we find that bank loans are a significant source of independent shocks to private demand, while funds from securities markets and public loans are not. The impulse responses in Figure 7.3 indicate that innovations to bank loans unconnected with interest rates and demand have a large and significant impact on private demand, with a ¥100 increase in bank loans leading to a ¥50 increase in real demand. By contrast, independent increases in funds from securities markets or loans from public institutions have no significant impact on demand. In the case of securities markets, this appears to reflect their limited importance in financial intermediation (comparing the size of own responses, the typical innovation to funding from securities markets is only two-fifths that of bank loans). For public sector loans, which are a more important component of the financial transmission mechanism, the results show that a rise in public loans is followed by reduction in privately-sourced funds. In other words, increases in public sector loans are almost entirely offset by subsequent reductions in bank loans and securities markets funding—public loans substitute for private credit, helping to explain why they have little impact on demand.

## Bank Lending

This section examines the role of banks in the monetary transmission mechanism by adding to the basic model the main components of bank assets, namely loans and holdings of securities. Including banks' balance sheets in the analysis yields the following insights into the monetary transmission mechanism in Japan: shocks to bank loans have a positive and significant effect on private demand, even controlling for interest rates and broad money; the impulse responses of private demand to interest rate and money shocks are reduced when bank loans are treated as given, suggesting that bank loans are an important transmission channel; and the addition of relative bank stock prices to the VAR suggests that bank loan shocks may largely reflect innovations to bank strength.

The bank lending VAR includes private demand, prices, interest rates, broad money, bank loans, and banks' holdings of securities. The impulse responses for the basic model variables are generally similar to the results reported previously, with the overnight call rate having a significantly negative effect—and broad money a significantly positive effect—on private demand. The response of private demand to a broad money shock is somewhat smaller to that in the basic model, suggesting that part of the broad money shocks in the basic model reflect bank lending shocks (Figure 7.4). Turning to the impact of the additional variables on private demand, a shock to bank loans has a positive, significant, and long-lasting effect—a ¥100 increase in bank lending increases private demand by more than ¥50—while shocks to securities have no significant short-term impact.

153

## Figure 7.4. Impulse Responses for Bank Lending Model
*(Responses to 1 SD innovations)*

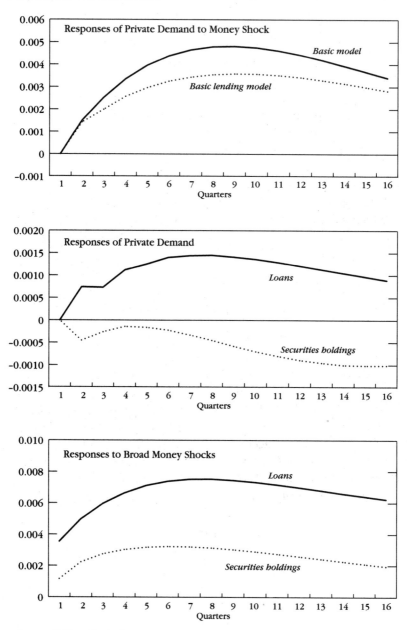

Source: IMF staff calculations.

Bank loans and securities both respond negatively to an interest rate shock and positively to a money shock.[12] The fact that the immediate reactions of bank loans and securities are so large, accounting for more than four-fifths of the shock to broad money, shows that a shock to the main component of bank funding (broad money) cannot be immediately offset with a change in other liabilities. In turn, this suggests that banks do not face a perfectly elastic supply of funds and thus need to make an immediate adjustment in assets. Our results show that bank loans and securities respond in similar ways to monetary shocks, which is not consistent with the idea that banks use their relatively liquid assets (securities) as a temporary shock absorber and adjust their loans over the longer run.[13]

The role of bank loans in the transmission mechanism can be further examined by exogenizing bank loans in the calculation of the impulse responses, that is, treating the lagged values of bank loans as given in a smaller VAR with private demand, prices, the interest rate, broad money, and securities holdings. This procedure generates a VAR identical to the original, except that it blocks off any responses within the VAR that pass through bank loans, so comparisons of the impulse responses across the two models provide a measure of the importance of bank loans in the transmission mechanism. Exogenizing bank loans shortens the impulse response of private demand to an interest rate innovation, and dampens the response of a money shock (Figure 7.5). By contrast, exogenizing securities holdings does not have these effects. These results indicate that bank loans play an important role in transmitting interest rate and money shocks to economic activity.

Given the importance of bank loans in determining activity, it is useful to try to identify the nature of loan shocks, as distinct from interest rate and money shocks. Motivated by the idea that bank weaknesses could be pushing banks to contract lending (a credit crunch), we considered a market-based measure of bank strength, namely the

---

[12]When the VAR is run without broad money, the impulse responses of private demand to innovations in bank loans and securities are somewhat larger, consistent with the view that these variables to some extent capture money shocks.

[13]Bernanke and Blinder (1992) show that—in the U.S.—securities act as a shock absorber.

Figure 7.5. Role of Bank Loans in Transmitting Monetary Shocks
*(Responses to 1 SD innovations)*

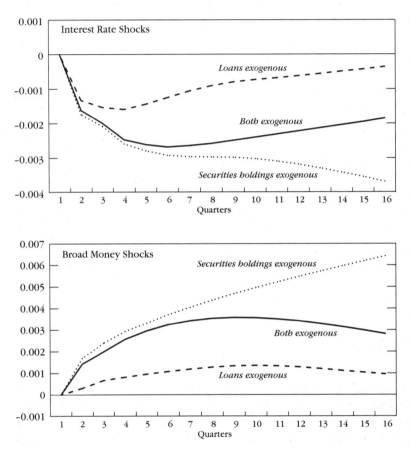

Source: IMF staff calculations.

relative value of bank stocks to the overall TOPIX.[14] When added to the VAR, this variable does a good job of anticipating movements in bank loans, and otherwise generates the anticipated pattern of re-

---

[14]Balance-sheet-based measures of bank strength, such as a bank's reported capital adequacy ratio, are not fully reliable. For example, Long-Term Credit Bank reported a capital adequacy of over 10 percent for March 1998, just a few months before it was found to have negative net worth equivalent to over 14 percent of risk assets.

sponses. The impulse response of private demand to bank strength is positive and significant. While private demand still responds positively and significantly to a shock to bank loans, the size of the response is now smaller. The responses of private demand to interest rate and money shocks are smaller, indicating that part of the impact of such shocks is captured by the measure of bank strength.

An interesting application of these results is to assess the likely impact of the recent decision to inject public funds into major banks on private credit and real demand. In the wake of the enactment of bank legislation in October 1998, which established the framework for the capital injections that eventually occurred in March 1999, bank stock prices recovered strongly—the bank strength variable rose by about 5 percentage points between the third and fourth quarters of 1998. In terms of the history of this variable, such an improvement is equivalent to a typical (one standard deviation) shock to bank strength. If we attribute this improvement exclusively to a previously unanticipated change in expectations about public capital injections, the estimated results suggest that bank loans will be about 0.5 percent of GDP higher than otherwise after about one year (and private demand about 0.35 percent of GDP higher).

## Summary Model

We now run a single VAR that summarizes our key findings about the role of banks in the monetary transmission mechanism, namely that banks are both a significant source of independent shocks to private demand and an important conduit for interest rate and broad money shocks. The summary VAR differs from the basic model in two crucial aspects. First, reflecting the particular sensitivity of business investment to monetary shocks, the summary VAR splits private demand into business investment and the remainder of private demand. Second, the summary VAR adds bank loans (ordered last).

The impulse responses of this model show that shocks to interest rates, broad money, and bank loans all have large and significant effects on business investment and the remainder of private demand (Figure 7.6). The reactions to these shocks of business investment and the remainder of private demand differ in two important ways: the reactions of business investment are two to three times larger, confirming that this component of private demand is particularly sensitive to

Figure 7.6. Impulse Responses for Summary Model
*(Responses to 1 SD innovations)*

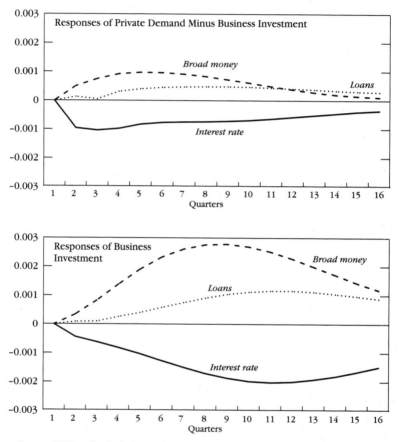

Source: IMF staff calculations.

monetary shocks; and the reaction to any given shock of business investment builds up more slowly than the reaction of the remainder of private demand, reaching their peaks about one to two years later, which is consistent with the idea that planning processes for business investment are longer than for other components of private demand.

The fact that shocks to bank loans have positive and significant effects on private demand, even controlling for interest rates and broad money, confirms that banks play an important independent role in the monetary transmission mechanism. This role of banks as lenders is distinct from that played by the monetary authorities (who determine the overnight call rate) and economic agents more broadly (who decide their demand for money). The fact that the impulse responses of private demand to interest rate and money shocks are reduced when bank loans are exogenized confirms that such shocks are transmitted—at least in part—through bank loans, suggesting an important role for a bank lending channel.

Finally, we use the results of the summary VAR to decompose the actual path of business investment from 1980 to 1998 into the part predicted by the exogenous variables (constants, time trends, and dummies) and the remainder (the shock). This total shock is then divided into the part explained by innovations in financial variables (overnight call rate, broad money, and bank loans) and that explained by innovations in "real" variables (remainder of private demand, business investment, and prices). The historical decomposition in Figure 7.7 indicates how the bubble in the late 1980s was driven by both real factors (including changes in business and consumer sentiment) and financial shocks, while the recession of the early 1990s reflected the reversal of both these sets of shocks. Conversely, the pickup in business investment in 1996–97, which helped Japan achieve the most rapid growth rate among OECD countries in 1996, was driven exclusively by real factors, with financial shocks remaining in negative territory. Similarly, the recent abrupt decline in business investment reflects a reversal of these real factors, possibly owing to adverse effects of the Asian crisis on confidence.[15]

Figure 7.7 also shows the individual components of the financial shocks to business investment: the interest rate shock, the broad money shock, and the bank loans shock. It is interesting that, at least according to our decomposition, interest rate policy was not surprisingly expansionary during the late 1980s—rather, the bubble was driven by money and loan shocks (possibly caused by irrational exuberance). The sharp swings in money demand in the early 1990s are difficult to explain, but could reflect in part the public's initial rush into bank deposits (accompanying the collapse of asset prices) followed by the realization that banks themselves were in difficulties.

---

[15]The results of the decomposition are similar if the VAR is reordered with the financial variables preceding the real variables.

Figure 7.7. Historical Decomposition of Shocks
to Business Investment

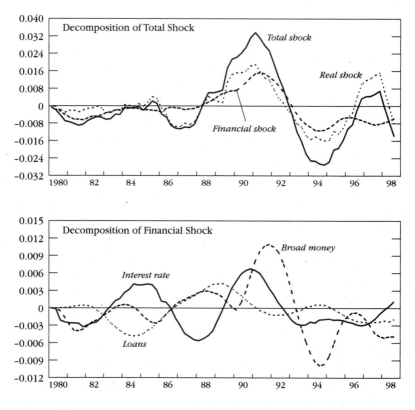

Source: IMF staff calculations

Although monetary policy more recently provided some positive sur-
prises, the public's confidence in bank deposits (money demand)
and banks' willingness to lend (bank loans) remained weak, underlying the urgency of further progress on bank restructuring.

# Conclusions

This chapter has used a series of VARs to examine the transmission
of monetary shocks to real activity in Japan. Starting from a relatively

simple specification that describes the overall mechanism, the role of the components of private demand, private sector funding, and bank lending were examined in turn by including relevant additional variables. Finally, a summary VAR was estimated that captures our main findings. The results of these exercises point to a transmission mechanism dominated by banks, in which bank lending is both an important independent source of shocks and an important conduit for the transmission of interest rate and broad money shocks to real activity. In a further experiment, we found that changes in the monetary base had relatively limited effects on real private demand, suggesting that in normal circumstances quantitative easing may provide limited benefits to activity.

The importance of bank loans in financial intermediation appears to reflect the lack of alternative sources of borrowing for much of the nonfinancial sector, with neither securities markets nor loans from public sector institutions providing a significant offset to changes in bank loans. In addition, independent disturbances to bank credit also appear to have a significant impact on private demand, and much of this effect can be captured by a measure of bank strength based on equity prices. By contrast, the potential benefits from increased loans by the public sector are negated by offsetting decreases in private sector credit.

The important independent role of bank loans in determining activity points to the fact that banking strains may have undermined the monetary transmission mechanism over the last few years. To the extent that banks have responded to their own difficulties by reducing their loans to the private sector, such behavior will have tended to offset the benefits of monetary easing. Indeed, the historical decomposition of the summary VAR shows that, while unanticipated monetary loosening has had a positive effect on business investment recently, shocks to bank loans have dragged down business investment, especially since 1996. Bank weakness explains a large part of the negative shocks to bank loans.

Looking to the future, the increasing role of private securities markets in financial intermediation likely to be created by the Big Bang financial deregulation initiative may well reduce the central role of banks in Japan's financial system, although such changes are likely to be gradual rather than rapid, particularly given the importance of small companies in Japan's industrial structure. In the meantime, the results presented here suggest that restoring the banking system to full health is essential both to revive the credit channel of monetary policy and to provide a direct boost to economic activity through increased bank lending.

## Appendix. Data Sources

Aggregate demand: Economic Planning Agency, *Annual Report on National Accounts.*

Consumer price index, broad money, bank loans and bank holdings of securities, overnight call rate: Bank of Japan, *Economic Statistics Monthly.*

Corporate and household funding: Bank of Japan, Flow of Funds Accounts, *Economic Statistics Monthly.*

Bank strength: Tokyo Stock Exchange (First Section) banking sector index divided by composite index (TOPIX).

## References

Aghevli, Bijan B., Tamim Bayoumi, and Guy Meredith (eds.), 1998, *Structural Change in Japan: Macroeconomic Impact and Policy Challenges* (Washington: International Monetary Fund).

Bayoumi, Tamim, 1999, "The Morning After: Explaining the Slowdown in Japanese Growth in the 1990s," IMF Working Paper 99/13 (Washington: International Monetary Fund).

Bernanke, Ben S., and Alan S. Blinder, 1992, "The Federal Funds Rate and the Channels of Monetary Transmission," *American Economic Review,* Vol. 82:4, (September), pp. 901–21.

Bernanke, Ben S., and Mark Gertler, 1995, "Inside the Black Box: The Credit Channel of Monetary Policy Transmission," *Journal of Economic Perspectives,* Vol. 9:3, (Fall), pp. 27–28.

Ito, Takatoshi, and Yuri Nagataki Sasaki, 1998, "Impacts of the Basle Capital Standard on Japanese Banks' Behavior," NBER Working Paper No. 6730, (September).

Kashyap, Anil K., and Jeremy C. Stein, 1997, "What do a Million Observations on Banks Say About the Transmission of Monetary Policy?" NBER Working Paper No. 6065, (June).

Krugman, Paul R., 1998, "It's Baaack: Japan's Slump and the Return of the Liquidity Trap," *Brookings Papers on Economic Activity: 2,* pp. 137–205, Brookings Institution.

Lipworth, Gabrielle, and Guy Meredith, 1998, "A Reexamination of Indicators of Monetary Policy and Financial Conditions," in Bijan B. Aghevli, Tamim Bayoumi, and Guy Meredith (eds.), *Structural Change in Japan* (Washington: International Monetary Fund).

Mishkin, Frederick, 1995, "Symposium on the Monetary Transmission Mechanism," *Journal of Economic Perspectives* Vol. 9:3, pp. 3–10, Fall.

Morsink, James, and Tamim Bayoumi, 1999, "A Peek Inside the Black Box: The Monetary Transmission Mechanism in Japan," IMF Working Paper 99/137 (Washington: International Monetary Fund).

Woo, David, 1999, "In Search of Capital Crunch: Supply Factors Behind the Credit Slowdown in Japan," IMF Working Paper 99/3, January (Washington: International Monetary Fund).

# 8

# Financial Reorganization and Corporate Restructuring in Japan

*Joaquim Levy*

The Japanese corporate sector, the vitality of which appeared indisputable a decade ago, is currently under great stress. Since 1990, the performance of the Japanese corporate sector has lagged that of its counterparts in several large industrial countries. As a result, while a number of large export-oriented companies continue to be strong, concern has grown about the overall health of Japan's corporate sector. A perception has emerged that the average Japanese firm is highly leveraged and in a fragile situation, and that large corporations cannot expect their considerable accumulated wealth to substitute permanently for strong rates of return from core businesses. Indeed, in the absence of genuine restructuring, the gradual depletion of these resources and poor prospects of profits had until recently led to a persistent decline in Japanese equity prices. These factors also contributed to the lowering of the credit ratings of many top Japanese corporations, including several major trading companies.

At least three factors have contributed to the fragility of the corporate sector. First, the surge in investment that occurred in the late 1980s yielded very low real returns, in part because much of it was directed to sectors in which Japan did not have a comparative advantage, while the similar diversification strategies followed by many large companies led to an excessive number of entrants in many markets (Mitsuhiro, 1994, and Moriaki and Yoshinobu, 1997). Second, Japanese companies were adversely affected by cuts in credit availability and widening credit spreads linked to Japanese banks' at-

164

tempts to maintain adequate capital. Finally, the economic slowdown in Japan was accompanied by deflationary pressures that helped erode the revenue-to-debt ratio of Japanese firms.[1] These factors were compounded by weak accounting and financial control systems, and the cumulation of unfunded corporate pension liabilities.

The intensification of pressures on corporations spurred a string of announcements of restructuring plans. Increasing attention by banks to credit quality—in part because of tighter regulations and more rigorous bank supervision—together with a sharp decline in profits were accompanied by a surge in announcements of corporate restructuring plans in early 1999. Market reaction to these plans was generally positive, but guarded. This reaction reflects doubts about whether the degree of planned restructuring is on a par with the magnitude of the challenges.

During 1999, the government took a series of measures to facilitate the restructuring of corporate assets and liabilities, as well as the reallocation of resources across sectors. A three-pillar strategy emerged:

- tax incentives to encourage business innovation and restructuring, including the reduction of production capacity;
- mechanisms to address the debt overhang problem, such as bankruptcy law reform to provide more effective reorganization procedures, and changes in the commercial code and other legislation to facilitate debt-for-equity swaps, corporate spin-offs, and the exchange of stocks in connection with corporate restructuring; and
- reinforcement of the social safety net to reduce the problems associated with labor mobility.

This approach attempts to spread the adjustment effort over corporations, banks, and employees, with public funds used to cushion some of the costs. This use of public funds may help mitigate the short-term macroeconomic impact of corporate restructuring, although it could bring long-term risks, particularly if large corporate bail-outs aggravate an already difficult fiscal position, or if it creates moral hazard by reducing incentives for prudent corporate governance.

---

[1]The impact of the debt overhang on business investment is discussed by Ramaswamy in Chapter 4 of this volume.

This chapter analyzes the factors pushing Japanese corporations into restructuring and discusses the steps being taken in this direction. It describes the leverage of the corporate sector and increasing signs of financial strain in the sector. It goes on to discuss how much corporate restructuring is needed and recent restructuring steps. It also reviews some institutional impediments to restructuring and recent official initiatives. The chapter closes with a section discussing prospects and risks. An appendix provides a brief discussion of market reactions to recent announcements of corporate restructuring plans.

## Approaching the Crossroads

### Corporate Sector Leverage

Overall, corporate leverage is higher in Japan than in most other large industrial countries.[2] Large Japanese firms are less leveraged than their U.S. or German counterparts (Figure 8.1),[3] but the high leverage of small and medium-sized firms (around 600 percent) pushes up the overall figure for the Japanese corporate sector (top panel of Figure 8.2). It should also be noted that there is an increasing disparity in leverage ratios among large firms. For instance, the average net debt/equity ratio of the lower quartile (in terms of indebtedness) of firms listed in the first section of the Tokyo Stock Exchange (TSE1) has remained stable at around 50 percent in recent years, while the leverage of the top quartile rose from 500 percent to 700 percent (middle panel of Figure 8.2).

Banks have been the main source of corporate credit, although large firms have increasingly substituted bond issuance for bank finance in the last 15 years (bottom panel of Figure 8.2). Roughly 70 percent of bank corporate loans are now to small and medium-sized firms, which also rely significantly on intercorporate credit. Although banks are still an important source of financing to large corporations,

---

[2]Leverage is the ratio of net debt to equity.

[3]The average leverage of companies listed in the first section of the Tokyo Stock Exchange is 350 percent, compared with 450 percent for the U.S. companies included in the S&P Industrial Index, and 460 for large German non-financial corporations.

## Figure 8.1. Corporate Leverage and Nonfinancial Sources of Funds

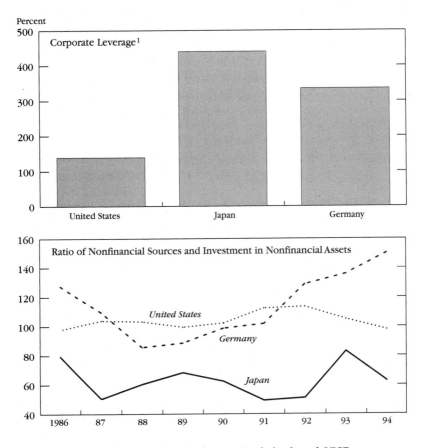

Sources: U.S. Federal Reserve; Bank of Japan; Bundesbank; and OECD.
[1]For the United States and Japan, leverage is defined as net worth (with assets at historical prices) divided by liabilities; for Germany, leverage is defined as own funds divided by liabilities to creditors.

the reliance of such firms on market instruments (such as bonds and CPs) is well illustrated by the high share of these instruments in the liabilities of firms belonging to the six largest economic groups (43 percent).

Corporate indebtedness also varies across the economy. As is typical in most countries, leverage in Japan is higher in nonmanufactur-

Figure 8.2. Selected Indicators of Corporate Leverage

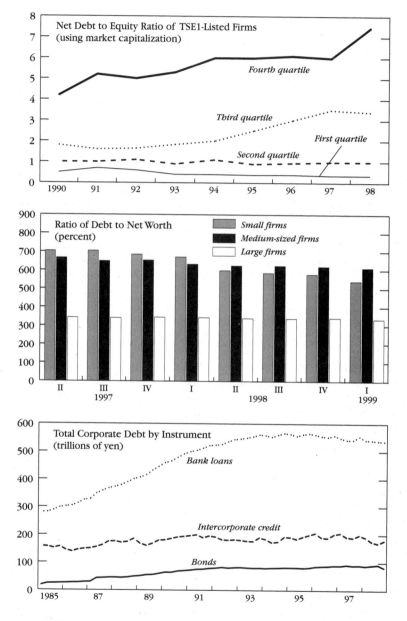

Sources: TSE1; and WEFA, Nomura database.

ing than in manufacturing (the consolidated net debt to equity ratio of large firms in the respective sectors is 250 percent and 60 percent). Within the manufacturing sector, large parent companies actually tend to have negative net debt. Among large firms, the average leverage has been pushed up by increases in the construction sector (the net debt to equity ratio rose fourfold since 1990), in the retail and trading sector, and in some segments of the manufacturing sector (such as electrical machinery, and pulp and paper).

The high leverage of Japanese corporations reflects in part the widespread reliance on external funding. For most of the postwar period, retained earnings were insufficient to finance the heavy investment schedules pursued by Japanese firms. Internal funds still accounted for less than 60 percent of corporate investment in nonfinancial assets in the late 1980s (a share that increased somewhat in the 1990s as the economy slowed down and investment rates declined); by contrast, in Germany and the United States, internal funds are typically almost as large as the amounts committed to fixed investment in years of strong economic growth, and exceed these flows when the economy slows.

Partial financial liberalization and a surge in land prices spurred the expansion of Japanese corporate balance sheets in the 1980s. Partial financial liberalization starting in the early 1980s granted large firms greater access to capital markets and allowed them to increase sharply their financial assets (top panel of Figure 8.3). This shift also prompted banks to substitute small and medium-sized firms for these borrowers and resulted inter alia in a 90 percent increase in long-term loans.[4] The loosening of monetary policy after 1985 and the ensuing rise in the price of land (which was the prime collateral for bank loans) compounded these forces. Overall, corporate debt increased by about 60 percent in the second half of the 1980s (close to 50 percent at constant prices). A drive toward corporate diversification fueled a 60 percent rise in the stock of reproducible fixed assets, which was mirrored by a roughly similar expansion in corporate financial assets.

The aggregate book value of the Japanese corporate sector continued to grow after the bursting of the "asset price bubble" in 1990,

---

[4]The traditional restriction excluding city banks from offering long-term loans was also weakened.

Figure 8.3.  Selected Indicators of Corporate Liquidity
and Equity Value

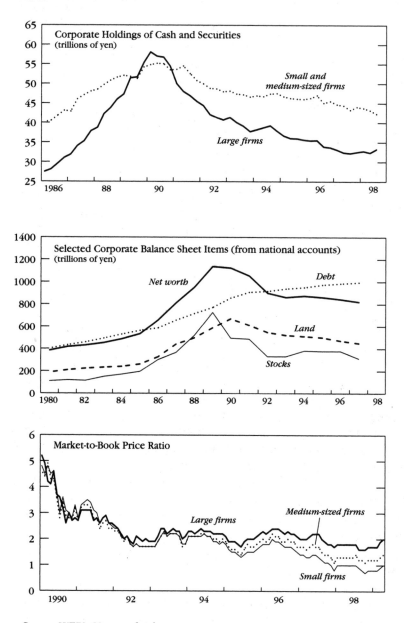

Source: WEFA, Nomura database.

## Table 8.1. Combined Balance Sheet of the Nikkei 300 Non-Financial Companies

*(Trillions of yen, unless otherwise indicated)*

|  | 1990 | 1998 | Percentage Change | Contribution to the Change in the Balance Sheet (percent) |
|---|---|---|---|---|
| Total assets | 284.5 | 359.8 | 26.5 | . . . |
| Current assets | 159.0 | 169.8 | 6.8 | 14.3 |
| Cash & Deposits | 42.6 | 28.9 | –32.1 | –18.2 |
| Marketable Securities | 12.7 | 16.2 | 27.2 | 4.6 |
| Inventories | 33.9 | 43.5 | 28.2 | 12.7 |
| Fixed assets | 125.3 | 188.6 | 50.6 | 84.1 |
| Tangible fixed assets | 80.7 | 130.6 | 61.8 | 66.3 |
| Investment & other assets | 44.6 | 58.0 | 30.2 | 17.8 |
| Liabilities | 213.7 | 267.8 | 25.4 | . . . |
| Current liabilities | 129.5 | 150.8 | 16.5 | 28.3 |
| Short-term debt | 42.7 | 48.2 | 12.9 | 7.3 |
| Fixed liabilities | 81.1 | 111.5 | 37.5 | 40.4 |
| Bonds | 46.3 | 62.9 | 35.8 | 22.0 |
| Long-term debt | 22.5 | 36.6 | 62.4 | 18.7 |
| Equity | 70.8 | 92.0 | 29.8 | 28.2 |
| Capital | 16.0 | 18.8 | 17.1 | 3.7 |
| Capital reserves | 17.8 | 20.3 | 14.1 | 3.3 |
| Legal revenue reserves | 2.0 | 3.3 | 67.7 | 1.7 |
| Other surplus | 28.1 | 41.2 | 46.7 | 17.4 |
| *Memorandum items:* |  |  |  |  |
| Net Debt/Equity | 90.9 | 113.0 | 24.3 | . . . |
| Liabilities/Equity | 3.02 | 2.91 | –3.6 | . . . |

Source: Goldman Sachs.

supported in part by the revaluation of latent capital gains on land- and stock-holdings. Despite the economic slowdown that followed the collapse of asset prices in 1990, the aggregate liabilities of the 300 largest firms listed in the TSE1 rose by 25 percent in 1990–97, while the book value of their equity increased by some 30 percent (Table 8.1). This increase was underpinned by a 60 percent rise in the book value of fixed assets, stemming in part from the revaluation of land. Stockholdings were also subject to a similar revaluation process, notably in the banking sector. Although an official study prepared in 1999 suggests that the top 50 firms still have sizable unrealized gains on land (the last mandatory revaluation of land occurred in 1952), the process of systematic revaluation of stockholdings appears to have run much of its course.

The progressive depletion of latent reserves has been reflected in the decline of the market-to-book value ratio of Japanese firms in recent years. In contrast with figures emerging from the aggregation of firms' book values, national account estimates of firms' assets and liabilities at market prices indicate a 25 percent decline in the net worth (equity value) of Japanese firms in 1990–93 (middle panel of Figure 8.3). The contribution of land to this decline is substantial, as land accounted for one-third of Japanese firms' assets in 1990 (land accounts for about 10 percent of the balance sheet of U.S. corporations) and the overall value of these holdings has declined by around 30 percent subsequently. The conflicting trends of book values boosted by revaluations of latent reserves and the decline in the market value of the assets underlying these reserves have been reflected in a 75 percent decline in the market-to-book value of Japan's corporate sector since 1990 (bottom panel of Figure 8.3). The market-to-book-value ratio of TSE1 firms dropped by half from 1990 to 1992. Since 1996, there has been a further decline of that ratio, especially among the smaller firms. While the market-to-book-value ratio of the largest, oldest firms is still close to 2.0, the ratio for the smallest firm in the TSE1 has fallen around one.

## Signs of Increasing Strain

Until recently, the growing fragility of corporate balance sheets was cushioned in part by the relief provided by declining interest rates—a trend now being reversed. Average interest rates on loans declined from 8 percent to 2 percent in 1991–97, allowing the proportion of gross interest expenses to sales to decline by 40 percent, despite the deterioration of firms' revenues during the period (top panel of Figure 8.4). From late 1997, however, financial turbulence and the tightening of regulatory standards by the supervisory authorities have driven a widening of credit spreads, while credit lines were curtailed. With the economy entering a prolonged downturn, sales declined 6 percent and profits dropped by roughly 30 percent in 1998. Despite the decline in market interest rates through 1998, the ratio of interest payments to sales began to increase.

Widespread corporate losses and troubles in the banking system have resulted in an erosion of the traditional sources of mutual support among corporations and in the deterioration of the credit

Figure 8.4. Selected Indicators of Firms' Cash Flow and Bankruptcy

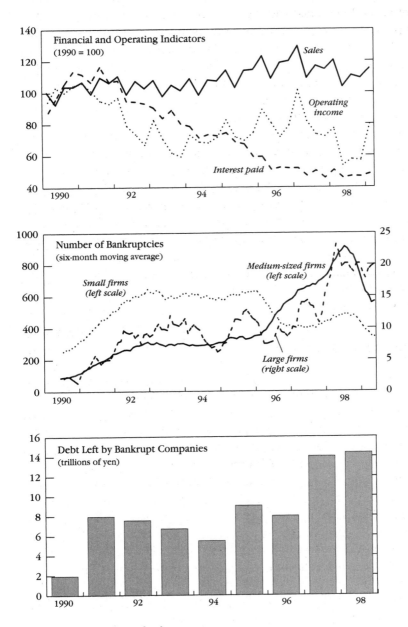

Source: WEFA, Nomura database.

173

rating of the Japanese corporate sector. In the past, firms belonging to an economic group (*kigyio shudan* and associated *keiretsus*) could count on support from their peers, parents, and main banks when facing distress.[5] The deterioration of banks' financial standing in recent years and the increasingly widespread weakening of corporate balance sheets have provoked changes in this behavior. With the ratio of loss-making firms increasing by about one-third,[6] and the depletion of reserves of large firms, it became harder to predict whether a distressed company would receive financial support from these traditional sources. For instance, several *keiretsu* companies refused to help related companies to raise capital or issue bonds when bank credit became scarce in 1997–98. With companies having to increasingly stand by themselves, credit agencies warned that the relationship between the ratings and corporate leverage of Japanese firms would converge toward that of U.S. companies. Moody's downgraded 82 Japanese nonfinancial corporations between February 1998 and March 1999, while Standard & Poor's downgraded about two dozen companies over the same period.

Corporate fragility has been manifest in a steep rise in the number and size of corporate bankruptcies. The number of corporate bankruptcies started to accelerate in 1997, with the year-on-year growth rate of new corporate bankruptcies approaching 35 percent in May–July 1998 (middle panel of Figure 8.4). Moreover, because for the first time large firms started to go bankrupt, the debt left by failing companies rose by 70 percent in 1997–98, compared to 1995–96 (bottom panel of Figure 8.4), about three times faster than the growth of the number of bankruptcies over this period. In the second half of 1998, however, the authorities took several steps to sustain credit to the corporate sector, and the number of bankruptcies subsided. Most important among these measures were the substantial public funding provided for widespread loan guarantees for small and medium-sized enterprises, and special credit lines for

---

[5]The structure of the typical Japanese large economic group comprises a set of top companies in different fields (*kigyio shudan*), which are the head of the vertical structures grouping their respective affiliates (*keiretsu*).

[6]The increase in FY1998 compared to FY1997 was 50 percent in the case of listed companies, with more than ⅓ of the companies declaring negative net profits.

## Table 8.2. Timetable for Japan's Accounting Reforms

| Adoption Deadline | New Standard | Old or Current Standard |
|---|---|---|
| March 31, 1998 | Mandatory disclosure of valuation profit/loss on financial derivatives holdings. | Disclosure is optional. |
| March 31, 1999 | Mandatory disclosure of miscellaneous liabilities, such as debt guarantees, on a consolidated basis. | Disclosure is optional. |
| March 31, 2000 | Mandatory use of consolidated financial statements, including affiliates over which the company exerts "effective control," even if it owns less than 20 percent of the affiliate. | Individual firms' returns are the primary reporting vehicle; consolidation based on majority shareholding. |
| | Mandatory consolidation of cash-flow statements. | Disclosure of six-month expected cash flow of parent firm. |
| | Recognition of R&D expenditures as a current expense when they are made. | No clear rule. |
| March 31, 2001 | Semiannual consolidated reports. | Semiannual reports on individual firm basis. |
| | Compulsory use of tax-effect accounting. | Recommended but not required. |
| | Compulsory use of fair market values for all financial assets except cross-held shareholdings. | Lower of purchase cost or market value for many financial assets. |
| | Classification of receivables and implementation of hedge accounting. | Lax rules or bad rules; no rules on hedges. |
| | Recognition of post-employment benefits (e.g., pensions and severance payments) on an accrual basis. Up to 15 years will be allowed to make good any underfunded liabilities. | Allowance for 40 percent to 100 percent of pension liabilities. |
| March 31, 2002 | Compulsory use of fair market values for cross-shareholdings (landholdings will not be required to be marked to market). | Valued at purchase cost. |

Sources: Tatsumi Yamada, Chuo Audit Corporation, and *The Nikkei Weekly*, July 6, 1998, p. 13.

firms facing the imminent redemption of bonds issued in the late 1980s.

New accounting and reporting rules are making firms' vulnerabilities yet more evident. Several changes in accounting and reporting rules take effect in 1999–2002 (Table 8.2). These changes are increasing the transparency of corporate financial statements and, in part because of market pressures, motivating Japanese companies to address some problems that have until now received little scrutiny.[7] In particular:

- Consolidated accounts will help clarify the overall profitability of Japanese firms and their actual cost of capital (consolidation is mandatory as of March 2000).[8] In an environment of weak profits, consolidated accounts are expected to reduce the scope for cross-subsidization, prompting parent companies to close or restructure unprofitable subsidiaries and reduce guarantees to affiliates.

- Marking to market firms' financial assets will expose a firm's sensitivity to changes in the market value of their holdings of financial assets, including stockholdings. The double gearing provided by cross-shareholdings could thus become a source of profit volatility, encouraging companies (and financial institutions) to reduce the presence of these holdings in their books.

- The disclosure of corporate pension liabilities and the extent to which they are underfunded is expected to raise the recognized leverage of Japanese firms and put pressure on corporate earnings.

The exact amount of unfunded corporate liabilities is not known, but market analysts have estimated that in the case of large firms, it could be equivalent to one-fifth of firms' equity. Unfunded corporate liabilities are roughly equivalent to a net debt of the firm toward its employees, although in Japan firms are not legally bound to fulfill all pension commitments. Japanese firms are not currently

---

[7]The authorities have also expressed increasing interest in the quality and independence of corporate auditors. There is room for improvement in this area. The Fair Trade Commission, for instance, has recently reported that about two-thirds of the *external* auditors supervising the accounts of the major six economic groups and their affiliates were employees, former employees, or directors of companies belonging to the respective groups.

[8]The coverage of such consolidation will change to include affiliates and subsidiaries into which the parent company exerts "effective control," although it may not have a majority of capital. The appointment of managers, for instance, will be considered an indication of exercise of effective control. Many companies already publish consolidated accounts on a voluntary basis, but the lack of uniformity in methods sometimes renders the interpretation of these accounts difficult.

obliged to disclose the extent to which their pension liabilities are funded, but market analysts have prepared estimates based on disclosures made by Japanese companies listed in the United States, which file their annual reports according to U.S. standards.[9] Adjusted for the current low rate of return on Japanese assets and extrapolated to cover all companies listed in the first section of the Tokyo Stock Exchange, these figures suggest that on a consolidated basis the underfunding is in the ¥50–80 trillion range (Goldman Sachs, 1998).[10] This amount is equivalent to about 5–10 times the current profits posted by listed companies in FY1998 (current profits amounted to less than ¥10 trillion, and net profits were below ¥1 trillion). These estimates of liabilities, although large, may not be exaggerated, as suggested by the disclosure in the spring of 1999 of Nissan's unfunded liabilities, which amounted to ¥330 billion, or more than 25 percent of the firm's consolidated equity. Given the magnitude of these potential liabilities and the discretionary aspect of some pension commitments, some analysts have also raised the hypothesis that firms could also consider renegotiating these implicit contracts with workers.

---

[9]The issue of pension liabilities actually involves two aspects: underexpensing and underfunding. The distinction between the two is the following. Underexpensing is the failure to fully recognize the pension rights accrued, i.e., the amount of liabilities; underfunding is the difference between those rights and the assets accumulated to support them. Correcting underexpensing would have an immediate impact on firms' equity through an accounting charge-off, while correcting underfunding would not necessarily have such an impact, to the extent that the firm may already have recognized those liabilities and has borrowed against them (by not funding them). Correcting underfunding affects earnings because the firm has to "repay" the pension fund. The discrepancy between expensing and funding pension commitments is typically driven by tax considerations. Corporate contributions to pension funds are not tax-deductible in Japan and, given the very low rate of return on assets, it may be cheaper for the Japanese firms to defer those payments, i.e., borrow against the pension funds.

[10]Recent financial disclosures of Japanese companies that have adopted U.S. accounting standards for their financial statements indicate that the majority of these companies have started to reduce the discount rate used for projecting their pension benefit obligations. For the most part, these firms reduced the discount rate by 100 b.p. (to around 3–4 percent), which resulted in a 20–30 percent increase in the net present value of these obligations.

177

## Directions for Change

### How Much Corporate Restructuring Is Needed?

The deterioration of corporate financial indicators reflects the underlying problem of overcapacity. Return on equity in Japan has dropped from around 7.5 percent in the late 1980s to an average of 2.8 percent in FY1991–98 (top panel of Figure 8.5). Estimates of the total cost of capital suggest that many TSE1 companies have not generated enough income to adequately compensate the resources mobilized in support of their activities.[11] These financial indexes suggest the existence of significant overcapacity. Indeed, the capital-to-output ratio has been well above trend, and capacity utilization in the manufacturing sector has dropped to around 65–70 percent.[12] The slack is typically larger in those industries where capacity increased more in the 1990s (middle panel of Figure 8.5), and cannot be fully attributed to cyclical factors (see Chapter 4 by Ramaswamy in this volume). Although not easily measured, overcapacity is also severe in the nonmanufacturing sector, in part because partial liberalization of some subsectors has reduced rents, implying cashflows that have not validated early investments (Ooyama, 1999).[13]

---

[11]A typical measure of total cost of capital assumes that corporate debt should earn the risk-free interest rate (proxied by government bond yields) and equity should yield a 3 percent premium over that rate. Matsui, Suzuki, and Katayama (1997) show that, during 1984–96, the return on capital was systematically lower than the cost of capital in 8 out of 12 leading sectors in the Japanese economy. The problem of inadequate return on capital was identified many years ago. Kester (1991) noted that it amounted to a diversion of economic rents from suppliers of capital to other stakeholders. In his view, it resulted from managers' unwillingness to breach long-standing implicit contracts with key stakeholders, specially lifetime employment commitments, and firms' inability to execute past strategies of simply growing in their original business areas. Thanks to the discretion in the allocation of funds that Japanese managers had in the late 1980s, Japanese companies pursued unrelated diversification strategies and kept sustaining businesses that were either marginal or in areas where the economy could not remain competitive internationally, a process that could not be sustainable in a global economy.

[12]The Economic Planning Agency has suggested that the excess in production capacity is equivalent to a capital stock of ¥85 trillion.

[13]In the case of the retail sector, this problem was compounded by the decline in real estate prices, because investments in new stores often involved the purchase of land and the decline in land prices widened the gap between the actual value of firms' assets and debts.

## Figure 8.5.  Selected Indicators of Profitability and Capacity Utilization

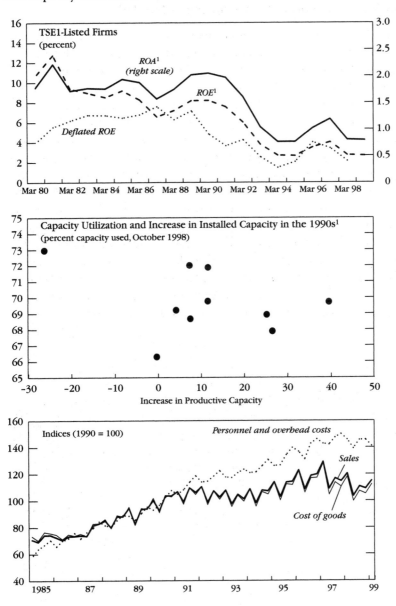

Sources: TSE1; MITI; and WEFA, Nomura database.
[1]ROA, Return on Assets; ROE, Return of Equity.
[2]Six-month average.

The burden of overinvestment has been compounded by a rise in labor costs that has outpaced economic growth. Corporate sales were 11 percent higher in 1998 than in 1990, while labor and overhead costs were 47 percent higher (bottom panel of Figure 8.5). Part of this increase in labor costs occurred in the early 1990s and, more generally, reflects the shift of the economy toward the service sector (which reduces the share of purchased goods in sales). Despite reductions in bonuses and overtime that have contributed to a decline in labor costs, the disconnect between costs and revenues has become more prominent with time. For instance, labor costs declined by 1 percent in 1998, substantially less than the contemporaneous 6 percent drop in nominal sales.

Raising the return on assets (ROA) of the corporate sector back to their historical average or to international levels would require an enormous effort. Since 1990, the ROA for the Japanese corporate sector as a whole has halved to roughly 2–2¼ percent (bottom panel of Figure 8.6), compared with 5½ percent for U.S. companies. The arithmetic of raising that ratio back to its historical average of around 3½ percent would require (assuming constant revenues) either an extraordinary reduction in assets or—given the share of labor cost in corporate revenues—a 15 percent reduction in such costs.[14]

## Institutional Factors and Recent Restructuring Steps

Recent restructuring efforts have been concentrated among large firms. Traditionally, corporate adjustment in Japan has followed a pattern in which large firms use the shelter provided by their intragroup ties to internalize costs (such as by hoarding and reshuffling labor), while small- and medium-sized companies either downsize or close. This pattern was broadly maintained until mid-1998, as suggested by the somewhat contrasting pattern of bankruptcies, investment, and employment among small and large firms (Figure 8.7).[15] Since then, there have been signs of new patterns of corporate restructuring. In particular, some large firms have undertaken significant efforts to restructure, while small and medium-sized firms have

---

[14]See Morgan Stanley Dean Witter (1999).

[15]The reduction in the leverage of small enterprises, which fell by 25 percent in the 12 months to early 1999, nevertheless continues.

## Figure 8.6. Composition of Costs and Return on Assets

Share of Costs and Operating Income in Total Sales
(Percent)

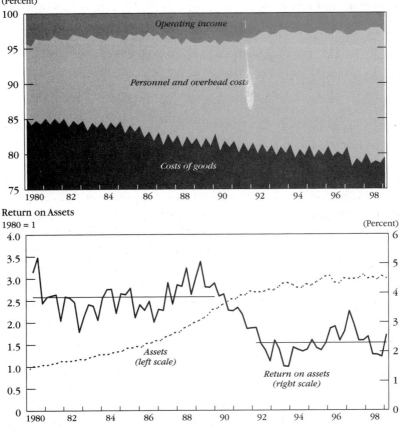

Source: WEFA, Nomura database.

generally benefited from special loan guarantees and other measures aimed at providing them with breathing space. This shift can in part be credited to large firms' expectation that the Big Bang financial reforms will continue to be implemented and bank supervision tightened. In such an environment, large, wealthy firms have strong incentives to reorganize their balance sheets, redeploying assets to raise profits and reduce liabilities.

Figure 8.7. Selected Indicators of Corporate Adjustment, 1997–99

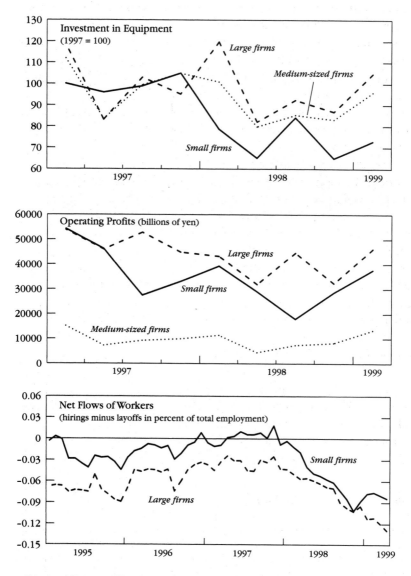

Sources: Ministry of Finance; and WEFA, Nomura database.

The number of announcements of corporate restructuring plans surged in 1999, with market reaction to announcements varying according to the type and scope of measures announced. The surge in the flow of announcements was in part attributed to the magnitude of losses many firms expected to incur in 1998–99 (Table 4.2),[16] and possibly in part to positive market reactions to the example set by a few large, profitable firms that have announced restructuring plans. A qualitative change was also perceived in some of these plans. In the past, the majority of restructuring plans aimed essentially at restoring the firm's near-term solvency rather than at deep corporate restructuring with a view to improving profitability on a sustainable basis. Restructuring plans consisted mainly of gradual reductions of personnel through attrition, and the occasional financial reorganization of subsidiaries (often with a component of debt forgiveness on the part of the parent company), without fundamental shifts in business strategy. By contrast, a number of more recent plans have included ingredients such as the establishment of clear lines of authority, improved accounting and financial control systems, withdrawal from noncore business, and the forging of links with foreign partners.[17] In the case of nonfinancial corporations, the announcing firm's stock price more often than not rose when markets viewed its plans as underpinned by genuine change (see Appendix).

Mergers and acquisitions involving foreign investors have become more common. The number of mergers and acquisitions by foreign companies in Japan doubled from 1996 to 1998, and is likely to have increased further in 1999. Although the absolute numbers are still small (75 in 1998), the size and nature of these deals have changed. For instance, several recent deals have involved large Japanese companies that are sectoral leaders, as the waning of the traditional sup-

---

[16]Recurrent profits of non-financial companies fell 26 percent and net profits dropped by 70 percent in 1998 vis-à-vis 1997.

[17]For instance, some plans took advantage of the upcoming introduction of consolidated accounts to simplify corporate structures and establish "in-house" units aimed at identifying cost and profit centers. These organizational changes are expected to help increase managerial accountability by allowing the timely evaluation of financial results of different units in a company. They are typically associated with a tilting of labor compensation rules toward giving greater weight to performance (e.g., by reducing the weight of seniority and raising the weight of stock options).

port elements has motivated firms to turn, albeit sometimes reluctantly, toward foreign partners. Such deals started in the financial sector, where foreign firms acquired bankrupt institutions (for example, Merrill Lynch acquired the branch network of the failed securities broker Yamaichi) or took a major stake in a profitable part of the business of Japanese firms (GE Capital opened a new venture with the insurer Toho, and Citicorp joined with Nikko Securities). More recently, foreign investments in the industrial sector have become more prominent, as illustrated by the acquisition of a large stake in a major automaker by a foreign company, as well as the purchase of a large tire company from a major *keiretsu* firm and the hostile takeover of a major telecommunication carrier by foreign investors.

Several informal debt workouts were concluded following a revision of the tax treatment of loan write-downs by banks in 1998 and the injection of public funds in major banks in March 1999. Bank-led informal reorganizations of companies, which had traditionally been the dominant form of corporate rehabilitation in Japan, were hindered by banks' weak capitalization through most of the 1990s.[18] In the first half of 1999, however, about a dozen midsized companies reached agreements with their bank creditors (Box 8.1). The announced plans involved write-downs in excess of ¥1 trillion, shouldered mainly by the firms' main banks, which typically contributed 50–85 percent of the total debt forgiveness. These workouts have been instrumental in averting bankruptcies (by contrast a leading glass-producing company that failed to complete a workout by the end of the fiscal year went bankrupt) and may presage a renewed reliance on informal mechanisms to facilitate corporate restructuring. Market analysts have, nevertheless, raised concerns that in some cases workouts have been geared more toward reestablishing the short-term solvency of the debtor than to allow the beneficiary firm to undertake a genuine restructuring plan.

Widespread corporate restructuring still faces institutional impediments, such as the high cost to firms of reducing employment. Job separation from large companies has historically been voluntary. Court rulings in the late 1970s made dismissals cumbersome (favoring the reshuffling of employees across subsidiaries), which led firms

---

[18]Discussed further in Chapter 9.

aiming at a real reduction in head counting to offer voluntary early retirement programs. Morgan Stanley Dean Witter (1999) estimated that the typical early retirement program has cost around ¥22 million (US$180,000) per worker, while noting that the payback period of eliminating redundancies through this mechanism was in some cases (such as in the oil industry) as short as 3 years. Despite this potentially short payback period, cash-strapped firms may have trouble financing such labor reductions.

Until now, tax and legal factors have not favored corporate restructuring. For tax purposes, Japanese firms can carry losses forward over five years. Owing to the structurally low profitability of Japanese firms, this relief may not, however, be a big incentive for firms to restructure: restructuring charges can easily exceed recurrent profits earned over five years. Other tax disincentives are associated with the taxation of events entailed by corporate restructuring, such as the transfer, securitization,[19] or revaluation of assets.[20] Bankruptcy laws, for their part, have been geared more toward firms' liquidation than their financial reorganization.[21] Although formal liquidation procedures are relatively common in Japan (some 2,000 petitions are filed every year), formal reorganization procedures are seldom used.[22]

Firms have responded to recent reforms to permit the creation of holding companies and to the expectation of a change in the basis of corporate taxation. Following the change in the antimonopoly law

---

[19]The passage of an asset-backed securitization law in 1998 and the special treatment of special vehicles have helped promote this type of operation, particularly in what concerns the securitization of low-credit-risk assets such as auto loans, receivables, and high-grade corporate loans, which have grown since. A few obstacles for the use of this technique still remain, however. For instance, there are still doubts about the effectiveness of existing perfection mechanisms (i.e., about the extent to which the securities are insulated from problems with the issuer). With respect to the securitization of real estate loans, the complex structure of the liens typically attached to the collateral of these loans and deficiencies in loan documentation continue to inhibit investors.

[20]Of course, there a ways to sidestep these problems (e.g., Ramseyer and Nakazato, 1999, pp. 232–44), but they are cumbersome.

[21]See Chapter 9.

[22]Only about 300 petitions are filed in a typical year, of which a large number are withdrawn before proceedings actually start. By contrast, some 20,000 petitions for reorganization under Chapter 11 of the U.S. Bankruptcy Code were filed every year in the United States during 1983–93.

---

Box 8.1. Recent Debt Workouts

About a dozen informal debt workouts benefiting midsized companies were announced in the first half of 1999. These agreements applied to five independent construction companies (plus a real estate subsidiary), two finance companies (one a captive company owned by a supermarket chain), and a major trading company (which had an extensive exposure to the real estate sector). These debt workouts reflected write-downs in excess of ¥1 trillion (top panel of Figure 8.8). The injection of public funds into 15 major banks appears to have been a key factor to the completion of several out-of-court debt workouts in the first half of 1999. Since late 1998, several of these companies had requested their bank creditors to provide them a degree of debt forgiveness. The expectation that the capital injection in major banks could facilitate these informal debt workouts was indicated by the large pickup in the prices of the shares of several of those companies observed on the day that those injections were announced in mid-March (for instance, the price of the stocks of the construction companies Sato Kogyo, Aoki, Haseko, and Fujita rose 60–100 percent).

The exact degree of debt reduction involved in these workouts varied by the extent to which parent companies assumed debts from their subsidiaries. For instance, one of the first workouts to be announced was that of the construction company Haseko, involving a debt reduction of ¥354 billion over four years. That reduction was equivalent to 86 percent of the parent company's bank debt at that time, but Haseko assumed ¥592 billion of debts from affiliates in late June. This was not a unique case, because most of the debt of Japanese companies is typically acquired by subsidiaries and does not appear on the parent company's books. Although information on the total indebtedness of companies on a consolidated basis can be fragmentary, a useful indication of this burden can generally be obtained by including in the parent companies' total liabili-

---

in late 1997 to permit the creation of holding companies, a number of firms have switched to this structure, reorganizing themselves along main business lines by transforming their divisions into subsidiaries under a holding company and consolidating subsidiaries. This process has accelerated since the beginning of FY1999 (the mandatory consolidation of accounts of publicly listed companies at ties the loan guarantees that they typically offer to their subsidiaries. Using this gauge, debt reductions in most of the debt workouts completed in 1999 entailed a 20–35 percent reduction in the company's total debt (bottom panel of Figure 8.8).

Debt workouts were accompanied by broad restructuring plans, a requirement for allowing banks to deduct the write-downs from taxable income. These plans typically involved the sale of completed units (e.g., condominiums) and a gradual reduction in the labor force. In some cases, such as that of the trading company, the plan involved a major refocusing of business on selected core activities, with a two-thirds reduction in the number of subsidiaries and in the number of employees at the parent company level.

Some market analysts have voiced concerns that some workouts have aimed more at restoring the near-term solvency of the beneficiary firm than allowing it to establish long-term viability. Analysts have noted that, irrespective of long-term prospects, main banks often had an interest in providing relief to those companies to avoid greater losses that would have resulted from the bankruptcy of those companies. Despite debt relief, however, beneficiary firms still face major challenges. First, given the decline in real estate prices, a 30 percent debt write-off may still leave a sizable gap between the market value of assets and the firms' liabilities. Second, support from non-main bank creditors remains limited. These banks have contributed little to the workouts (roughly 20 percent of their exposure). They have also expressed reluctance to continue to provide working capital to the companies, forcing companies and their main banks to resort to complicated mechanisms to raise short-term funds. Third, there is substantial overcapacity in the construction sector, and the restructuring plans agreed to in connection with the workouts may not guarantee the survival of the beneficiary firm in the medium term.

the end of the current fiscal year and the anticipation of the shift in taxation being contributing factors). These transformations have been particularly swift among large independent companies (including the leading telecommunications company). Firms belonging to the six top economic groups (*keiretsus*) appear to be somewhat lagging independent firms in this respect. This lag can be in part attributed to

Figure 8.8. Recent Out-of-Court Debt Workouts

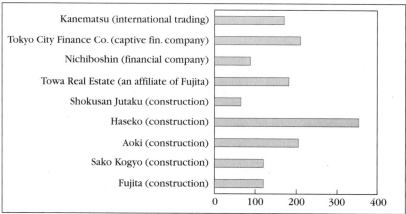

Amount of Debt Reduction Agreed
(billions of yen)

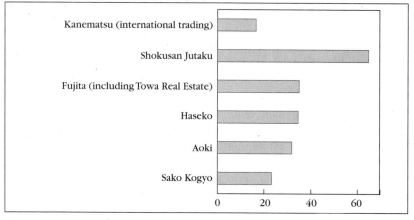

In Percent of Parent Company's Debts and Loan Guarantees

Sources: Bloomberg News, Kikkei, Goldman Sachs, Standard and Poor's; and IMF staff calculations.

the host of complex issues raised by this process in the case of the *keiretsu* firms (Box 8.2).

## Official Initiatives

The government has proposed several measures to facilitate corporate restructuring. Since mid-1998, two bodies have been set up to advise the government on corporate restructuring and have produced a wide range of proposals.[23] In particular, the many suggestions made by the Economic Strategy Council and the Competitiveness Commission helped shape later proposals made by the Ministry of International Trade and Industry. The following measures presented by the government beginning June 1999 reflected these proposals and were expected to be approved by the Diet.

- Temporary tax incentives to reduce production capacity and promote corporate reorganization. The measures include deferral of the taxation of capital gains realized in connection with the transfer or reorganization of subsidiaries and divisions; the extension of favorable tax treatment to land transactions such as in-kind transfers of land to newly incorporated firms or land sales to the public sector; the extension of the carryforward period for losses from five years to seven years, and the option of a one-year carryback of losses; and introduction of an accelerated depreciation schedule for replacement of equipment linked with the scrapping of capacity.[24] Firms will be allowed to apply for these tax benefits until late 2001, with MITI responsible for the approval of applications.

---

[23]The first of these groups was the Economic Strategy Council set up in August 1998. The Council, which was relatively autonomous in its deliberations, comprised 10 members from business and academia, and produced a comprehensive report in February 1999. In March 1999, the Competitiveness Commission comprising several Ministers, heads of agencies, and representatives from the business sector was set up. The Commission is chaired by the Prime Minister, with MITI being in charge of directing its agenda.

[24]These measures could help, for instance, a steel company to absorb the costs of closing a plant. The company could carry forward closing charges (including severance payments) for two additional years, reducing tax payments for up to seven years. In balance sheet terms, special treatment of capital gains on landholdings would help the firm to use its latent reserves to shore up its equity position, offsetting asset write-downs associated with the closedown of plants. Alternatively, steelmaker A could join steelmaker B to spin off specializing activities, consolidating them into a new firm. The new measures would reduce the cost to register the new firm and transferring the assets to it (payment on capital gains on these assets would be reduced until they are realized, and real estate acquisition taxes would benefit from a rebate). In addition, the new firm could benefit from a favorable depreciation schedule.

---

**Box 8.2. Changes in Corporate Structures in Japan: Some Implications for the Large Economic Groups**

The changing institutional environment in which Japanese companies operate is transforming corporate organization in at least three dimensions. These include a shift away from the lifetime relationship between employees and their firms, compensation practices to increase the link to performance, and a reordering of the ties between firms. A growing number of companies are becoming holding companies, transforming existing divisions into subsidiaries under their direct control and consolidating affiliates in which they have a minority interest only.

Although these changes are affecting most Japanese companies, they can have special implications for the firms belonging to the six major economic groups. There are many large independent companies in Japan, but there are six major economic groups that are prominent, among other reasons, because they are present in most economic sectors (they account for 16 percent of net corporate assets) and each has close links with individual city banks. Also, the organization and behavior of many other companies are in part modeled after these groups.

Current reforms could help reduce the ambiguity of these groups' governance mechanisms. The organization of major economic groups typically comprises a set of top companies in different fields and their respective affiliates, and is centered around a trading company and a city bank, which still are a sort of "first among peers." Top companies themselves keep few formal direct links with each other (except for minority shareholdings). Corporate governance has largely been exercised in informal ways, including the exchange of views in the meetings of the "Presidents' Clubs," management rotation, and banks' control over credit. In recent years, the perception has emerged, however, that these mechanisms, although binding the groups together, are insufficient for effective managerial control. It has been felt that the reorganization of firms into more segregated and tightly controlled structures could increase managerial accountability and profits. The recent reforms have in part been inspired by this sentiment and are likely to push companies in this direction.

---

- Legal changes to facilitate corporate reorganization and change in corporate ownership structures. Measures include steps to permit banks to exceed the 5 percent limit on equity holdings

Top companies in the major economic groups have two main options to adjust to the new environment. They can become more independent, or they can try to coalesce under a very large holding company, somewhat along the lines of the structures existing before World War Two (the *zaibatsu*). Although three of the current six major economic groups originate from *zaibatsus*, and membership in a large conglomerate could provide a sense of protection to many firms, there are institutional obstacles to the resurgence of *zaibatsus*. The changes in the antimonopoly rules to allow holding companies, or those recently proposed with a view to easing the restrictions on corporate mergers, appear to fall short of permitting the establishment of full-fledged *zaibatsus*. The agency in charge of enforcing the antimonopoly law (the Fair Trade Commission, FTC) has established that holding companies are in principle not to be allowed to control the largest firms in more than a few economic fields. Also, the FTC needs to be consulted whenever a merger would result in a firm controlling more than a certain fraction of the domestic market. The proposals to weaken the latter rule are aimed mainly at facilitating consolidation in mature sectors (e.g., steel) and need not extend the scope of holding companies.

Financial liberalization can promote more independence among group members and facilitate the merger of city banks. Insofar as laws effectively limit excessive ownership, greater emphasis on profits and increasingly open financial markets are likely to provide incentives for top companies in major economic groups to use the new organizational options to increase their individual identity, e.g., by becoming holding companies themselves and asserting their control over their subordinated *keiretsu*, while reducing their links with other peer companies and their affiliates (a few recent episodes suggest—albeit weakly—that these incentives have started to operate). Greater independence may require and promote the unwinding (or dilution) of cross-shareholdings, for example, to accelerate divestment of noncore activities. This process of increasing (financial) independence could also facilitate mergers between city banks by reducing the impact of such mergers on companies belonging to different economic groups.

in a nonfinancial firm in the event of a swap of debt for equity; the easing of antimonopoly laws to permit Japanese companies competing in the global economy to hold a large share of the

Japanese market;[25] and changes in the Commercial Code to facilitate changes in ownership structures.[26]

- Use of public funds, such as a public lending facility to finance capacity reductions at special interest rates; subsidies to firms that increase employment (in designated sectors); and training program for dislocated workers.[27] An extension of the eligibility periods for unemployment benefits (restricted to workers laid off as a result of capacity reductions) has also been considered. The official policy remains, however, one of helping firms not to reduce their workforce and to devise short-term steps to provide support for middle-aged workers who have been laid off (as stated in the white paper issued by the Labor Ministry on July 2, 1999).

The authorities are also amending bankruptcy laws with the aim of increasing their effectiveness. Specifically, the Ministry of Justice has announced the acceleration of plans to supplement the law typically applied to small and medium-sized companies with a new Financial Rehabilitation Law.[28] The latter would incorporate several provisions paralleling those in Chapter 11 of the U.S. Bankruptcy Code, aimed at increasing the protection against secured creditors and the use of the debtor-in-possession principle (this principle typically translates into allowing incumbent management to maintain control of the firm

---

[25]Previously, the Fair Trade Commission had to be consulted on any merger in which the resulting company would hold more than 25 percent of the domestic market (10 percent if the resulting company is the largest in the market). The new criteria would look at resulting shares in the global rather than local market.

[26]These changes aim to increase the ability of corporate boards to dispense with a general shareholders' meeting when deciding on the sale of businesses or other restructuring steps; to force minority shareholders to sell their shares when a bidder has acquired over 50 percent of company shares or when they disagree with a spin-off; and to allow the acquiring company to pay shareholders of the target company with its own shares.

[27]These measures build on a system introduced in December 1998 that entitles workers who complete a training program designated by the Ministry of Labor to be reimbursed for up to 80 percent of the associated expenses (to a maximum of ¥200,000). The main distinction between the new programs and the traditional approach is that support will now be provided directly to the individual rather than to the employer.

[28]See Chapter 9.

during the procedure). The law would also permit debtors to satisfy secured claims by paying the current (estimated) value of the claim's collateral and lumping the residual part of the claim with other unsecured debts. This provision is likely to facilitate the renegotiation of real estate loans (for example through debt-for-equity swaps), because it reduces the extent to which secured creditors can cling to their original claims in the expectation of capturing a future upside in the real estate collateral.

## Prospects and Risks

Initial strides toward genuine corporate restructuring need to be followed by resolute actions, because a half-hearted process of corporate restructuring could dampen economic growth for many years and contribute to an unsustainable fiscal position. Particularly, progress is being made with large corporations, while small- and mid-sized companies have been given some breathing space. This two-tiered approach could prove effective if large firms undergo a genuine restructuring process, and recent measures to foster start-up firms and the reallocation of resources to the service sector succeed in providing some dynamism to the economy. Some observers have noted, however, the risk that the positive reaction of markets to recent announcements of corporate restructuring, or signs that the worst of the recession is now over, might result in complacency. If top-tier corporations, including those in mature or labor-intensive sectors, do not undergo a deep restructuring, the current approach could add new strains to a fiscal scenario already burdened by the effects associated with the projected shifts in the Japanese demography.

The government has recognized the importance of establishing an environment conducive to corporate restructuring, while ensuring that primary responsibility for initiatives rests with individual firms. Fiscal incentives are being introduced to encourage large firms to adjust and stimulate small and medium-sized firms. In addition, legal impediments to reorganization are being reduced, while steps are being taken to help dislocated workers to find new jobs. Tax incentives can be a powerful and cost-effective tool, helping the corporate sector to absorb some of the costs of restructuring, although it will be important to ensure that their application is nondiscriminatory and based on clearly defined conditions, rather than on ministerial discretion. Moreover, tax incentives can cushion the burden on banks, and possibly reduce the magnitude of the public injections of capital necessary to maintain the stability of the bank system. On the expenditure side, the proposed public funding of training programs could help cushion the shock of dismissals and facilitate the needed reallocation of labor within the corporate sector. The subsidization of jobs in designated sectors, on the other hand, has the potential to introduce distortions into the market mechanism.

Effective corporate governance will be an important factor in promoting restructuring of the corporate sector. Big Bang financial reforms are expected to gradually enhance market discipline and the impending changes in accounting rules will impart a higher degree of transparency to corporate accounts. An increasing number of Japanese companies have professed that their main goal is to maximize shareholders' value. Nevertheless, mechanisms to enforce management accountability remain limited. In particular, the high degree of corporate cross-shareholdings still limits the scope for "hostile takeovers." The unwinding of such cross-holdings is expected to be encouraged by upcoming rules requiring firms to mark them to market. On the other hand, some proposals that would allow companies to shift the ownership rights of these holdings to trusts (set up in order to fund corporate pension commitments), but retain the associated control rights, could help to perpetuate the problem.

Recent measures that facilitate the vertical integration of economic groups are also an attempt to respond to concerns about corporate governance. The law permitting the creation of holding companies was in part a response to a growing perception in Japan that the present system of governance can be too diffuse to allow for effective management in a more competitive environment, in which official guidance does not have a role and maximization of shareholders' value is becoming the priority. Together with the possible introduction of consolidated corporate taxes, this reform could encourage large firms to adopt a more tightly controlled structure, which could increase managerial accountability and corporate profitability.

Corporate specialization could be a key ingredient to enhance the efficiency of Japanese companies. International experience since the 1980s suggests that improvements in profitability and economic growth have often been associated with specialization and the streamlining of conglomerates. In most countries, asset reallocation has resulted both from voluntary divestment of affiliates in sectors outside the conglomerate's core businesses and from "hostile" takeovers. Although often involving intermediate steps, hostile takeover activity in the United States generally resulted in the allocation of assets to firms in the same industries as the targeted assets (Bhagat, Shleifer and Vishny, 1990). Gains would typically result from consolidation of (sometimes declining) industries.

The development of a market for noninvestment grade bonds could facilitate the streamlining of existing *keiretsus* and corporate specialization. In the United States, corporate restructuring has been facilitated by the development of a market for noninvestment grade (speculative) instruments that provide scope for increased competition in the market for corporate control. In Japan, limitations in financial disclosure standards have been a deterrent to the development of a market for such instruments. Expected improvements in corporate accounting and the new options of saving vehicles offered by the Big Bang reforms could now foster such a market and facilitate an aggressive divestment policy on the part of the *keiretsus*. The development of such a market could also provide a potentially lucrative advisory business to banks.

Proposed changes to encourage debt-for-equity swaps could play an important role in supporting financial reorganization in Japan, particularly if other constraints on corporate restructuring are addressed. These swaps could be instrumental in reducing firms' debt overhang, while allowing creditors to share in the gains from improved performance. Banks could be reluctant to engage in such operations, however, when firms are limited in their ability to shed labor or take other measures needed to improve their performance. Banks' reluctance will be heightened by the fact that, after FY2001, equity holdings will be marked to market. In these circumstances, banks will have an interest in ensuring a rapid turnaround of firms in which they have taken equity (or, at least, in establishing a sound profit profile for those firms), so that equity claims can be sold without incurring additional losses.

In summary, there are encouraging signs on both the official and private fronts, but challenges remain large. Firms are increasingly committed to change and the authorities have shown growing resolve in advancing this process. Labor unions have also in many

195

cases expressed some support for change, focusing demands at times more on the provision of mechanisms facilitating job search and improved training than on insisting on absolute job protection. Although corporate restructuring could have a negative short-term impact on aggregate demand, the government can alleviate this impact and its associated social costs by ensuring an adequate social safety net and effective means for corporations to seek financial rehabilitation. On the other hand, if complacency were to take hold following a rise in economic activity or stock prices, a prolonged period of half-hearted corporate restructuring could result in yet more years of mediocre economic growth and considerable fiscal costs.

## Appendix. Market Reaction to Restructuring Plans

During the first three months of 1999, several listed Japanese firms announced restructuring plans, often coinciding with the forecast of large losses for the fiscal year. The ultimate effectiveness of these plans was difficult to discern, although, at least on the surface, they appeared more ambitious than the wave of announcements that followed the appreciation of the yen in 1995. Changes in stock prices in reaction to announcements are one way to gauge the potential effectiveness of these plans, because they provide insight into the market's reaction to these announcements. This appendix reports an event study, based on a sample of about 60 announcements made in the first two-and-a-half months of 1999.

Event studies are a standard method to identify the information content of market news by measuring abnormal returns on stocks around corporate actions or announcements. In these studies, the actual return on a share within a time window around the event day is computed and compared to the prediction of some benchmark model such as the Capital Asset Pricing Model (CAPM) portfolio model. Here, abnormal returns are also computed against the average returns in the second half of 1998, in order to address the possibility that the results using the CAPM might be biased by the cumulative effect of announcements on overall market sentiment.

Variables that reflect the nature of the announced plan, recent changes in the firm's profitability, and the firm's industry sector are used to assess market reactions. Plans were grouped into five categories, and firms were grouped in three sectors: manufacturing (37 observations), finance (13 observations), and other sectors (construction, services, and light industry) (20 observations). Two financial variables were used; the percentage change in earnings per share between FY1998 and FY1999, and a discrete variable indicating whether or not the 1999 dividend was expected to be zero. The allocation of plans into the five categories was based on news reports and comments by market analysts from major investment banks in Japan, which unavoidably involved some judgment. For instance, major restructuring plans typically involved reductions in the labor force and divestment in non-core activities, and divestment of single lines of business could be considered a merger and acquisitions activity. Results were, however, broadly unchanged by the reclassification of some plans that had ambiguous features. Also, the results using the CAPM and those based on historical average returns were similar.

The results suggest that markets were in general cautious about restructuring announcements, particularly those of financial institutions (Table 8.3). Only a small fraction of announcements resulted in cumulative abnormal returns during the subsequent four days that were in excess of two standard deviations from those predicted by the CAPM or from the average return on individual stocks in the second half of 1998. It is noteworthy that some of the largest increases were associated with an announced acquisition by a foreign firm. The low significance of stock price changes around announcements could also reflect information leakage, market skepticism, and simply the high level of volatility of Japanese stock prices in recent months owing to macroeconomic factors that are not captured fully by the CAPM.

An alternative to the above approach is simply to assess the qualitative reaction of markets rather than attempt to assess the magnitude of these effects. A Probit model was used for this purpose (it predicted the right sign of the change in stock prices in two-thirds to three-quarters of the cases, depending on the specification used). A main finding from the Probit analysis is that an announcement by a financial institution involving a reorganization plan was viewed by the market, more often than not, less positively than those made by other companies. A second finding is that announcements of major restructuring plans, mergers and acquisitions, and the sale of non-

**Table 8.3. Stock Price Response to Recent Restructuring Announcements**

| | OLS | | | | | Probit | | | |
|---|---|---|---|---|---|---|---|---|---|
| | | CAPM | | Average Return | | | CAPM | | |
| Variable | (1) | (2) | (3) | (4) | (5) | (6) | (7) | (8) | (9) |
| Percent change in earnings per share | -2.E-04 (.393) | | -4.E-04 (.068) | -2.E-04 (.336) | -4.E-04 (.122) | -7.E-04 (.031) | -4.E-04 (.091) | | -7.E-04 (.011) |
| No dividend in 1999 | | -0.20 (.755) | | | | | | -0.31 (.556) | |
| Financial sector | -1.01 (.071) | -0.85 (.165) | -0.84 (.185) | -0.80 (.105) | -0.72 (.147) | -1.32 (.004) | | -1.10 (.029) | -1.18 (.034) |
| Industry[1] | | | | | | | 0.69 (.071) | | |
| Attrition | -1.65 (.014) | | | -1.23 (.035) | | -2.24 (.001) | -2.24 (.001) | | |
| Governance | | 1.32 (.066) | 1.59 (.155) | | 1.46 (.168) | | | 1.32 (.039) | 2.06 (.022) |
| M&A | | 1.99 (.004) | 2.39 (.024) | | 1.88 (.020) | | | 1.22 (.038) | 2.21 (.008) |
| Divestment | | 0.95 (.190) | 1.24 (.001) | | 2.32 (.066) | | | 1.49 (.018) | 2.29 (.004) |
| Major restructuring | | 2.40 (.010) | 2.70 (.084) | | 1.18 (.002) | | | 1.61 (.042) | 2.39 (.003) |

Source: IMF staff estimates.
Note: The numbers in parentheses indicate the significance ratio of the coefficient (i.e., .050 means different from zero at the 5 percent level).
[1]Industry excludes construction and beverages.

core business were generally viewed favorably by the market, while plans based on attrition were associated with a decline in stock prices. The coefficient on the variable indicating plans based mainly on a multi-year reduction in the workforce through attrition was significantly negative in all model specifications. In contrast, the coefficient associated with plans based on other strategies was uniformly positive. A third finding is that financial variables appear to suggest that market discipline contributed to more rigorous corporate restructuring; expected declines in earnings per share were negatively correlated with changes in stock prices.

# References

Bhagat, S., A. Shleifer, R. Vishny, 1990, "Hostile Takeovers in the 1980s: the Return to Corporate Specialization," *Brookings Papers, Microeconomics,* pp. 1–84 (Cambridge: Massachusetts, NBER).

Goldman Sachs, 1998, "Tsunami Alert: the ¥80 Trillion Pension Funding Wave," *Portfolio Strategy,* Goldman Sachs Japan, Tokyo, October.

James, Christopher, 1996, "When do Banks Take Equity in Debt Restructurings," *The Review of Financial Studies,* Vol. 8:4 (Winter), pp. 1209–34.

————, 1996, "Bank Debt Restructurings and the Composition of Exchange Offers in Financial Distress," *The Journal of Finance,* Vol. 50:2 (June), pp. 711–27.

Kester, C., 1991, *Japanese Takeovers, the Global Context for Corporate Control* (Boston: Harvard Business School).

Matsui, K., H. Suzuki, S. Katayama, 1997, "EVA®: Theory and Practice, Implications for Japan," *Portfolio Strategy,* Goldman Sachs Japan, Tokyo, July.

Mitsuhiro, Seki, 1994, *Beyond the Full-Set Industrial Structure: Japanese Industry in the New Age of East Asia* (Tokyo: LTCB International Library Foundation).

Morgan Stanley Dean Witter, 1999, *Japan Restructuring* (Tokyo), May.

Moriaki, Tsuchiya, and Konomi Yoshinobu, 1997, *Shaping the Future of Japanese Management: New Leadership to Overcome the Impending Crisis* (Tokyo: LTCB International Library Foundation).

Ooyama, T., 1999, "Stagnation and Structural Adjustment of the Non-Manufacturing Industries in the 1990s," *Monthly Bulletin,* February, Bank of Japan (in Japanese) (also found at http://www.boj.or.jp/en/index.htm).

Ramseyer, M., M. Nakazato, 1999, *Japanese Law, an Economic Approach* (Chicago: University of Chicago Press).

# 9

# Reform of Japan's Insolvency Laws

*Joaquim Levy*

The traditional interplay between corporate law and business custom and practices in Japan is gradually changing, including with respect to bankruptcy law. Custom plays an important role in corporate relationships in Japan, where recourse to the judicial system is generally less prevalent than in some Western countries, notably the United States. The effectiveness of some of these customs has been eroded, however, and the growing inability of firms to count on traditional business methods has increasingly exposed the weakness of existing legal procedures. To a large extent, this is the case with insolvency laws. The Japanese authorities had for some time recognized that these laws needed to be reformed and had studied alternative approaches. The task became more urgent, however, because of the increasing ineffectiveness of customary approaches to deal with corporate financial distress.

The basis of the traditional informal approach to corporate financial reorganization has eroded since the 1980s. Until that time, firms' access to credit was dictated in large part by affiliation to economic groups built around major banks. Under these conditions, banks had privileged knowledge of a borrower's prospects and strengths, and could, when they felt appropriate, lead an informal debt workout. Insolvency procedures were used mainly in connection with the liquidation of small and medium-sized firms, which depended largely on specialized banks and intercorporate credit and had little access to commercial bank credit. Partial financial liberalization in the 1980s, however, permitted large firms to reduce their reliance on bank loans and prompted commercial banks to look aggressively for new customers, mainly among small firms and nonmanufacturing companies (notably in the real estate sector), changing the functioning of the system.

When the financial bubble burst in 1990, major banks were often neither in a condition nor willing to intervene in ailing companies. Banks' own balance sheets were too weak to face the losses from real estate loans, and banks did not have the advantage of a long-term relationship with many of their borrowers. As banks were not pressured by regulators to deal decisively with their bad loans, the problem of deteriorating corporate balance sheets was left festering, and the orientation of insolvency laws toward liquidation remained a secondary issue.

Bankruptcy law reform has become a priority because obstacles to the renegotiation of debts have increasingly become a potential source of inefficiency to the economy. Following the financial turbulence of 1997, the rate of corporate liquidations increased dramatically as banks faced tighter regulatory standards and the economy slowed down. The liquidity crisis that occurred made apparent the fragility of corporate balance sheets and motivated firms to accelerate their restructuring efforts. Corporate financial reorganization, however, continued to face many obstacles. Banks generally continued to grant or deny support to debtors based less on their assessment of the viability of the debtor than on considerations related to their own capitalization, notwithstanding the boost provided by the injection of public funds into their capital base. Formal insolvency procedures, on the other hand, were not providing effective means to restructure over-indebted but still viable firms for a variety of reasons, including the insufficient protection against secured creditors they typically afford and the difficulties in securing unanimous creditors' approval of reorganization plans.

Faced with this situation, the Japanese authorities decided to accelerate bankruptcy law reforms, focusing on creating a new legal instrument for corporate rehabilitation, drawing on mechanisms that have proved to be effective in fostering corporate financial rehabilitation in other countries. Although some of these mechanisms already existed in Japanese legislation, they were scattered over several laws, and hence were not fully operational. The new Financial Rehabilitation Law is expected to gather these mechanisms under one single procedure, which could permit debtors to strengthen their position vis-à-vis creditors. By offering a realistic option for debtors to successfully emerge from a formal reorganization procedure, the law could also increase the odds for financially distressed companies to persuade creditors to participate in informal debt workouts.

The rest of this chapter discusses in more detail the existing laws, the reasons why a reform became necessary, and the prospective features of the Financial Rehabilitation Law.[1]

## Existing Legal Procedures

There are five insolvency procedures in Japan, of which three aim at the financial reorganization of the firm and two at liquidation (Table 9.1). The laws governing these procedures draw on legislation from several countries and date from different periods. The Bankruptcy (*hasan*) and Composition (*wagi*) Laws of 1922 draw on old German Codes. The sections of the Commercial Code dealing with Corporate Rearrangement (*kaisha seiri*) reflect prewar British legislation on receiverships. The Corporate Reorganization (*kaisha kousei*) Law of 1952 mirrors the old U.S. Bankruptcy Code, albeit amended in the 1970s. The Bankruptcy Law (as well as sections of the Commercial Code not discussed here) deals with liquidation procedures, while the three other texts deal with reorganization procedures.

Procedures under the Composition Law typically aim at providing a reduction or rescheduling of unsecured debt, not at promoting the reorganization of the firm. Compositions, which can be filed only by the debtor, are aimed at serving small and medium-sized firms. They are often used just to provide the debtor with breathing space to seek an out-of-court resolution with short-term creditors.[2] Indeed, about

---

[1]The discussion does not address the issue of the compatibility of Japanese international insolvency law with international practice. For a review of this particular issue, see Matsushita (1998).

[2]Compositions provide little protection against secured creditors, but they help to avert the presentation of promissory notes. The latter feature is valuable in Japan, because the failure to honor two promissory notes within six months leads to the suspension of business transaction with banks and the virtual death of any business (Matsumura and Ryser, 1994).

half of the petitions filed are withdrawn before the actual commencement of the case. For those few cases that go through, a 50 percent debt reduction is typically achieved. Although that reduction covers only unsecured debts, outcomes appear to be efficient, in the sense that the promised repayment is on average 2.5 times larger than the estimated liquidation value of the firm (Eisenberg and Tagashira, 1994).

Corporate rearrangements have a broader scope, but the approval of reorganization plans requires unanimous consent from creditors, and failure to satisfy that restriction often leads to liquidation. Corporate rearrangements are also a relatively flexible procedure in which incumbent management retains most of the control of the firm (court involvement in the firm's daily management is minimal, being limited to steps to prevent managers from dissipating the firm's assets). The procedure can provide for some temporary protection against secured creditors (at court discretion), but it requires unanimous consent for the adoption of the reorganization plan (which is usually drafted by the debtor). This requirement is aimed at protecting creditors in view of the limited role of the courts, in particular in the implementation of the reorganization plan. It tends, however, to heighten the resistance of secured creditors, who often stall negotiations. Because liquidation is mandatory when, after a statutory period, there is no prospect for reorganizing the company, courts tend to respond to such delays by forcing the firm into liquidation.

The Corporate Reorganization Law, which applies only to large firms, provides comprehensive protection against creditors, but the rigidity of its provisions limits its effectiveness in promoting corporate restructuring. The law provides for automatic protection (stay) against secured creditors. Such a provision reduces the chances of essential assets being stripped from the firm. Also, a qualified majority of creditors, rather than unanimity, is required for the approval of the reorganization plan.[3] The procedure, however, includes a number of

---

[3]Approval of the plan requires two-thirds or more of the unsecured creditors' aggregate voting rights, three-fourths or more of the aggregate voting rights of the secured creditors if the maturity of their claims is changed, and four-fifths or more if other modifications are involved, and generally the simple majority of shareholders.

Table 9.1. Legal Procedures for Insolvent Companies

| Procedure | Liquidation | | Reorganization | | |
|---|---|---|---|---|---|
| | Bankruptcy *Hansan* (under the Bankruptcy Law of 1922). | Liquidation *Tokubetsu-seisan* (Section 432 et. seq. of the 1899 Commercial Code). | Composition *Wagi* (Composition Law of 1922). | Corporate rearrangement *Kaisha-seiri* (Section 381 et. seq. of the Commercial Code, modified in 1938 to add features of U.K. laws). | Corporate reorganization *Kaisha-kousei* (Corporate Reorganization Law 1952, revised in the 1970s). |
| Application | Similar to Chapter 7 in the U.S., although inspired by German law. Can be transformed into a reorganization. Conversely, it may result from the failure of reorganization efforts. | Applicable to companies being wound up, but which are considered to be insolvent. Any joint stock company may use it. It is more efficient than bankruptcy if the creditors are cooperative. | Popular system where an arrangement with creditors can allow the firm to continue in business. | Reorganization occurs under minimal supervision by the court. Can be used only by unanimous agreement among creditors. Typically applied to small and medium-sized companies. | Similar to Chapter 10 of the old U.S. Bankruptcy Code, or the Administration Order under the U.K. Insolvency Act. Typically used by large corporations; it often takes a long time to be completed. |
| Control of the firm | A trustee (a lawyer) is appointed, who will liquidate the company independently of the creditors and distribute money pro-rata. | A former director of the company is chosen as liquidator; no trustee is appointed. | An appointed trustee retains the power of administration over the firm's assets (management retains some control over ordinary business actions). | The company retains its administrative powers, except if the court decides otherwise. | A reorganization trustee is appointed, who holds all necessary management powers. |
| Secured credits | May be executed separately. | Separate execution may be restricted by court order. | May be executed separately. | Separate execution may be restricted by court order. | May be executed only through the procedure. |

| | | | | | |
|---|---|---|---|---|---|
| Unsecured creditors | Participate in the procedure; seniority rights not absolute. | Equality is required by law, but may be adjusted reflecting agreement by a majority of creditors. | Absolute priority subject to trustee's decision. | Individual execution of claims is suspended, but the firm may repay specific debts (preference). | All creditors participate in the procedure. |
| Voting | . . . | Votes equivalent to ¾ of claims required. | Votes equivalent to ¾ of claims required. | Unanimity. | Qualified majority by class of creditor. |
| Power to ratify plans | Amounts recovered are divided by the court; typically they add to less than 10 percent of the claim. | Payments will be made according to a convention approved by the legal majority of creditors, after approval by the court. | The court approves the sharing arrangement, subject to agreement by creditors. | The firm has discretion on which payments it makes, subject to agreement by creditors. | The scheme of reorganization should be agreed by the majority of creditors. The scheme itself and execution are subject to the supervision of the court. |

Source: Sakai (1998), Shea and Miyake (1996), Eisenberg and Tagashira (1994).

provisions that reduce the scope of its use, as well as its attractiveness to the debtor:

- The procedure can be initiated only if the firm is about to default because payment would seriously impair its operation, or it is otherwise facing the risk of bankruptcy, limiting its usefulness in promoting early reorganizations.[4]
- The law calls for the dismissal of incumbent management. This is a strong disincentive for its early use, especially in the case of large firms in which entrenched management is likely to be able to protect its tenure against shareholders' interests.
- The debtor may borrow new money only with the court's approval, limiting the ability of financially distressed firms to continue operations (when the court approves the issuance of new debt, the new money is granted first priority).
- Firms under reorganization cannot be sold. Although a piecemeal sale of assets may be done under court approval, the firm cannot be sold as a whole. This limitation reduces the scope for using the market to reallocate resources and can contribute to dissipation of the value of the firm.
- The reorganization plan is drafted by the court-appointed trustee.

Because the simpler procedures provide little protection against creditors, and Corporate Reorganization is too rigid and penalizes management, formal reorganization procedures are used only sparingly in Japan. In a typical year, only about 2,000 corporate insolvency procedures are initiated in Japan, of which about 85 percent aim at the liquidation of the firm. The number of initial petitions for entering into any of the three reorganization procedures hovers around 300, of which a few dozen correspond to corporate reorganizations or rearrangements, with compositions accounting for about 80–85 percent of the total (Tables 9.2 and 9.3). By contrast, in the 1980s and early 1990s some 20,000 applications for reorganization

---

[4]Article 30 of the law states that the procedure can commence only when "a company is unable to pay its obligations that are due without exceedingly impeding continuation of its business" or "where the facts comprising causes of bankruptcy are likely to take place with respect to the company" (Shea and Miyake, 1996). The court, creditors, and debtors may all file for Corporate Reorganization (Sakai and Jacobson, 1998).

Table 9.2. Number of Insolvency Procedures

|  | 1995 | 1996 | 1997 |
|---|---|---|---|
| Corporate liquidations | | | |
| Filings | 2,838 | 3,489 | 4,349 |
| Compositions | | | |
| Filings | 255 | 244 | 279 |
| Withdrawals | 98 | 102 | 125 |
| Commencements | 129 | 112 | 119 |
| Corporate rearrangements | | | |
| Total | 33 | 20 | 18 |
| Corporate reorganizations | | | |
| Filings | 36 | 18 | 31 |
| Completions | 30 | 36 | 23 |
| Pending[1] | 202 | 184 | 192 |

Source: Matsushita (1999).
[1]Includes plans that have already been approved and are under execution.

were filed in the United States every year (under Chapter 11 of the Bankruptcy Code), in addition to hundreds of thousands of petitions for liquidation (under Chapter 7).[5]

# Transformation of the Main Bank System and its Impact on Corporate Reorganization

In the past, under the "main bank" system, major banks were in a good position to monitor firms' behavior. Under this framework, firms usually borrowed from many banks, but the main bank was the syndicate leader and the bank responsible for monitoring that particular loan. The main bank was expected to prove its commitment to this task by shouldering the bulk of the cost of any reorganization. As a consequence, the bank would also use its leverage (based in part on the limited sources of external finance available to firms) to influence firms' investment decisions, and charge relatively high interest. This arrangement was possible because, until the 1980s, access to credit was dictated in large part by affiliation to economic groups built

---

[5]Owing to the current strength of the U.S. economy, the number of Chapter 11 filings has declined to around 8,000–10,000 per year.

Table 9.3. Number of Corporate Bankruptcies and Filings for Court Protection in Selected Industrial Countries

| Country | United States | | Japan[2] | Germany | United Kingdom | France[3] |
| | Nationwide | California Court[1] | | | | |
| --- | --- | --- | --- | --- | --- | --- |
| Year | 1993 | 1993 | 1997 | 1992 | 1993 | 1993 |
| Insolvencies | . . . | . . . | 16,365 | 15,734 | . . . | . . . |
| Formal procedures | | | | | | |
| Filings of liquidations | . . . | 68,992 | 3,900 | 3,691 | 18,237 | 4,913 |
| Filings of reorganizations | 24,624 | 2,228 | 330 | 63 | 2,991 | 1,746 |
| Confirmed by court | 5,505 | . . . | 114 | . . . | . . . | . . . |

Sources: Teikoko Data Bank; Matsushita 1999; Franks et al. 1994; and Kaiser, 1994.

[1]Figures from the Central District of California Bankruptcy Court illustrate that the number of filings for liquidation (Chapter 7) is typically much larger than that of filings for reorganization (Chapter 11); also only about 30 percent of the cases filed under Chapter 11 are confirmed (the rate of confirmations for small firms, i.e., those firms with assets valued at less than US$ 0.5 million, is around 10 percent).

[2]There is no official figure for total bankruptcies in Japan. Information is collected by Teikoko Data Bank and the Federation of Banker's Association. According to Teikoko Data Bank, the number of bankruptcies actually initiated (rather than just filed) in 1997 was less than two thousand (2,617 in 1998). Among the total insolvencies, about 12–15 percent result in informal debt workouts.

[3]In France, although the initial presumption of any filing is to achieve a reorganization, courts can order an immediate liquidation upon accepting the case. Of the cases closed in 1993, there were 782 liquidations in addition to the 4,913 immediate liquidations, 177 sales, and 146 successful reorganizations.

around major banks. This relationship allowed the firm's main bank to have a privileged knowledge of the firm's prospects and strengths. As a result, firms belonging to a *keiretsu* were generally able to raise more money from banks than other "independent" firms.

Several incentives supported this delegated monitoring scheme (Sheard, 1994). First, the main bank's participation in the group firms' equity would tend to align its objectives with those of shareholders, while providing additional monitoring mechanisms such as the appointment of senior management and of members to the firms' board of directors. Second, each bank could free ride on loans monitored by other main banks. Therefore, the arrangement allowed banks to minimize duplication of efforts. Finally, a close-knit banking system and the expectation of suasion on the part of the authorities could act as effective enforcement mechanisms.

When distress did occur, support from main banks helped to minimize the disruption to the affected firms. On these occasions, the

firm's main bank typically put pressure on suppliers (often group-related firms) to continue dealing with the distressed firm, while shouldering most of the financial cost of the rescue by easing its own
credit terms to the distressed firm and paying off other bank creditors. The bank would also often intervene by appointing new directors and managers to the firm. In some cases, such arrangements allowed group-related firms to continue to invest even in periods of
negative cashflow, and otherwise reduce their susceptibility to financial distress or a debt overhang (Hoshi, Kashyap, and Scharfstein,
1990). The evidence is not, however, unanimous (Hayashi, 1997).

During the 1980s, financial liberalization dramatically changed the
environment in which Japanese corporations and banks operated. Although loans continued to be syndicated in the traditional way, the
basic tenets of the main bank system were undercut by growing
competition. In particular, the foundation of what could be seen as
an implicit "insurance" system eroded when banks became unable to
collect the economic rents they had grown accustomed to. With new
sources of capital market financing becoming available, large corporations grew increasingly unwilling to pay a premium for an "insurance" that often limited their profitability and expansion prospects,
preferring to tap the capital markets (Nakatani, 1984; Weinstein and
Yafeh, 1998).[6] Over a period of few years, those corporations were
able to cut the share of bank borrowing in their balance sheet by
half.

This loss of business prompted banks to look for new customers
and venture into the relatively uncharted territory of loans to small
firms and to nonmanufacturing companies. In the case of loans to the
real estate and construction sectors, credit was extended mainly
through banks' nonbank subsidiaries. Major banks often relied more
on the pledging of collateral than on careful screening when extending credit to these new borrowers. While banks were equipped
to monitor a relatively limited set of large firms with which they had

---

[6]A spectacular relaxation of the requirements imposed on firms wishing to
issue domestic unsecured debt occurred after the Foreign Exchange Control Law
was revised in 1980 to allow firms to issue unsecured bonds abroad. Only two
firms met those criteria in 1979. By 1989, about 300 were entitled to issue unsecured debt, and 500 to issue unsecured convertible bonds (Japan Securities Research Institute, 1998).

close links, they were probably not prepared to extend that effort to cover a much larger and less known universe. Thus, when the asset price bubble burst in 1990, banks had little incentive to provide significant support to customers that were difficult to monitor or control, and from which the scope for extracting long-term rents was limited.

The rate of bankruptcies among large firms was contained during most of the 1990s by the weak balance sheets of the major banks. Although banks were not in a condition or willing to rescue ailing companies, they feared to force them into bankruptcy. Loan syndication had made every bank vulnerable to each other's actions. Foreclosing on a marginal loan could help shore up the balance sheet of Bank A, but was likely to affect other banks, which might have large exposure to that particular borrower. This could lead to retaliation, i.e., another bank could threaten a major borrower from Bank A. Any unilateral action against a given firm was thus viewed as potentially triggering a chain reaction of forced loss recognitions that could quickly wipe out the sector's capital. Banks considered themselves in a "prisoner's dilemma" and, absent major pressures from supervisors, chose mainly to roll over their loans, without forcing debtors into restructuring. The decline in interest rates reinforced this choice by reducing the carrying cost of nonperforming loans.

In the aftermath of the financial turbulence of 1997, the need to restructure the banking sector changed the debtor-creditor dynamics again, this time underscoring the vulnerability of creditors. After the failure of three large financial institutions in late 1997 and a tightening of regulatory standards, banks reassessed their strategies and started to curtail credit, not necessarily only on the basis of the riskiness of the borrower. The number of bankruptcies soared in the following months and started to decline only after the authorities took several measures to support credit, including the expansion of a program of loan guarantees to small and medium-sized enterprises and special loans to large firms facing the redemption of bonds. In most cases, bankruptcies led to liquidations, with only a few companies entering into formal reorganization procedures.

The injection of public money into major banks in 1998–99 and changes in tax rules have increased the scope for out-of-court debt workouts, but the restructuring completed to date has mostly aimed at restoring the debtor's near-term solvency rather than providing for fundamental financial reorganization. Following a ¥7.5 trillion injection of public money into the major banks in the spring of 1999, several construction companies, as well as one of the top trading companies, succeeded in renegotiating their bank debts (see Chapter 8). The amount of debt forgiveness entailed by these agreements approached ¥1 trillion, being borne mainly by the respective main banks (the contribution of main banks typically accounted for 40–85 percent of the total written off). Generally, the debt reduction—equivalent to 20–30 percent of the liabilities of the firm—was estimated by market analysts to be insufficient to fully solve the problems of the beneficiary company. Indeed, some of the agreements appeared to have been prompted mainly by the desire of main banks to avoid the need to fully provision those loans in the event the company was inadvertently pushed into bankruptcy. In the case of legal bankruptcy procedures, write-offs might have reached 60–70 percent of the face value of the loans, reflecting the decline in real estate prices since the early 1990s.

Informal debt renegotiation is likely to remain rare as long as debtors possess too few options to compel creditors into collective negotiation. Independent of the still low capitalization of major banks, debt workouts face several hurdles. The tax treatment of debt forgiveness is still somewhat uncertain, and bank managers have expressed the concern that by forgiving debts they could incur the risk of being sued by shareholders.[7] Also, securitization is still at an early stage, reducing the chances of banks to sell bad loans to specialized agents that could have more means to negotiate with debtors.[8] More generally, many debtors in Japan do not face just a liquidity problem, being instead close to insolvency or insolvent. This weakness tends to render debt workouts difficult by heightening the chances that

---

[7]It is difficult to gauge this specific risk, because court actions are not as common in Japan as in the United States, and corporate governance in general is exercised somewhat differently in the two countries. The expression of this concern, nevertheless, probably also reflects banks' perception of some uneasiness on the part of stakeholders and possibly society at large with the use of public money to bail out companies that have or had close ties to political parties.

[8]Although a new securitization law was adopted in 1998, investors have still balked at investing in bad assets, in part because deficiencies in loan documentation continue to exacerbate the problems raised by the complex web of liens usually attached to loan collateral in Japan.

some creditors will hold out against renegotiation.[9] In this situation, debtors have little leverage against creditors. A threat to file for court protection is not credible, because under the current laws the ensuing procedures are likely to result in the liquidation of the firm or, at the least, the dismissal of management. An attempt was made in 1998 to address some of these problems by establishing ad-hoc panels to mediate the resolution of real estate loans. Concerns about the perception by the public that those panels could result in the bailing out of politically connected construction companies, following the recapitalization of banks with public money, led the authorities to abandon this approach.

## Directions for Reform: the International Experience and Academic Views

Since the late 1970s, several industrial countries have overhauled their bankruptcy laws to increase the use of formal procedures and promote efficiency. Starting with the overhaul of the United States code in 1978, new bankruptcy laws were introduced in the United

---

[9]The holdout problem is a coordination failure that emerges when marginal creditors realize that their own claims tend to become more valuable after claims of the main creditors are relinquished. The problem is less severe when the debtor is facing mainly a liquidity crisis, because in this case the on-going value of the firm is typically much higher than its liquidation value, making it easier to pay off creditors holding out. When larger sacrifices are required, reliance on legal procedures is more likely. For instance, Franks and Torous (1994) find that write-offs are relatively small and junior and senior debts are reduced by broadly the same proportion in the case of debt workouts, while legal bankruptcy is associated with larger write-offs, ones in which junior creditors absorb much larger losses than senior creditors. Although high-leveraged firms in the United States tend to prefer workouts to legal bankruptcy (Chatterjee, Dhillon, and Ramirez, 1996), this is typically explained by the fact that, in the United States, high leverage is associated with high interest payments. Highly-leveraged firms thus tend to default after relatively small shocks to their revenue flows, i.e., they often face more of a liquidity crisis than insolvency. In Japan, interest rates have been low and the disciplining effect of leverage has largely not been in operation (Jensen, 1986). Firms facing default are thus likely to have already depleted much of their assets and be close to insolvency, and their problems may be less easily addressed by informal bilateral workouts.

Kingdom, France, and Germany. In Germany, reform was prompted in part by a transformation of the financial landscape similar to that which occurred in Japan, which reduced the effectiveness of the traditional methods for dealing with corporate financial distress (notably the weakening of the *Hausbank* system, which shared some similarities with the Japanese main bank system).[10] Most of the new laws attempted to be more "debtor friendly," with some making a larger effort to give priority to the (*ex post*) efficiency principle that states that insolvency procedures should preserve those distressed firms with an on-going value greater than the liquidation value.[11] (Box 9.1 provides a summary of the aspects that help to characterize bankruptcy laws.)

Chapter 11 has achieved a remarkable success in fostering formal reorganizations in the United States. Chapter 11 replaced Chapters X and XI of the old U.S. Bankruptcy Code, introducing many features that are credited with having contributed substantially to the success of corporate restructuring in the United States (Table 9.4). The number of formal reorganizations increased by 85 percent in the first full year after the introduction of the new code and did not decline until the mid-1990s. Among the features of Chapter 11 that have contributed to its popularity are:

- Automatic protection against secured debtors, and the granting of seniority to new debt.
- Approval of reorganization plans that depends on the consent from a majority of creditors.
- The ability of courts to "cram down" creditors, that is, force a class of creditors to accept a plan in which it will not be worse off than in liquidation.
- Firms can be sold while undergoing financial reorganization.

However, some practitioners and academics believe that Chapter 11 has an excessive bias in favor of incumbent management. This

---

[10]German law was heavily tilted toward liquidation. Similar to Japan, most liquidations and reorganizations proceeded out of court, in part because stringent screening mechanisms would bar most firms from applying to enter a legal procedure. In a typical year, only 60 petitions for compositions were accepted.

[11]See also IMF, 1999 for a comprehensive economic analysis of key issues surrounding insolvency procedures. Ex ante efficiency, i.e., the extent to which the law affects contracts and credit, has until recently received less scrutiny.

**Table 9.4 Features of Reorganization Procedures in the United States and Germany and the Prospective Financial Rehabilitation Law in Japan**

| Country | United States | Germany | Japan |
|---|---|---|---|
| Procedure | Chapter 11 of Bankruptcy Code | 1994 Bankruptcy Code | (Prospective) Financial Rehabilitation Law |
| Main objective and application | Reorganization of the firm as an ongoing concern; only indirect consideration for stakeholders other than the debtor. | Liquidation, reorganization (composition), or possible auction; some consideration for "social" and other external objectives. | Financial rehabilitation of individuals, unincorporated firms, and corporations through a streamlined procedure. |
| Solvency and other requirements | Firm needs not be insolvent; protection is often sought by debtor. | Firm cannot meet payments or is overindebted. It needs to prove it has enough funds to pay for procedural costs (after netting out secured assets). | Solvent firms can apply if debt burden becomes excessive; prepayment of court costs is likely to still be required. |
| Control rights and authority to propose a reorganization plan | Debtor in control: in 50 percent of cases, previous managers retain control; in remainder, new managers are appointed by debtors. Managers have 120 days after the filing (extendable by the court) to present reorganization plan. The 1995 reform somewhat increased the power of creditors to reject that plan. | Power is shared. Court appoints a creditors' committee and an administrator, who proposes a reorganization plan to the creditors' assembly within three months. If the plan is rejected, the administrator may be allowed to propose a new plan or a chance can be offered for the debtor to take the lead. | DIP principle is embraced; similar to current practice under the Commercial Code, incumbent managers may retain control of the firm, with some supervision from the court, and propose the reorganization plan. Implementation of the plan will be overseen by court, but without deep involvement. |
| Automatic stay against creditor claims | Most creditors' claims and the service of those claims are stayed (with exceptions such as lease payments). | Automatic minimum three-month stay for all claims; stay can be extended by creditors' assembly. | Stays against secured creditors are not automatic, but are expected to be granted liberally and expeditiously by courts (comprehensive stays will substitute for the current system where the debtor has to seek individual injunctions against each creditor). |

| | | | |
|---|---|---|---|
| Renegotiation of liabilities and voting rights | Great discretion to renegotiate debt contracts. Impaired creditors vote by class; plan is approved by simple majority by number and ⅔ majority by claim, subject to court confirmation. Court can "cram down" junior creditors. | Ample scope for renegotiation (in the past, essentially only the repayment schedule of claims could be renegotiated). Creditors vote by class; plan is approved by simple majority by number and by size of claim, and subject to court confirmation. | Creditors are likely to vote as one class, with plans to be approved by a qualified majority by number and size of claim. Firms will be able to be sold as going concerns during the procedure. |
| New financing | New financing is easily accommodated because it has priority over existing claims, under the debt-in-possession (DIP) statute. | New senior financing allowed (it was the case in the old code). | New financing to receive senior status. |
| Preservation of residual claims on equity holders and deviations of absolute priority | Equity often retains value, usually through creditor's consent, and sometimes through a court "cram down." Junior creditors may be paid while senior creditors may not be paid in full, when the latter were undersecured, or made concessions. | Deviations can be proposed, but must be agreed by a creditor's vote. In compositions, they tended to occur. | Deviation from absolute priority expected, e.g., debtors will be able to satisfy the claims of secured creditors by paying off the actual value of the collateral (arbitrated by a third party) and debt-for-equity swaps will not require the wiping out of shareholders' wealth. |
| Other options for distressed firms and their main objectives | **Prepackaged Chapter 11** (in which impacted creditors agree on a plan before filing); **informal debt workouts**, including through the exchange of claims; **liquidation under Chapter 7** of the Bankruptcy Code | The new code combined the compulsory liquidation (*Konkursordnung*) and composition (*Vergleichsordnung*) procedures; **informal debt workouts** most common. | All existing legislation (**Composition, Rearrangement, and Corporate Reorganization Laws**) will remain in place until they are fully revised and possibly unified within a 3–5 year horizon. |

Source: Franks and others (1996), Paulus (1998), Matsushito (1998).

## Box 9.1. Specific Features of Bankruptcy Laws

Five general aspects of bankruptcy law determine the balance between the protection granted to creditors and to debtors. They also indicate the extent to which the law favors the liquidation of the firm, its sale (as an ongoing concern or after a breakup), or its financial reorganization under the incumbent or a new management team. These aspects can be summarized as follows:

Screening mechanisms: Stringent screening requirements tend to reduce the number of bankruptcy petitions accepted, while increasing the proportion of those being completed (e.g., it is easy to enter into Chapter 11 in the United States, but less than 15 percent of the filings result in a confirmed reorganization plan). Liquidations can usually be initiated by creditors after default on payment or other covenant (e.g., a financial ratio). They can also be initiated by the court based on the insolvency of the firm (in some countries, the debtor who fails to report an insolvency may be prosecuted), or by the debtor. Reorganization procedures can usually be initiated by creditors or the debtor. In some countries, their acceptance by courts would depend on the court estimating the value of the firm to be sufficient to cover the cost of the judicial process, and the court may decide to convert the procedure into liquidation if over time it comes to believe that the reorganization will not be successful.

Stays of proceedings: Staying proceedings means to stop the repayment of claims, an action that increases the firm's chances of survival. The absence of an automatic stay against senior secured debt may lead to the hasty sale of some assets of the firm. That may hamper the ability of the firm to continue operating, reduce the firm's sale value, or impinge on the value of remaining assets. More generally, the stay allows information about the firm to be shared among claim holders and the court, i.e., it gives a breathing space before the decision on whether the firm should be reorganized or liquidated is taken.

Preservation mechanisms: These can operate in many ways. For instance, they include court supervision of managers to deter the dissipation of assets, as well as the granting of seniority to debt issued after the firm files for court protection, as a means to provide liquidity to the firm and help it continue operating. In some countries, the administrator is required to approve the granting of seniority to reduce the risk of an unviable firm being kept operating at the expense of the original creditors.

Control rights and power to design and implement the reorganization plan: In the United States the *debtor-in-possession* principle leaves these rights in the hand of incumbent management, and the flexible stance taken by the courts with respect to the observation of absolute priority, has contributed to raise the chances of the firm to apply for court protection and to continue operating afterwards (absolute priority means that junior claimholders are paid only after senior creditors are paid in full). Those privileges are not, however, an unmitigated good, because they can lead to overinvestment, especially when combined with the super seniority granted to debt acquired after the beginning of the procedure. Assigning these rights to a subset of creditors can also be distortionary; e.g., the receiver under U.K. law may favor a quick settlement that covers the claims he represents, over another plan that would maximize the value of the firm as a whole. The consequences of assigning those rights to a court-appointed administrator depend on the incentives and constraints faced by such administrator. It may bias procedures toward liquidation and, depending on the complexity of the procedures, entail large administrative costs. More specifically, complex rules may help avoid fraud and the undue treatment of individual creditors, but they may erode the value of intangible assets. For instance, suppliers may stop extending credit, customers may shun the products of the company fearing that it will eventually fold, and employees with particular expertise may leave the company when faced with the prospect of a long period of judicial intervention.

Voting powers: A requirement of unanimity among creditors usually makes the approval of reorganization plans difficult, biasing procedures toward liquidation. A common method to address this problem is to parse creditors who hold similar claims in specific groups. Approval may then require just the support of a majority of claimholders within each group. In the United States, only claimholders who are not being repaid in full can vote. Moreover, although support from all eligible groups is in principle required, when at least a class of creditors accepts a reorganization plan, courts may force claimholders to accept it as long as those claimholders receive at least what they would have received in liquidation. Together with the voting power granted to shareholders, that practice tends to bias procedures in the U.S. toward the reorganization of the firm.

perceived bias is reflected in the rather lengthy "exclusivity period" in which the debtor is the only party that can file a plan of reorganization, and to some extent in the "debtor-in-possession" provisions that allow the debtor (and, in about half of the cases, incumbent managers) to retain the control of the firm. Both tend to strengthen the hand of managers and can, when unchecked, slow down the pace of corporate restructuring and lead to inefficient outcomes.[12] Indeed, many firms that emerge from Chapter 11 continue to experience poor operating performance and more than one-third of them must undergo a second restructuring (Hotchkiss, 1995), in part because managers insist on not allocating corporate resources to their highest-valued uses (Bradley and Rosenzweig, 1992).

The potential "pro-management" bias of Chapter 11 has in part been balanced by the existence of a strong market for corporate control in the United States. The existence of active capital markets in the United States provides mechanisms to help investors (including outside investors) to eject managers and can deter excessive management entrenchment (management turnover, although not exceptionally high after entrance in Chapter 11, is higher than among healthier firms). The sale of the firm as a going concern during the procedure is another method to change the way the company is operated, while often increasing the chances of its survival. Evidence of the sale of U.S. publicly traded firms in bankruptcy, for instance, suggests that such a market-based mechanism fostered an efficient reallocation of resources, often also contributing to the success of sectoral corporate restructuring (Box 9.2).

Several academics have also proposed the conversion of debt into tradable contingent claims as a means to foster efficient outcomes, but except for debt-for-equity swaps these alternatives have not been adopted in recent codes. A number of proposals have been made in

---

[12]The most cited case in which lenience toward incumbent managers afforded by the code has proved very costly is that of Eastern Airlines. When the company filed for bankruptcy it had $3.7 billion in assets, which was enough to repay its $3.4 billion in debts. After a year in Chapter 11, the company offered its creditors $1.6 billion, and in its final proposed plan it offered only $0.8 billion. The company was eventually liquidated, with creditors receiving less than a tenth of the firm's stated value on entering bankruptcy (Neish, 1995). The Code was amended in 1994 to allow creditors to appeal against the extension of privileges to the debtor, but these changes were, on the whole, marginal.

---

**Box 9.2. Acquisitions of Bankrupt Firms Under Chapter 11**

Recent research finds that takeovers of distressed firms have the following characteristics (Hotchkiss and Mooradian, 1998).

- The majority of buyers of bankrupt firms come from the same or
  related industries. This result supports the argument that potential
  buyers with the highest valuation of a bankrupt firm usually come
  from the same sector, even if industry conditions may constrain
  these potential bidders, who may themselves be distressed (Shleifer
  and Vishny, 1992). Firms from the same sectors will tend to know
  how best to operate the firm. They may also have had prior relations with the firm, reducing the problem of asymmetric information (i.e., they do know the strengths and weaknesses of the firm).
  Nevertheless, "vulture" investors, i.e., deep-pocket investors who
  specialize in the acquisition and the temporary management of distressed companies, tend also to be active in this market. More generally, vulture investors appear to have on balance facilitated corporate restructuring in the United States. For instance, Betker (1997)
  finds that the direct costs of Chapter 11 are lower when vulture investors are involved in the restructuring.
- Most firms showed marked operating gains. These gains generally
  stemmed from reductions in operating expenses and employment.
  Ratios such as that of expenses to sales improved, while revenue
  increases lower than those observed industrywide suggested reductions in capacity.
- Stock markets reacted positively to those acquisitions. Acquisitions
  usually led to abnormal stock returns for the bidder and the bankrupt target at the announcement of the acquisition.

---

recent years that seek to avoid the costs, uncertainties, and delays
that usually result from the effort creditors must undertake to arrive
at a consensual plan. Typically, they include the transformation of all
claims into equity and options on equity (Aghion, Hart, and Moore,
1992; Roe, 1983; Branch, 1998) under an order from the court (a formal procedure is usually necessary to address the holdout and free
rider problems that would affect voluntary exchanges). In most of
these schemes, senior debtholders would receive all the equity of the
firm, and junior claimants would receive calls on those shares. The

strike price on those calls would be set in a way that junior claimholders would be paid only after senior creditors were repaid in full.[13] The issue of control is not, however, always solved by these schemes—and some voting structure may still be needed—because if control is vested in senior creditors (who received all the equity) and their repayment is bounded by the options on that equity, a situation similar to that arising in receiverships may occur (that is, the senior creditors may focus on recouping their own investment, not necessarily in maximizing the value of the firm). In standard debt-for-equity swaps in which returns are not bounded, senior creditors are more likely to focus on the overall maximization of firm value. Debt-for-equity swaps have been relatively common under Chapter 11.

The new German Code, which incorporates many features of Chapter 11, attempts to promote efficiency also by providing several mechanisms to foster coordination among parties. The code was introduced in 1999, although an early version had been applied in eastern Germany for some years. In the code, debtor-friendly provisions are balanced by the prominent role given to the creditors' committee.[14] Such a committee is appointed at the beginning of the procedure and can help the trustee draw up the reorganization plan (if the debtor has not proposed one, or the one proposed is deemed inadequate). Subsequently, the general assembly of creditors votes on this plan. If the assembly rejects the plan, it can ask either the trustee or the debtor to draw up a new one. Such coordination mechanisms, and the ample and timely production and dissemination of information among parties, can have an instrumental role in promoting effi-

---

[13]A cascade of call options on call options could replicate the absolute priority structure, with the original shareholders exercising their call if a residual was left after all debtholders were paid. Proposals usually allow these securities to be traded before maturity, with the maturity time being set with a view to permit claim holders to exchange enough information to facilitate the rational exercise of their rights (e.g., after a full year of operation, or a detailed audit of the company).

[14]Provisions akin to those in Chapter 11 include automatic stays against secured creditors, the division of creditors in classes for voting purposes, the sufficiency of majorities for the approval of plans, and the ability of the debtor to submit a reorganization plan when petitioning for protection. The code also allows incumbent management to remain in charge of day-to-day operations, although at the creditors' discretion and under court supervision.

cient outcomes. They help expedite the procedure, while avoiding letting the debtor, creditors, or a court-appointed trustee monopolize decisions. Building on German tradition, the code also provides mechanisms to facilitate the takeover of distressed firms.[15]

Bankruptcy law reform has not been uniformly successful, reflecting the difficulty of striking the right balance between being "debtor-friendly" and being able to deal with firms that should close. For instance, the 1985 French law appears to have tried to reconcile too many conflicting goals in an effort to keep firms alive and preserve jobs. As a consequence, an excessive number of firms typically undergo repeated reorganizations.[16] By contrast, the 1986 British Corporate Voluntary Arrangement (CVA) forces the transfer of the control of the firm away from the firm's directors and is seldom used. Its inadequacy, as well as the drawbacks of other U.K. bankruptcy laws (such as receiverships), contributed to the prominence taken by the London Approach to debt workouts in the 1990s. That approach evolved as a response to the financial difficulties faced by many U.K. companies at the onset of the 1989 recession, and the transformation of the role of banks following financial liberalization in the United Kingdom—which made even strongly capitalized banks less able or willing to support distressed firms on a bilateral basis.[17] Under this

---

[15]An aspect of the code that could also be of some interest in Japan is the attempt made to address the problem of dealing with labor redundancies following acquisitions through negotiations with employee representatives. This problem can be serious in Germany, where workers enjoy far-reaching employment protection.

[16]The code was amended in the 1990s, but the problem to an extent still persists.

[17]Under the London Approach, the Bank of England has attempted to be a catalyst to create a generally agreed framework and to help corral banks into unanimity, where this was a precondition for restructuring packages (Kent, 1997). The financial and legal expertise and its deployment in particular situations was left entirely to the financial institutions involved, as well as the company in difficulty. Ingredients of the London Approach include the commitment of banks not to initiate legal action against the troubled firm, rather keeping their credit lines open; efforts to keep the decision-making process collegial; and attempts to balance the respect for absolute priority with the desire to share the cost of rescuing the firm in a fair way. The Bank of England has been involved with over 160 workouts, a small proportion of the workouts that occurred under that framework but without the Bank's involvement.

approach, the Bank of England took the role of an "honest broker" between parties, exerting some moral suasion, but leaving to the private parties the onus for designing and implementing the required restructuring strategies.

## The Proposed Financial Rehabilitation Law

The project to reform Japanese insolvency law gained momentum in 1999. An Advisory Committee for the Reform of Insolvency laws was established at the Ministry of Justice in October 1996. The committee published a first document for discussion in December 1997. This document suggested that efforts should focus on drafting a law to facilitate the financial rehabilitation of small and medium-sized companies in order to carry out a comprehensive reform of all insolvency laws.[18] Responding to the deterioration of the economic situation and the recognition of the importance of facilitating corporate restructuring, the pace of preparation accelerated in 1999, and legislation was proposed to the Diet in the fall of 1999.

The prospective features of the new Financial Rehabilitation Law tend to increase debtors' bargaining power and extend some market mechanisms. The proposed law includes key provisions paralleling those in Chapter 11. In particular:

- Courts will have discretionary power to provide stays against secured creditors, reducing the risk of the firm ending up in liquidation after being stripped of essential assets; the stays will not be automatic, although courts are expected to be liberal in issuing them. The law also envisages the issuance of comprehensive injunctions, saving the debtor from the current burden of requiring an individual injunction against each creditor.
- The debtor-in-possession (DIP) principle will apply. Incumbent management will be entitled to remain in control of the firm during the procedure and propose the reorganization plan.

---

[18]The document also gave priority to the development of laws covering individual bankruptcies and to reform international bankruptcy procedures. Although the new law is expected to supplement the composition law, all existing laws will remain in place until the original reform project is completed.

- Debts acquired after the commencement of the procedure will be granted seniority over previous claims.
- Approval of reorganization plans will require the support of a qualified majority of creditors, rather than their unanimous consent. Creditors will not, however, be divided by classes for the purpose of voting on the plan, and it is thus not clear if a mechanism similar to the ability of the court to "cram down" creditors will be available.
- Debtors will be able to satisfy claims of secured creditors by paying off the current (estimated) value of the collateral and lumping the residual part of the loan with other unsecured debts. This provision extends the protection granted by the Corporate Reorganization Law, which states that any deficiency of collateral shall be treated as an unsecured claim.
- Firms will be allowed to be sold as a going concern during the rehabilitation procedure, an option usually blocked under the Corporate Reorganization Law (there are mechanisms to sidestep this restriction, however, as illustrated by the quick sale of Japan Leasing Co., an affiliate of Long-Term Credit Bank (LTCB), even before a formal reorganization plan was approved).
- Rules would be changed to permit debt to be converted into equity through the issuance of additional equity, rather than by replacing existing equity, which will tend to facilitate debt-for-equity swaps.

The new legislation will thus feature the stronger protection against creditors found in the Corporate Restructuring Law and the autonomy provided to the debtor found in the Composition Law and the Commercial Code. By combining features of all three laws, the new text may become more operational, leading to an increase in the number of petitions. The authorities expect the number of cases to double or triple. An effort has also been made to simplify procedures. For instance, although the authorities have been favorable to the creation of creditors' committees, their structure and exact role are likely not to be codified.

The authorities are also considering changes in connected legislation. The implementation of measures such as the promotion of debt-for-equity swaps will require changes in other laws that are being carried out. Exemptions to the Commercial Code, for instance, are being considered to permit the reduction of the capital of the firm without the need of shareholders' approval. Also, the Antimonopoly Law is being changed to permit a bank to hold more than 5 percent of the equity of a firm. Indeed, small changes in ancillary legislation and rules are likely to be instrumental to any increase in corporate financial reorganizations.

The ultimate objective of overhauling the texts of the insolvency laws in the medium term was not altered. Plans still call for a comprehensive reform of the insolvency laws in a 3–5 year horizon, as well as the connected changes in other laws, notably those referring to provisions in the Commercial Code.

## Issues and Challenges

The accelerated introduction of new rehabilitation procedures can prove useful. The early passage of legislation supplementing current laws and addressing a relatively narrow set of problems can be helpful on two counts. First, it can provide an effective vehicle for corporate rehabilitation, thus helping to relieve strains on the economy from corporate distress, including liquidation. Second, it can work as a "pilot" for at least some sections of the final law. This was the strategy followed in Germany after reunification. Reform had been discussed in western Germany for many years, permitting the law of the former East Germany to be quickly modernized. The resulting temporary statute was used as a "test drive" for some of those concepts before the enactment of the new code for the unified country in 1994 (Paulus, 1998).

Promoting corporate restructuring, while reducing the risk of management entrenchment, is likely to require a delicate balance. The objective of facilitating the financial reorganization of the largest possible number of firms could lead to the preservation of inefficient firms. In this respect, international experience indicates the importance of avoiding an excessive relaxation of the criteria for evaluation of reorganization plans. The rights of minority shareholders as well as those of small creditors should also be safeguarded.

With respect to larger firms, the experience in the United States suggests that a strong market for takeovers can act as a balance against management entrenchment. Permitting this mechanism to develop can be crucial to ensure efficiency, especially if the desire not to overburden the law results in the exclusion of the formal checks and balances that, for instance, characterize the new German Code. There are indications that the ongoing financial reform and upcoming changes in accounting and disclosure rules could help the development of such a market.

Successful legal reform is also likely to promote a growing number of informal debt workouts. By providing new options to debtors, the reform could induce creditors to engage in out-of-court negotiations. It is often mentioned, for instance, that banks are reluctant to resolve or renegotiate real estate loans because a title on those loans is akin to holding an option on the value of the land collateral, and low interest rates make that strategy cheap. The provision under the proposed law permitting debtors to satisfy the secured part of those claims by paying cash for the current value of collateral essentially curtails this option under a legal reorganization proceeding, and creates an incentive for banks to renegotiate. If the ability to revert to formal procedures remains remote, however, the threat embodied in these provisions will not be effective.

International experience points to the importance of the judicial infrastructure in the success of bankruptcy reform. In the United States, a factor behind the success of Chapter 11 was the creation of a body of qualified private trustees to serve in bankruptcy cases and relieve the judge of much of the administrative responsibility (Morse and Shaw, 1988). In Japan, a review of court procedures and manpower available could also prove necessary. Revisiting the issue of restrictions on the role of foreign lawyers may be helpful in enlarging the pool of experience available to support the financial reorganization of Japanese firms.

Summing up, bankruptcy law reform can make a valuable contribution to the restructuring process by providing a fair and transparent legal framework for sharing losses between creditors and debtors, while protecting firms' value as going concerns. While trade-offs will need to be made between the interests of different parties, experience in other countries provides some useful pointers as to how best to marry efficiency and equity considerations. Thus, with skillful handling, new bankruptcy laws could help unleash forces that would find fruition in a renewed dynamism in the Japanese economy.

# References

Aghion, P., D. Hart, and J. Moore, 1992, "The Economics of Bankruptcy Reform," *Journal of Law, Economics and Organization,* Vol. 8, pp. 523–546.

Betker, B., 1997, "The Administrative Costs of Debt Restructurings: Some Recent Evidence," *Financial Management,* Vol. 26:4, (Winter), pp. 56–69.

Bradley, M., and M. Rosenzweig, 1992, "The Untenable Case for Chapter 11," *Yale Law Journal,* Vol. 101, pp. 1043–95.

Branch, B., 1998, "Streamlining the Bankruptcy Process," *Financial Management,* Vol. 27:2, (Summer), pp. 57–69.

Chatterjee, S., U. Dhillon, and G. Ramirez, 1996, "Resolution of Financial Distress: Debt Restructurings via Chapter 11, Prepackaged Bankruptcies, and Workouts," *Financial Management,* Vol. 25:1, (Spring), pp. 5–18.

Eisenberg, T., and S. Tagashira, 1994, "Should We Abolish Chapter 11? The Evidence from Japan," *Journal of Legal Studies,* January, pp. 111–157.

Franks, J., and W. Torous, 1994, "A Comparison of Financial Recontracting in Workouts and Chapter 11 Reorganizations," *Journal of Financial Economics,* Vol. 35, pp. 349–422.

Franks, J., K. Nyborg, and W. Torous, 1996, "A Comparison of US, UK, and German Insolvency Codes," *Financial Management,* Vol. 25:3, (Autumn), pp. 86–101.

Hayashi, F., 1997, "The Main Bank System and Corporate Investment: An Empirical Reassessment," NBER Working Paper No. 6172, September.

Hoshi, T., A. Kashyap, and D. Scharfstein, 1990, "The Role of Banks in reducing the Costs of Financial Distress in Japan," *Journal of Financial Economics,* Vol. 27, pp. 67–88.

Hotchkiss, E., 1995, "Post-bankruptcy Performance and Management Turnover," *Journal of Finance,* Vol. 50, pp. 3–21.

Hotchkiss, E., and R. Mooradian, 1998, "Acquisitions as a Means of Restructuring Firms in Chapter 11," *Journal of Financial Intermediaries,* Vol. 7, pp. 240–262.

International Monetary Fund, 1999, *Orderly and Effective Insolvency Procedures: Key Issues,* Legal Department, International Monetary Fund.

Japan Securities Research Institute, 1998, *Securities Markets in Japan, 1998,* Tokyo.

Jensen, M., 1986, "The Agency Costs of Free Cash Flow: Corporate Finance and Takeovers, *American Economic Review,* Vol. 43, pp. 401–32.

Kaiser, K., 1994, "European Bankruptcy Laws: Implications for Corporations Facing Financial Distress," *Financial Management,* Vol. 25:3, (Autumn), pp. 67–85.

Kent, Pen, 1997, "Corporate Workouts: A U.K. Perspective," in Masciandaro and Riolo (eds.), *Crisi di Impresa e Risanamento,* Fondazione Rosselli, Milan (also found in the Bank of England web site).

Matsumura, T., and M. Ryser, 1994, "Revelation of Private Information about Unpaid Notes in the Trade Credit Bill System in Japan," The Institute of Social and Economic Research, Osaka University, Discussion Paper No. 341.

————., 1998, "Present and Future Status of Japanese International Insolvency Law," *Texas International Law Journal,* Winter.

Matsushita, J., 1999, "Current Japanese Insolvency Law and the Comprehensive Reform Project," presented at the *Current Issues & Future Directions for Bankruptcy Reform in Indonesia* conference, Jakarta, April 29–30.

Morse, D., and W. Shaw, 1988, "Investing in Bankrupt Firms," *The Journal of Finance,* Vol. 43, pp. 1193–1206.

Nakatani, I., 1984, "The Economic Role of Financial Corporate Grouping," in Aoki (ed.), *The Economic Analysis of the Japanese Firm* (Netherlands: Elsevier Science Publishers).

Neish, S., 1995, "Is the Revised Chapter 11 Any Improvement?" *Corporate Finance,* Vol. 124, (March), pp. 37–40.

Paulus, C., 1998, "The New German Insolvency Code," *Texas International Law Journal,* Winter.

Ramseyer, J., and M. Nakazato, 1999, *Japanese Law and Economic Approach* (Chicago: University of Chicago Press).

Roe, M., 1983, "Bankruptcy and Debt: A New Model for Corporate Reorganization," *Columbia Law Review,* (April), pp. 527–602.

Sakai, H., and Jacobson, C., 1998, *Guide to Insolvency in Japan* (Tokyo: Law Offices of Hideyuki Sakai).

Shea, P., and K. Miyake, 1996, "Insolvency-Related Reorganization Procedures in Japan: The Four Cornerstones," *UCLA Pacific Basin Law Journal,* Spring.

Sheard, P., 1994, "Reciprocal Delegated Monitoring in the Main Bank System," *Journal of the Japanese and International Economies,* pp. 1–21.

Shleifer, A., and R. Vishny, 1992, "Liquidation Values and Debt Capacity: A Market Equilibrium Approach, *Journal of Finance,* Vol. 47, pp. 1343–1366.

Weinstein, D., and Y. Yafeh, 1998, "On the Costs of a Bank-Centered Financial System: Evidence from the Changing Main Bank Relations in Japan," *The Journal of Finance,* Vol. 52:2, pp. 635–72.

227

**DATE DUE**

| | | | |
|---|---|---|---|
| | | | |
| | | | |
| | | | |
| | | | |
| | | | |
| | | | |
| | | | |
| | | | |
| | | | |
| | | | |
| | | | |
| | | | |

Post-bubble blues